IN THE WAKE OF THE SURGE

Michael J. Totten

Michael J. Totten is a foreign correspondent and foreign policy analyst who has reported from the Middle East, the Balkans, and the former Soviet Union.

He's a contributing editor at *City Journal* and writes regularly for *Commentary*. His work has also appeared in the *New York Times*, the *Wall Street Journal*, *The New Republic*, *Slake: Los Angeles*, *Pajamas Media*, the *New York Daily News*, *City Journal*, *LA Weekly*, the *Jerusalem Post*, Beirut's *Daily Star*, *Azure*, and *Reason*.

He won the 2007 Weblog Award for Best Middle East or Africa Blog, he won it again in 2008, and was named Blogger of the Year in 2006 by *The Week* magazine for his dispatches from the Middle East. He lives with his wife in Oregon and is a former resident of Beirut.

Visit his blog at www.MichaelTotten.com

ALSO BY MICHAEL J. TOTTEN

The Road to Fatima Gate

IN THE WAKE OF THE SURGE

MICHAEL J. TOTTEN

First American edition published in 2011 by Belmont Estate Books

Cover photo by Zoriah Miller

Manufactured in the United States on acid-free paper

FIRST AMERICAN EDITION

Totten, Michael J.
In the Wake of the Surge
ISBN-13: 978-0615508405
ISBN-10: 0615508405

For my parents

Contents

Introduction

I raq made fools of just about everyone.

Those who thought the U.S.-led invasion in 2003 was a good idea were chagrined to discover that Iraq's dictator Saddam Hussein didn't have stockpiles of weapons of mass destruction after all. The most convincing explanation I've heard yet for why so many intelligence agencies goofed it came from the tyrant himself. He needed to pretend that he didn't have them to avoid being attacked by the West, but he also, at the same time, needed to convince the Persians next door in Iran that he *did* have them to deter an attack from the east. So he told the world that he was defenseless, but he didn't dare let international weapons inspectors comb through his country to prove it.

So it goes in Iraq, and in the Middle East generally, where almost nothing is at it appears on the surface. Most Westerners who live there and work there eventually learn this the hard way. Most American presidents have to learn it the hard way, as well, if they ever, in fact, learn it at all.

The war opponents were right then, or at least partly, and at least for a while. For not only did Saddam Hussein not have caches of chemical and biological weapons, American and British soldiers found themselves sucked into an overlapping series of additional wars in Iraq, against the regime's former loyalists, against Abu Musab al Zarqawi's Al Qaeda in Iraq, and against an array of Shia militias backed by Iran. The country held free and fair elections for the first time in its history, but that did not stop it from disintegrating into something that looked more like Afghanistan and Somalia than a model Arab democracy.

By 2006 almost everyone, including me, thought if something radical didn't happen—and fast—that it would be best for the U.S. to just cut its losses and leave.

Something radical did, however, happen, and just at the last moment, too. After suffering a humiliating mid-term election loss based at least in part on the American public's Iraq war fatigue, President George W. Bush changed everything by placing a little-known general named David Petraeus in command. Not only did Petraeus send a "surge" of additional troops to Iraq, he transformed the American strategy there out of all recognition.

This time it was the opponents of the war who failed to see what was coming. Most figured the Petraeus strategy was doomed to fail just like everything else that had been tried. Some declared his effort a failure before he even had time to get started. Yet he led the American and Iraqi forces, against all odds and most expectations, to something that looked a great deal like victory.

I wrote the dispatches and essays that make up this book between 2006 and 2009 in *City Journal, Reason, Azure,* and on my blog, which you can find at www.MichaelTotten.com. You may notice some subtle shifts in tone as you read them. In 2006 I assumed, like most people did, that the U.S. was going to lose and that Iraq would be conquered by guerrilla and terror militias. Yet when I embedded with some of General Petraeus' units in Baghdad, it struck me at once that he might pull this thing out of the fire. If anyone could fix Iraq, Petraeus could fix Iraq. And if Petraeus couldn't fix it, I doubted anyone could. I said so in print and caught some flack for it at the time, but hey, I was right. Or at least it seemed I was right for a while.

By 2009, my mood darkened somewhat again. Iraq remained a mind-boggling dysfunctional place even after the insurgency was more or less beaten. When I wrote the last piece that makes up this collection, I was not convinced that the country was truly out of the wilderness. Yet by the time this book was published, Iraq looked like an island of sanity and stability all of a sudden. Arab revolts had just swept away tyrants in Tunisia and Egypt while open rebellions met ruthless repression in Syria and Libya. Hardly anything was happening in Iraq. Not everyone liked the prime minister, but at least, unlike most other heads of state in the region, he was elected. And he did not have absolute power. Back in 2006, when the first of these dispatches was published, hardly anyone would have thought that Iraq would be one of the most stable countries in the entire Middle East five years later, but that's what happened.

I edited most of these dispatches slightly. They were written as stand-alone pieces, and I found, when rereading them all in one sitting, that some of the same background information came up again and again. I couldn't assume that everyone who read one piece in particular had read all the others, but I can now that they're here in one place. So for the sake of readability, I took out my scalpel and cut.

I also made a few aesthetic adjustments, nipping some little things here and tucking a bit over there. For the most part, though, the material here appears as it did when I wrote it.

No one can know what comes next in Iraq, but I can tell you what I saw and what I heard during seven trips to that long-suffering country shortly before, during, and at the end of the surge. Together these seventeen snapshots of places in time tell the story of the Kurds, the Arabs, and the Americans in Iraq at a violent and wrenching time in that country's history.

One reviewer described my first book, *The Road to Fatima Gate*, as a love letter to Lebanon. No one will think *In the Wake of the Surge* is a love letter. As Tony Horwitz wrote in *Baghdad Without a Map*, no one makes love to Iraq. I sincerely hope, though, that one day its people will emerge from the darkness and flourish.

Portland, Oregon
July 2011

PART ONE

KURDISTAN

One

Iraq Without a Gun

Iraq is one of the last places in the world a normal person would want to visit. Until just a few months ago Baghdad had the only international airport in the country and you risked your life just taking a taxi to the kinda-sorta halfway "safe" Green Zone from the terminal. Today you can fly directly to Erbil (known as *Hawler* in Kurdish), the capital of Iraqi Kurdistan in the north, where the war is already over.

So I took a charter flight from Beirut with a dodgy little outfit called Flying Carpet Airlines. I paid as much for that ticket as I would have paid to fly from Lebanon to the United States, but it beat the logistical pain of driving in over the land border from Turkey.

Erbil's tiny international airport—with its tiny little customs booth and its tiny little luggage rack—doubles as a military base. Civilian craft only started landing there a few months ago. Civilian cars aren't allowed anywhere near the terminal for security reasons, so I took a bus to a checkpoint a mile or so away where my pre-arranged driver Mr. Araz picked me up.

Driving to the center of any city from an airport rarely leaves a good first impression. The only exceptions I can think of are the trips into Tunis and Istanbul. But my fifteen-minute ride to the Erbil International Hotel (aka, "The Sheraton," even though it isn't really a Sheraton) was much less pleasant than usual. The city didn't look like anywhere I wanted to be. Most of the buildings and houses are run-down, dun-colored, flat-roofed utilitarian structures utterly devoid any aesthetic characteristics. Erbil desperately needs a makeover. (As I later found out when I could explore the city properly, it is getting one.)

"Today is Friday," Mr. Araz said. "The city is more quiet than normal."

Friday is the Muslim holy day when almost everything closes, but I had a hard time believing Erbil could ever look like a place with much activity. Such are rides from the airport. I hadn't seen downtown yet, though, and I tried not to make too much of the first things I saw.

Security at my hotel set up a circular perimeter of thick concrete bomb-blast walls. I would have taken a photograph, but I decided not to help Googling terrorists with any logistical plans by publishing what the place looks like. Armed security guards made me get out of the car while they opened the trunk, rifled through everything, pulled out the spare tire, and checked under the chassis for bombs.

"Is it safe to walk around here?" I asked Araz.

"No," he said. "I do not recommend it."

Great, I thought. *What the hell am I doing in this country?*

"Why, exactly, isn't it safe?" I said. I hoped he would say that I might get lost or be menaced by crazy drivers.

"I don't personally know of any incidents that have happened," he said. "But I never see foreigners like you walking around without a local person."

I didn't plan on spending much time alone anyway. I had already decided to hire a driver and translator. It's always best, though, to explore foreign cities on foot whenever possible, and I certainly wasn't happy that Araz was warning me that I shouldn't.

There was something fishy about the man, though. Yes, Erbil is part of Iraq, but it's also in Kurdistan. The war is over in Kurdistan. He was the guy who was going to supply me with a driver and translator, and he wanted 350 dollars a day for that service, but the Kurdistan Development Corporation told me I shouldn't have to pay anywhere near that much. I suspected Araz was trying to scare me so I would pay his exorbitant fee.

After I checked in at the desk I asked him if he would lower the rate.

"I will have to see about that and get back to you later," he said. I quietly decided not to hire him. All I had to do was call the Kurdistan Regional Government's public relations office and ask them to set me up with someone more reasonable.

Night fell as a storm came in. Rain lashed against my hotel room window. I heard a solitary boom of thunder and, later, a jet that sounded distinctly military.

Erbil, like the rest of Iraq, does not have a functioning electrical grid. Residents of the city get two hours of power each day if they're lucky. I stood at my window and looked out over the dark city as feral dogs howled at something unseen. I felt okay, and I was oddly happy to be there, but I couldn't get it out of my mind: *I'm in Iraq I'm in Iraq I'm in Iraq I'm in Iraq.*

I met the *Guardian* reporter Michael Howard in the lobby. He and I have a friend in common, and he kindly gave me a solid welcome and introduction to Iraq and its politics. He has spent most of the past three years in the country, and he knows it better than most Westerners do.

I would have more than enough time to get a grip on the politics. What I needed to know right up front was how safe (or not) Iraqi Kurdistan really is.

"Realize that this hotel is a primary target," he said. "Last year a bomb went off only 100 meters from here. Dozens of people were killed. Chunks of flesh were picked out of the garden near the front entrance."

"What about kidnappings?" I said. "Correct me if I'm wrong, but to my knowledge not a single person has been kidnapped in Kurdistan."

"That's true," he said. For the first time since I arrived in the country somebody said something that made me feel better.

"So can I walk around by myself?" I said. I'm not afraid of bombs that explode once a year. In some parts of the country they explode every day. But when kidnappers target Westerners, and when I'm one of perhaps only 100 Western civilians in a 50-mile radius, I can't afford to be naïve or stupid. "I need to know how to behave in this country, and right now I'm not sure. What do you do? Do you walk around by yourself?"

"I'll walk the main streets," he said. "But I don't walk any side streets. You don't have to worry much in Sulaymaniyah or Duhok. I'll go anywhere in those cities. But Erbil is a little more dangerous."

Last year's attack near the hotel wasn't the only terrorist incident in the city. In 2004 Sami Abdul Rahman, the deputy vice president of the Kurdistan Regional Government, was assassinated by a suicide bomber along with dozens of other people.

"I lost five friends that day," Michael told me. "I missed that explosion myself by only five minutes."

Just a few days after I arrived, a memorial to the dead in that attack would be dedicated in the city park. I had plans to meet Bayan and Vian Rahman, the daughters of the murdered deputy prime minister, for dinner the next day. I hadn't even been in the country for eight hours yet, and the violence felt close already. I tried not to let it frighten me much. Terrorists recently killed more people in a Madrid train station than have been killed in Erbil since the start of the war. And who is afraid to visit Madrid? Nobody I know.

My logic didn't always make me feel very much better. Abu Musab al-Zarqawi's Al Qaeda in Iraq is terrifying to think about when you're *in* Iraq, whether or not the Kurdish armed forces, the Peshmerga ("Those Who Face Death"), stand in the way. The bloody city of Mosul was just down the road. I could hail a taxi and be within easy reach of head-chopping killers in 45 minutes.

Later a man from the Kurdistan Regional Government rescued my nerves when I told him what Mr. Araz had said to me about the dangers of walking around by myself.

"He told you *what*?" he said.

"He told me it wasn't safe to walk around Erbil by myself," I said.

He was literally taken aback, and he flung himself ramrod straight against the back of his chair. His face flushed red. "Who is this man?" He pulled out his notebook. "What is his name and what is his phone number?"

I told him. "He also wanted to charge me 350 dollars a day for a driver and translator."

"*How* much?" he said. "He is lying to you. He is lying to you so you will pay him more money. I can't believe he is scaring visitors like that. I am going to report him." To whom, I wondered? "You are safe here. You are as safe here in Kurdistan as you are in any American city."

I believed him, partly because I wanted to believe him, but also because it lined up with everything I had heard and read about Kurdistan before I got there. Yes, it's Iraq, but the war is in a different part of the country. There are no Kurdish insurgents. The Peshmerga guard Kurdistan's de-facto border with ruthless effectiveness. Those who attempt to cross away from the checkpoints and the roads are ambushed by border patrols. Anyone who doesn't speak Kurdish as their native language stands out among the general population.

Iraqi Kurds, out of desperate necessity, have forged one of the most watchful and vigilant anti-terrorist communities in the world. Terrorists from elsewhere just can't operate in that kind of environment. Al Qaeda members who do manage to infiltrate are hunted. This conservative Muslim society did a better job protecting me from Islamist killers than the U.S. military could do in the Green Zone in Baghdad.

I did what I wanted and needed to do. I threw myself into their society, without a gun and without any bodyguards, and trusted that they would catch me. And catch me they did. I trusted the Kurds with my life. No trust in the world is greater than that, especially in a blood-spattered place like Iraq.

February 2006

Two

The Kurds Go Their Own Way

Two hours into my first tour of Erbil, my guide for the day taught me to feel lucky. "If we were doing this in Baghdad, we would be dead by now," he said.

Our driver nodded vigorously.

"It's *that* dangerous?" I asked.

"With your face," my guide replied, "and with our Kurdish license plates on the car, we could not last two hours."

So goes the capital of Iraq. But I was touring the capital of Iraqi Kurdistan.

A hard internal border between the Kurds' territory and the Arab-dominated center and south has been in place since the Kurdish uprising at the end of the 1991 Gulf War. Cars on the road heading north are stopped at a series of checkpoints. Questions are asked. ID cards are checked. Vehicles are searched and sometimes taken apart on the side of the road.

The second line of defense is the Kurds themselves. Anyone who doesn't speak Kurdish as their native language—and Iraq's troublemakers overwhelmingly fall into this category—stands out among the general population. There is no friendly sea of the people, to borrow Mao's formulation, that insurgents can freely swim in.

In a region where rule by reactionary clerics, gangster elites, and calcified military dictatorships is the norm, Iraqi Kurdistan is, by local standards, an open, liberal, and peaceful society. Its government is elected by a popular vote, competing political parties run their own newspapers, and the press is (mostly) free. Religion and the state are separate, and women can and do vote. The citizens here are tired of war, and they're doing everything in their power to make their corner of the Middle East a normal, stable place where it's safe to live, and to invest and build.

But to carve out their breathing space, the Kurds have adopted discriminatory policies that would make any liberal-minded Westerner squirm. It remains to be seen how the contradictions will sort themselves out in the long run. But the outcome is important, especially if Kurdistan reaches the day—and it seems increasingly likely that it will—that it breaks entirely free of Baghdad and declares independence.

Only 200 U.S. troops are stationed in Iraq's Kurdistan region. Even those are mere tokens. The Kurdish armed forces, the Peshmerga, are in charge of security. They do a remarkable job. Since Saddam Hussein's Baathist regime was toppled, only a handful of violent attacks have taken place in their part of the country.

Granted: In 2004 a suicide bomber killed Sami Abdul Rahman, the deputy vice president of the Kurdistan Regional Government, along with more than 100 other people. Last year another suicide bomber self-detonated just outside the perimeter of the fake knock-off "Sheraton" hotel. Bits of flesh splattered the flowers near the front door.

Those were major attacks. But not much else has happened. Meanwhile, the rest of the Kurds' country—if we can still think of Iraq as their country—is the most terrorized place in the world.

For that reason, among many others, Iraq might not survive in one piece. The overwhelming majority of Iraqi Kurdistan's people are packing their bags for independence. Most have already said goodbye.

Not one Iraqi flag flies in Erbil. The national flag does appear above government buildings in the eastern city of Sulaymaniyah. But it's the old flag, the pre-Saddam flag, the one that doesn't have *Allahu Akbar* ("God is Great") scrawled across the middle of it. The only reason it's flown in Sulaymaniyah at all is that the city is headquarters to Jalal Talabani's political party, the left-wing Patriotic Union of Kurdistan, and Talabani is the president of Iraq. (Note: The prime minister, not the president, is head of the government.)

In January 2005 the Iraqi Kurds held an informal referendum on

independence. More than 80 percent turned out to vote, and 98.7 percent
of those voted to secede. The Kurds have long dreamed of self-determination; today, when they look south, they see only Islamism, Baathism,
blood, fire, and mayhem. To them, Baghdad is the capital of a deranged
foreign country. The only people I met who thought of Kurdistan as "Iraq"
were the foreigners. When a Palestinian-American aid worker warned
me about security, he told me, "*Never* forget that you're in Iraq." But the
Kurds kept saying, "This isn't Iraq."

I f Middle Easterners had drawn the borders themselves, Iraq wouldn't
even exist. Blame the British for shackling Kurds and Arabs together
when they created the post-colonial, post-Ottoman map. The Kurds do.
Like the English, they refer to a toilet as "a W.C."—but they insist the letters stand for "Winston Churchill."

Arab Iraqis who want to "keep" Kurdistan should thank the heav-
ens for Talabani, Iraq's president. He belongs to the 1.3 percent of Iraqi
Kurds who at least say they want to remain tied to Baghdad. Meanwhile,
Masoud Barzani, president of Kurdistan and chief of the "conservative"
Kurdistan Democratic Party, is playing the bad cop. While Talabani is in
Baghdad trying to forge a federal Iraq with official Kurdish autonomy,
Barzani broods in his mountain palace and openly threatens secession.
"Self-determination is the natural right of our people," he said early last
year. "When the right time comes, it will become a reality."

It's hard to overstate just how long and how badly the Kurds have
wanted out. Barzani's father, the guerilla leader Moula Mustafa, once told
Jim Hoagland of *The Washington Post*, "We can become your 51st state
and provide you with oil." That was back in 1973.

Indeed, the dream of an independent Kurdistan dates back to the
dissolution of the Ottoman Empire at the end of World War I. The League
of Nations promised the Kurds a homeland of their own. Instead their
homeland was broken into shards and parceled out to Iraq, Turkey, Syria,
and Iran. Only in Iran, where the local Kurds call the Persians "cousins,"
do they feel much kinship with their nominal countrymen.

The Kurds have had their own de facto independent state here for the
last 15 years. Most of Kurdistan north of Sulaymaniyah was protected by

the U.S. and U.K. "no fly" zones during the interim between the first and second Gulf Wars. Young Iraqi Kurds have no memory of living under Saddam, no memory of ties to Baghdad, no memory of associating with Arabs, no memory of the oppression, the genocide, or the war. They see no point in *creating* ties with Baghdad that haven't existed in living memory—especially when Baghdad is burning.

Sidqi Khan Bradosti, whose family owns the Zozik Trading Company, put it more mildly than anyone else. "We have nothing to do with Baghdad," he said. "And I don't *want* to have anything to do with Baghdad if it can't be part of a federal rule-of-law democracy." The comments of English teacher Birzo Abdulkadir were more typical: "We have nothing to do with the rest of Iraq. It was inflicted on us. What do we have to do with Arabism?"

Most Kurds are moderately conservative Sunni Muslims, but their religious tradition is historically more liberal and lenient than many others in the Middle East. "I speak and read Arabic fluently," Abdulkadir told me. "I have read the Koran in its original language. I know it's more flexible than most Arab imams admit."

Their isolation has produced a you-leave-us-alone-and-we'll-leave-you-alone mentality. The mayor of Halabja, the city where Saddam used chemical weapons to massacre thousands in one day, wanted to make sure I understood this. "We never terrorized anyone in any country," he said. "We occupied no one's land. We defended ourselves with humble military force against a powerful enemy. We consider our nation a protector of human rights."

The president of Duhok University, Asmat M. Khalid, whose office is in that city's old Baath Party headquarters, told me the Kurds intend to build a new country with this idea as its foundation: "We have a different way of thinking here. We believe the key is to be civilized....We don't want our new generation to be aggressive. We don't want them to have to fight. It is not our habit to kill." The Kurdistan Democratic Party (KDP) does what it can to broadcast this message to Arab Iraqis on its Arabic-language satellite station *Il Takhi. Il takhi* means *brothers.* There is no Arabic equivalent of such a channel in Kurdish.

I did sometimes hear Kurds expressing racist comments. Iqbal

Ali Muhammad of the Kurdistan Islamic Union, a relatively moderate Islamist organization that is the third largest party in Iraqi Kurdistan, bluntly said, "The Arab, he is wild. He is not a civilized person."

Funny place, Kurdistan. I have defended Arabs before. But I never expected to do so in front of a Middle Easterner who described himself as an Islamist. Iqbal patiently listened to what I had to say in defense of Arabs generally, if not in defense of Saddam Hussein's campaign of black Arabism and genocide. I could tell I didn't convince him.

Arab Iraqis might not mind Kurdish independence as much as some expect. The Baghdad-based blogger Omar Fadhil wasn't allowed to meet me in Erbil because he's an Arab (more on that later), so he told me in an e-mail that maybe he could meet me someday when I "visit *Iraq.*" It isn't just the Kurds who have come to internalize the border between this region and the rest of the country.

Schoolteacher Raz Rasool lived for a while in Baghdad before returning to Sulaymaniyah. She thinks that if the Kurds decide to secede most Arab Iraqis will shrug and say, "Fine then, get out"—at least as long as they don't try to take Kirkuk's oil fields with them. (Granted, that's a big *if.*)

"Arab Iraqis don't care about any of our problems in Kurdistan," Rasool said. "They think of our problems as our problems, not theirs. They don't care that the Turkish military has soldiers stationed in parts of northern Iraq. That's because they don't think about Kurdistan as part of Iraq. They only care about Kirkuk, and they only care about Kirkuk because of the oil."

Many Arab Iraqis aren't even aware that Saddam's regime committed genocide against Kurds. "A gum-smacking teenage Arab girl from Baghdad recently visited the genocide museum here," Rasool told me, referring to an old Baath Party dungeon that has since been converted into a monument to the tortured and the dead. The girl had no idea hundreds of thousands were murdered. She had no idea 5,000 villages were completely annihilated. She didn't know that thousands, including children, were tortured to death in the prison blocks.

"She broke down in tears," Rasool said. "She only knew that Kurds were supposedly troublemakers. She said she was so sorry, that she was ashamed to be an Arab."

Some Middle Eastern countries—Egypt, for instance—are grim, depressing places that feel like they're circling the drain. Iraqi Kurdistan is optimistic, full of hope, infused top to bottom with a go-go, build-build attitude. Vast tracts of lovely new housing developments are under construction all over the major cities. Sulaymaniyah, the region's cultural capital, has doubled in population in the last three years. It's up to around 800,000 now, although no one is sure how many people actually live there. Like all cities that undergo rapid urban migration, most of the newcomers live on the outskirts. Unlike most Third World cities that explode in population, the outskirts of Sulaymaniyah are more prosperous than the old inner city.

Urban beautification campaigns are under way everywhere. Freshly cut bricks are being laid into sidewalks. Enormous new parks, some so large you might need a car to get from one end to the other, can be found in both Erbil and Sulaymaniyah. Highways are well-signed and in perfect condition. Advertisements for DSL Internet connections line the road from Erbil to the resort town of Salahhadin. There are no statues of tyrants, dead or alive. Most of the statues I saw were of poets. It's a different world from the shattered country below. It's easy to imagine the place as a reasonably well-functioning conservative democracy, a moderately prosperous Utah of the Middle East.

The longer central Iraq burns, the more distant the Kurds feel from Baghdad. But while the Kurds may not feel like they belong to Iraq, they don't pretend they aren't still shackled to it.

Erbil's international airport is built with one-way glass. Step outside, turn around, and you'll find that you can't see a thing inside the terminal.

Every time I walked into a government office in Sulaymaniyah, security guards asked if I had any guns. I didn't, but there was always a pile of them on a table that others had dropped off before they were let inside.

I expected the Peshmerga to let me blow through the checkpoints with minimal hassle because I'm American. Instead, they scrutinized me just like everyone else. A couple of times I got pulled out of the line for even closer inspection. The soldiers were cold, serious professionals. The only people who have an easy time at these checkpoints are those who perfectly speak Kurdish with a local accent. That's the one trait that can't easily be faked, and it's the only trait that can be trusted.

Kurds love freedom, but they love checkpoints too; in general, they see them as the barrier that holds back the horrors from the south. People don't merely trust and appreciate the security. They *feel* it. A detached garden restaurant on the grounds of the "Sheraton" has all-glass walls on three sides. The only wall made of metal and stone is the one behind the well-stocked bar. Suburban Sulaymaniyah is a wonderland of brand-new modern shiny glass buildings. No one in their right mind in Baghdad would build brand-new structures like these.

During Beirut's civil war the profits of window and glass companies perfectly tracked the rise and fall of the level of violence. When people felt safe from the chaos of war, they replaced the windows blown out from bullets, rockets, and car bombs. When they felt under siege and pessimistic, they didn't bother. Iraqi Kurds are so optimistic they're putting up new glass buildings for the first time in their history.

There is some disgruntlement. I met a university professor who got so wound up in his opposition to both major parties I thought he might have a heart attack. "They are all corrupt!" he said as he flailed about in his chair. "All of them!" There is, indeed, an enormous amount of corruption. Leaders and functionaries in both parties take a cut from almost every business that matters. "And they want everyone to become a Peshmerga!" the professor exclaimed. "We have more generals than the Red Army!"

Perhaps the security apparatus is a bit overdone. Few Kurds are in the mood to take any chances, though. The Peshmerga are in charge of security here; the Iraqi army has been infiltrated by Baathists and isn't allowed anywhere inside the autonomous zone. Like most people, the Kurds believe a modern civilized country needs a state with a monopoly on the use of force. But they don't think the state in Baghdad is civilized yet.

The Peshmerga offered to patrol the roads in and out of Kirkuk, which is just outside Kurdish government territory. But the U.S. authority on the ground wouldn't have it. Arab tribes in the area might get twitchy about being policed by the Kurds.

The Kurds took the pushback in stride. The minister of the interior in Sulaymaniyah laughed out loud when I asked him how well they get along with the American military. "Ha ha ha, our relationship is *very* good," he said.

It's certainly better than their relationship with Arabs. The Kurds may be the most liberal of Iraq's three dominant ethnicities, but they're the quickest to impose illiberal laws on everyone else. I learned that when Omar and Mohammad Fadhil, the famous bloggers behind *Iraq the Model*, drove up to Kurdistan from Baghdad to meet me at my hotel. They never made it. The Peshmerga told them Arabs were not allowed to enter the region without a Kurdish escort.

It was racial profiling at its worst. The Fadhils did nothing at all to deserve that kind of treatment. Two upstanding citizens were not allowed to visit a region in their own country for no reason except that they're Arabs. The *Economist* Intelligence Unit's Index of Political Freedom ranks Iraq the third freest Arab-majority country, after Lebanon and Morocco. Yet freedom of movement, one of the most basic freedoms, still doesn't exist. It's a one-way limitation too: Kurds can visit the north, center, and south of Iraq whenever they feel like it—not that most want to.

Meanwhile, the Kurdistan Regional Government actually provides money and housing for Arab Christians who want to pick up and resettle in the north. The overwhelming majority of Kurds are Sunni Muslims. Yet they discriminate against their fellow Sunnis in favor of "infidels."

Arab Muslims aren't barred from the region. They can visit as tourists, and they can buy new homes there. But they must have connections if they want to settle in Kurdistan, and they must prove they aren't a security threat before they can even show up.

And then there's Kirkuk. Perhaps nothing in all Iraq poses a bigger challenge to Western liberal principles than this city.

Kirkuk sits atop one of Iraq's biggest oil fields. It has always been an ethnically mixed city on the southernmost fringe of Iraqi Kurdistan. Today it lies just beyond the Kurdistan Regional Government's autonomous zone. From 1986 to 1989 Saddam Hussein ethnically cleansed a good portion of the Kurds who refused to change their ethnicity to "Arab," then moved more Arabs, Stalin-style, into the Kurds' former homes.

No ethnic group dominates the city today. Kurds, Sunni Arabs, Shia

Arabs, Turkmen (Turkic Iraqis who speak their own dialect of Turkish), and Assyrian and Chaldean Christians live cheek by jowl. It's a little Lebanon where everyone is a minority. And it's one of the worst tinderboxes in all of Iraq. Two violent incidents, from terrorism to kidnapping to sniping, occur every day in that city.

The Kurds want it back. They don't want to leave Iraq without the city they call "Our Jerusalem." Nor will they tolerate a federal Iraq that doesn't include Kirkuk in their autonomous zone.

I asked KDP Minister Falah Bakir what "Our Jerusalem" was all about. Is Kirkuk some kind of cultural capital? Is there a historic significance to the city that Westerners aren't aware of?

"No," he replied. "Kirkuk is part of Kurdistan. But it isn't 'Jerusalem.' Kirkuk is Kirkuk, just as Erbil is Erbil and Mosul is Mosul." It's just another Kurdish city, in other words. It was dubbed "Our Jerusalem" by Jalal Talabani as part of a P.R. campaign.

The Peshmerga could take Kirkuk militarily any time the order is given, but they're holding back. The Kurdistan Regional Government says it wants to take the city peacefully and with honor.

Trouble is, first they want to kick out the Arabs moved there by Saddam. Not all the Arabs. Those who lived there before the Arabization campaign, those who are actually from there, are welcome to stay. The Kurds swear they have no interest in creating an ethnic-identity state. They merely want, they insist, to make the city as safe and secure as Erbil, Sulaymaniyah, and Duhok.

South of the Peshmerga line, some towns with Sunni Arab majorities are forcibly evicting Shia Arabs at gunpoint, with rocket launchers, and without compensation. The Kurdistan Regional Government, by contrast, says it will financially compensate everyone asked to leave. Even so, reversing one population transfer with another isn't right. The Kurds seem to understand this, given that they're offering to pay damages to the evicted. They might not even care about the city's ethnic composition if Kirkuk weren't wracked with violence. But the city is a dangerous place, and the aftershocks of Saddam's divide-and-rule strategy are still explosive.

Guardian reporter Michael Howard knows the city well. "Many of the

Arabs I've spoken to in Kirkuk are aware that they are in someone else's territory," he told me. The overwhelming majority of Kirkuk's residents eschew violence no matter what their politics might be. But there are just enough people who don't to turn the city into a looming mini-Yugoslavia.

It's hard to say what will come next. The Kurds seem to know what they want, but even they have no idea what their next move is. If they declare independence today, Turkey very well may invade; the Turks dread nothing more than Turkish Kurdistan attaching itself to Iraqi Kurdistan. Or open war could break out between Kurdistan and what's left of Iraq. No one wants to lose the black gold mine in the earth beneath Kirkuk. Even the U.S. might not recognize an independent Kurdish state for the trouble it may cause if Ankara and Baghdad aren't persuaded to go along first.

The Kurds are patiently biding their time, but make no mistake: they aren't waiting to decide if they want to remain part of Iraq. They're waiting for just the right moment to jump.

Racialist policies may or may not outlast the war. Iraqi Kurds want to be protected from predominantly Arab terrorists. More than anything, though, they want self-determination for Kurds. How they treat their own ethnic minorities if they ever achieve independence will be a crucial first test. Are they really the kind of people they think they are?

On February 1, I had lunch in a restaurant in Duhok with my driver and translator. A music video played silently on a TV in the corner: a beautiful woman with flowing black hair singing what seemed to be a slow, quiet song.

"Is she a Kurdish singer?" I asked my translator.

"Look," he said. "She is at the oil fields of Kirkuk."

He was right. A flame shot out the top of a well.

"What's she singing about?" I asked.

I expected a heavy dose of Kurdish nationalism, but he surprised me. "A long time ago," he said, "before the Kurds knew Islam or science, when we still worshipped fire, Kirkuk was a mystical place. We did not know then what oil was. Flames came out of the earth."

On screen, the singer swayed slowly and sadly. "People used to go there and pray when they hoped to give birth to a son," he said. "She is there now asking for peace."

Reason Magazine
August 2006

Three

No Friends But the Mountains

O ver the past few years, I have traveled and worked in Iraqi Kurdistan frequently, often staying there for long periods of time, and have always moved about freely, without need of a gun, body armor, or bodyguards. Americans can go there on holiday, if they so desire, and feel just as relaxed as they would in Canada. Even more so, perhaps: The Kurds are friendlier, and more pro-American, than Canadians. Thomas Friedman wrote a few years ago that "after two years of traveling almost exclusively in Western Europe and the Middle East, Poland feels like a geopolitical spa. I visited here for just three days, and got two years of anti-American bruises massaged out of me." I felt much the same in Iraqi Kurdistan.

Indeed, it is hard to overstate how pro-American the people of Kurdistan are. They are possibly more pro-American than Americans themselves. If Bill Clinton was America's first "black" president, people in at least one part of the world say George. W. Bush is the first "Muslim" one: He is sometimes referred to in Kurdistan as "Hajji Bush" (meaning that he made the Muslim pilgrimage, or Hajj, to Mecca), an undeniably high honor for a Republican Christian from Texas. Kurdistan is not a "red state," and Kurds are not Republicans. Nor does it occur to most of them to prefer America's conservatives over its liberals. Rather, their warm feelings of gratitude and friendship extend to all Americans and both political parties for having liberated them from the totalitarian dictatorship of Saddam Hussein.

If you ask them, it was a real liberation—but one need not ask. Any reference to the Iraq war as an invasion will be quickly corrected. The United States destroyed the Hussein tyranny in 2003, but the slow-motion liberation of Kurdistan in truth began a decade before. After the 1991 Gulf War, the United States , the United Kingdom, and France imposed no-fly zones over Iraq's Kurdish north and Shia south. American, British, and, initially, French pilots patrolled the skies and threatened to shoot down any Iraqi aircraft they encountered.

Massive uprisings began in the south and north. The Shia were beaten by the regime, as they had always been beaten. Horrible war crimes and atrocities followed. But the Kurds were a force to be reckoned with. They had mountains, disciplined organizations, and battle-hardened fighters with years of experience in guerilla warfare. Civilians fled en masse from the cities to the mountains, Turkey, and Iran, thus clearing the battlefield for the Kurds' final, epic battle against Saddam Hussein. The Peshmerga then descended from above and fought the Iraqi army in the streets. After bloody clashes, the Iraqi army finally withdrew in 1991. Kurdish villages, neighborhoods, and cities, and eventually all of Iraq's northernmost provinces were cleared of Baath soldiers and agents. The Kurds have been strictly autonomous ever since, and have lived, to one extent or another, under a protective Western umbrella the entire time.

The Kurds have "no friends but the mountains," or so an old saying goes. It is hard for Westerners to grasp just how isolated the Kurds feel: They are hated by almost everyone in the region, and ignored by or unknown to almost everyone else in the world. That partly explains their fanatical pro-Americanism: A friend, at last! Israelis, perhaps, can relate.

Iraqi Kurds, though, are much more aggressively pro-American than Israelis. They arguably take their pro-Americanism to the point of absurdity. Fake McDonald's restaurants with names like "MaDonal" pop up in Kurdistan nearly as fast as real McDonald's chains devour the landscapes of Western cities. Teenagers wear United States Army uniforms, T-shirts, and pants as a fashion statement—and they do so without irony. Even some of the waiters in restaurants wear button-up shirts with the words *U.S. ARMY* stitched above the breast pocket.

During Saddam Hussein's genocidal Anfal Campaign in the late 1980s, Iraq's Kurdish cities were devastated by air strikes, artillery, and chemical weapons. Forests were clear-cut. Concrete was poured into wells. Between 100,000 and 200,000 people were murdered in massacres, and 85 percent of Kurdish villages were destroyed. Tens of thousands, including children, were tortured to death. "All of Iraq suffered terribly during those years," wrote Christopher Hitchens in *Vanity Fair* of his first trip to Iraqi Kurdistan after the 1991 Gulf War. "But its Kurdish provinces were among the worst places in the entire world—a howling emptiness of misery where I could catch, for the first time in my life, the actual scent of evil as a real force on earth."

Since that era of horror, however, Kurdistan has seen nothing less than a renaissance. It is now the safest, freest, and richest place in the country, and it's obvious why the Kurds reject what passes for politics in Baghdad: Iraq's Baath Party was the most brutal and thoroughly oppressive Arab Nationalist party in history, and no one suffered at its practitioners' hands more than the Kurds. Their rejection of Arabism does not stop at politics, though. Most reject the prevailing interpretation of Islam as well. Many blame religion itself for what ails the Iraqis, but the Kurds are as Muslim as anyone else. And the Baath Party—whose remnants make up some part of the insurgency—is brutally secular.

Religion is an important part of the texture of every society, but religion alone doesn't determine a society's course. Ethnic traditions matter too, which is what the Kurds mean when they say *We are Kurds*. Abdullah Mohtadi, secretary general of Iranian Kurdistan's Komala Party, puts Kurdish exceptionalism into historical context: "Kurds were one of those rare nations which resisted to the end the Arab and Islamic invasion," he told me. "They defended their land, and they also defended their own religion. Our loyalty to our Kurdishness is much more important than our loyalty to Islam. In official national anthems we say we are Kurds before we are Muslims. It's a general belief. The Kurds—and also the Persians, but especially the Kurds—are the only nation [in the region] apart from Israel where Islamic fundamentalism has no real roots. Kurds are not fanatic in their religion. When I was a child before the Islamic Revolution in Iran, most of the people, the young generation, they didn't pray. They didn't fast during Ramadan. People made jokes about religion, about God, about everything. They were so relaxed. They were not bigots about religion. I don't know why, but that was the case. And that still is the case."

Even so, most Iraqi Kurds are conservative Muslims. Theirs is undoubtedly a man's world, and on average less than a quarter of the people out in public are women. Even in Sulaymaniyah, Iraqi Kurdistan's most liberal city, around half the women wear the headscarf. Boys and girls are schooled separately, nightclubs are taboo, and while alcohol is available, outside of Sulaymaniyah most of its vendors are Christians. At the same time, though, the Iraqi Kurds aren't as culturally foreign to the West as they first appear. Political extremism of every conceivable variety is discouraged. Even a self-described Islamist said in an interview, "Extremes are bad, the middle is better."

"Kurds don't get upset about religion," English teacher Birzo Abdulkadir told me. "We believe in arguments based on reason, not emotion. If people don't agree with me about something, I'm not going to get mad at them. We will just have different opinions."

Sadly, the two major Kurdish political parties, the Patriotic Union of Kurdistan and the Kurdistan Democratic Party, are corrupt political machines. They own most of the media, and they have their own intelligence agents who sometimes spy on civilians. But there are third, fourth, and even fifth parties as well. They also run in elections and hold seats in parliament. They own newspapers and magazines and operate freely. There is certainly a great deal of corruption in Iraqi Kurdistan, and it is one of the most acknowledged problems among the Kurds themselves—but at least no one has a monopoly on it. No single party or clan, let alone person, holds all the power. And part of the reason is that Iraqi Kurdistan isn't a police state. The people there grouse about their elected officials, and they do it openly. Indeed, if Kurdistan-style graft were the scourge of Baghdad rather than death squads and car bombs, Iraq would be showcased as a smashing success and a model for the entire Middle East.

Perhaps the most refreshing thing about Kurdistan is that, its name notwithstanding, it is not an ethnic-identity state. Arabs can and do move there from the center and south of Iraq. As of May 2007, seven thousand Arabs per month are permitted to relocate to Kurdistan after they clear internal security checks. Of course, not everyone is happy about Arabs moving in, but most nonetheless contort themselves like good Western liberals to avoid expressing their thoughts in racial terms. They stress that many Arabs are fine people, that they do not mean to conflate a culture's worst elements with the whole. It is a strange thing to behold in a region where political correctness and racial sensitivity do not, as a rule, exist.

Perhaps it is not surprising, then, that Kurdish culture in Iraq is uncorrupted by terrorism. Unfortunately, the same cannot be said of Kurdish culture in Turkey. There, the Marxist-Leninist Kurdistan Workers Party (PKK) has been waging a low-level guerilla and terrorist war against the government and civilians for years. By contrast, Iraqi Kurds never murdered Arab civilians in Iraq or anywhere else—even though Saddam's regime was incomparably more oppressive than Turkey's. "Abdullah Ocalan was our own Yasser Arafat," one Kurd told me, referring to the PKK's former leader, who was at one time supported by some Iraqi Kurdish parties. "The difference between us and the Palestinians is that we learn from our mistakes."

And here we come to the most striking thing of all about the Iraqi Kurds, the thing that shows just how different they really are from most of the region: The Kurds are all right with the Jews.

Hatred and distrust of Jews in Kurdistan is but a whisper compared to what festers in the Arab world. I have not knowingly encountered a single anti-Semitic person in Kurdistan, even after spending months there talking to people about regional politics. Of Kurdish bigotry against Jews, I have heard only secondhand.

"Is *Jew* the right word to use to describe Jewish people?" my translator asked me.

"Yes," I said. "Jews call themselves Jews. Why do you ask?"

"I want to make sure I'm not using an offensive word," he said, all but bristling with political correctness. "Some people use Jew as a bad word."

Who? I wanted to know. I never heard anyone in Kurdistan use "Jew" in the pejorative.

"Just some old people," he said.

"Never young people?" I asked.

"No, not at all," he said. "Young people have no reason to think Jews are bad people."

He could have been describing attitudes in the United States, which, after Israel, is probably the least anti-Semitic country in the world. In fact, young and old alike in Kurdistan both have reason to distrust those who think Jews are bad people: Saddam Hussein routinely libeled Iraq's Kurds as Zionist agents—which only encouraged them to think more highly of Zionism. Nor did that canard die with Saddam. "The Arabs call us a second Israel all the time," Peshmerga colonel Salahdin Ahmad Ameen told me. "They instigate their people and say we want to make a second Israel here in the middle of their area."

Arab nationalists and Islamists have been at war with the State of Israel since its founding, and at war with the presence of Jews in the Middle East before then, during the period of *aliya* in the late nineteenth and early twentieth centuries. In Iraq, they have been at war with the Kurds for almost as long, and for many of the same reasons. So it is quite natural that the Arab-Israeli conflict looks different from the vantage point of Kurdistan than from, say, Damascus or Cairo. Indeed, Kurds and Israelis have something very important in common—they are, and have long been, besieged minorities in the Middle East, and at war with the same people.

But the Kurds have something important in common with the Palestinians, too—statelessness. One might imagine, then, that Kurdish culture would be more or less equally divided on the matter of the Arab-Israeli conflict, or that individual Kurds might be conflicted internally, or even that Kurdish opinion would naturally side with fellow Muslims rather than with Jews. And indeed there are many Kurds who are conflicted when it comes to the Arab-Israeli dispute; you can find individuals who sympathize more with Israelis, and you can find, in principle, individuals who sympathize more with Palestinians. But every Kurd I have met supports the Israelis.

It is not hard to understand why: No one in Iraq can forget that Saddam Hussein's staunchest apologists in the Arab world were the Palestinians. In the run-up to the 1991 Gulf War, President George H.W. Bush assembled a coalition that included numerous Arab and Muslim countries, but Palestinian leader Yasser Arafat sided with Saddam Hussein. And the Kurds know that the primary weapon in the Palestinians' fight against Israel is terrorism—the one violent act Kurds in Iraq refused to commit, even when they were victims of genocide. Palestinian terrorism may be explained away, even celebrated, in most of the Arab world, but in Kurdistan it is offensive.

I asked Peshmerga colonel Mudhafer Hasan Rauf if the Kurdish army or regional government has any relations with the Israelis. "We live in the Middle East," he said. "The Arab countries don't want to have a relationship with Israel. Many Islamic groups inside the Arab world regard a relationship with Israel as something unholy. We believe in Islam, but if you compare us and the Arabs we think of Islam as a religion of brotherhood and peace. The Arab chauvinists wronged the religion's direction and made it another thing."

"We would like to have a relationship with Israel," Colonel Ameen said. "We have the same destiny. We are secretly their friends. We have many Jewish Kurds there now. They write articles for our magazines."

"The problems in the area are because of a misunderstanding of each other's religion," Colonel Rauf concurred. "Between the Jews and the Muslims and the Christians. I believe in the Koran. I know that Allah is the only God. God orders people and nations to have relationships with each other. But the fundamentalist Muslims don't think like this."

A member of the Kurdistan Regional Government explained that the Kurdish government is compelled to publicly split the difference between Arabs and Israelis because Baghdad demands it. "Right now we have to follow Baghdad on foreign policy. But at the same time, we say we have nothing to do with the Arab-Israeli conflict. If you told me you were Israeli I wouldn't have any problem with that. Most people here would rather meet an Israeli than an Arab. Arabs murdered our people." Thus is Kurdish affection for Israel an open secret.

Kurdistan Regional Government President Masoud Barzani said more or less the same thing on *al-Arabiya* earlier in the year: "The constitution does not give us the right to maintain ties with any country," he said. "Diplomatic relations are the exclusive authority of the federal state. If an Israeli embassy were opened in Baghdad, we would no doubt open an Israeli consulate in Erbil. If diplomatic relations are not established between the Iraqi and Israeli states, there will be no relations between the Kurdistan provinces and Israel. But, in fact, as I have said in the past, I do not consider relations with Israel to be a crime or something forbidden… I support the rights of the Palestinian people, but at the same time I am against driving Israel into the sea. This is impossible… this policy is wrong, illogical, and unreasonable. Why annihilate a people? I do not believe in annihilating the Israeli people."

I asked General Rostam why the Kurdistan Regional Government does not simply cooperate with Israel clandestinely, since both have few friends and many common enemies. "We don't have enough relations to be able to cooperate or discuss," he said. "But we expect to have that in the future. We will have relations and cooperation." It is unclear whether Rostam means he expects Baghdad to come around, which would mean that Erbil could cooperate openly, or if he expects Kurdistan to declare independence, in which case it will do whatever it wants. But one can make an educated guess.

If Kurdistan is a nation in all but name, Iraq is a nation in name only. The belief that northern Iraq is actually a nascent Kurdish state is so widespread, in fact, that the only people one meets there who think of Kurdistan as "Iraq" are from somewhere else.

The dream of an independent Kurdistan dates back to the dissolution of the Ottoman Empire at the end of World War I, when Arab and Turkish nationalism were born as well.

And nowhere do Kurds feel more distant from their fellow citizens than in Iraq. Old people's views of Baghdad are colored by memories of brutal oppression, genocide, and war, but young people have no memories of living under Saddam, no memories, in fact, of living among an Arab majority. Most do not even speak Arabic; English is now the second language taught in schools. The defiance of the Kurds may be quiet, but it is strong and hardening.

Kurdistan Regional Government officials, when they are speaking on the record, say they support federalism in Iraq and do not seek independence. Privately, though, they say they are simply stalling. Even that puts them out of step with most Kurdish citizens—but everyone knows they are not sincere. Maintaining nominal relations with Baghdad is a pragmatic, temporary, and likely prudent position for them to take.

Better, they think, to hold off on declaring independence until their nation is strong enough—or until that independence can be guaranteed by foreign powers.

"The Kurds have now stepped onto the stage of Middle Eastern history," Christopher Hitchens wrote, "and it will not be easy to push them off it again. You may easily murder a child, as the parties of god prove every single day, but you cannot make a living child grow smaller."

The United States might withdraw from Iraq before the fighting is finished. American public opinion may well demand it. But if that should happen, the war will simply rage on without the Americans, and the Iraqi government might not survive the post-withdrawal scramble for power from insurgents, militias, terrorists, and their foreign patrons. And if the government falls, there probably won't be another.

Iraq may end up resembling other regional weak-state anarchies, such as Somalia, which exist solely as geographic abstractions. Or it could go the way of Lebanon in the 1980s and divide into ethnic and sectarian cantons. Perhaps it will be invaded and picked apart by Turkey, Syria, and Iran, all of which have vital interests in who rules it and how. Iraq could even turn into a California-size Gaza, ruled by militants who wear black masks instead of neckties or keffiyehs.

But one certainty, at least, is that if Kurdistan declares independence and is not protected, one of two possible wars is likely to begin immediately. The first will involve Turkey; after all, few things are more undesirable to Ankara than Turkish Kurdistan violently attaching itself to Iraqi Kurdistan. The second will be about borders: Iraqi Kurdistan's southern borders are not yet demarcated. If Turkey doesn't invade, the Kurds will want to attach the Kurdish portions of Kirkuk Province, and possibly also Nineveh Province, to their new state.

Even if Kurdistan doesn't declare independence, there may still be more war on the way. "We believe if the Americans withdraw from this country there will be many more problems," Colonel Mudhafer said. "The Sunni and Shia want total control of Iraq. We are going to get involved in that. Iran is going to be involved in that. Turkey is going to be involved in that. Syria is going to be involved in that. The Sunni and Shia fighting in Baghdad will pull us in. We are going to be involved. Turkey and Iran will make problems for us. It is not going to be safe. All the American martyrs will have died for nothing, and there will be more problems in the future. Americans should build big bases here." For obvious reasons, the idea of the American military garrisoning its forces in Kurdistan is wildly popular among the Kurds.

It should be obvious by now why an American-guaranteed independent Kurdistan would benefit the Kurds of Iraq. But few Americans seem to realize that—after Kurdistan itself—no country would benefit more from this than the United States.

For starters, if the United States insists on cutting its losses in Iraq, it would be best to cut only its losses. And clearly, Kurdistan is not a loss. Indeed, it would be a waste and a disgrace if this eminently decent society is abandoned to war, terror, and mayhem. Certainly the Kurds would have to be crazy to trust, let alone work with, Americans ever again. Moreover, the complete and permanent liberation of Iraqi Kurdistan and its rehabilitation from mass grave to free state would surely be one of the great foreign policy successes in American history. It would rightly take its place alongside the democratic transformation of Nazi Germany and Imperial Japan, and the rescue of South Korea from the Stalinist starvation monarchy in Pyongyang. Losing Arab Iraq would be a partial loss, for sure. Yet no serious person says America unambiguously lost in Korea because only part of that country was saved.

Declaring partial victory isn't just a matter of pride. Al Qaeda has set up shop in Iraq and hopes to defeat America there, just as the Mujahadeen drove Soviet troops from Afghanistan in the 1980s. The Mujahadeen's defeat of the Soviets there has long been one of Al Qaeda's most effective ideological talking points and recruiting slogans, insisting (however wrongly) that the economic and military superpowers are in fact easily defeated facades. Osama Bin Laden insisted that America would be next, and millions of radical Islamists loved him for it. Many wished to help him and joined Al Qaeda.

And for a time, particularly in the weeks and months following September 11, it might have looked as though they were right. But they have been in decline ever since, unable to top their murder of three thousand civilians in New York and Washington. If they drive the American military out of Iraq, however, they will surely have topped themselves. They will no longer be in decline; they will, rather, be at a whole new peak. Bin Laden's old and dubious claim that America is "next" will look almost plausible, and he will have a new case in point when he says that America and the West are the "weak horse."

Now, a partial American victory in Iraq won't stop Al Qaeda from declaring its own partial victory. But a draw certainly beats a rout. If Al Qaeda manages to build a statelet in the Sunni Arab portion of Iraq—the only part of the country it could take over, even in theory—that statelet will exist right on the border of Kurdistan. How much better it would be if American troops were just minutes, and not time zones, away. Without a doubt, no better strategic location exists for American forces to disrupt or destroy Al Qaeda's new base—or, for that matter, to undertake future operations, should the need arise, in Iran or Syria.

As if more reason were needed, the odds of American soldiers facing a Kurdish insurgency are vanishingly close to zero. A few hundred troops are based there already, and not a single shot has been fired at them. In fact, Iraqi Kurdistan is where American soldiers go to relax on the weekend, a place where they can briefly take off their body armor. Nearby Arab countries—even those with friendly governments—are scarcely as welcoming: Most Kuwaitis, for example, don't mind hosting American troops, since it was America that liberated them from Saddam Hussein. But some Kuwaitis think it's time for American troops to go home now that Baghdad has a new government. American troops in Saudi Arabia also protected that country from an Iraqi invasion after Saddam swallowed Kuwait, but Osama Bin Laden cites that very protection as one of the grievances that triggered Al Qaeda's formation. Moving American troops to friendly Kurdish soil and away from hostile Arab soil will help put this long-standing problem to bed. American bases won't be needed in Saudi Arabia or Arab Iraq if they are re-located to Kurdistan.

And one thing is certain: The United States military needs bases it can use without walking into the minefield of regional politics. If radical regimes like those in Syria and Iran are more emboldened than ever in

the wake of recent American setbacks, new bases in Kurdistan may prove
their worth very quickly.

In the mid-1970s, the United States quietly armed and funded a Kurdish insurgency against Saddam Hussein. This was before America's
notorious yet temporary and cold strategic alliance with Iraq during that
country's war against the Islamic Republic of Iran.

Although the Iran-Iraq war broke out just after the 1979 revolution
that forced Shah Muhammad Reza Pahlavi into exile and brought Ayatollah Ruhollah Khomeini to power, hostilities had long been brewing:
The shah, an American client-state dictator, was no more enamored of
Saddam than the Islamic Republic would prove to be. So the United States
and the shah were all too happy to back Iraq's Kurds in their fight against
Baghdad. When the shah signed a peace treaty with Saddam, however,
American aid to the Kurds was cut off without warning. The Kurds were
left stranded, cruelly exposed to Saddam's murderous retaliation.

Between 150,000 and 300,000 Kurdish civilians were forced to flee to
Iran. Some sought asylum in the United States, but Washington refused
to grant them refugee status: "Covert action," said then-secretary of
state Henry Kissinger, "should not be confused with missionary work."
Indeed, Washington refused even to provide humanitarian assistance to
the people Congressman Otis Pike admitted were used as mere "tools."

Today, the Kurdistan Regional Government is bracing itself for
another round of more of the same. "As a military person, I am disturbed
by what is going on in America now," said General Karam. "They want to
withdraw their troops. We want the Americans to stay. Why are people
thinking like this? I want you, as a reporter, as a journalist, to get our
Kurdish voice to the American people so they know about Kurdish suffering in Iraq. We don't want the American army to leave this area. The
terrorists are excited about what is going on in the Congress."

True, the Kurds have a lot less to worry about than do most Arab
Iraqis. Those who work with the United States in the Iraqi government,
the Iraqi army, and the Iraqi police are already on the hit lists of numerous death squads, terrorist cells, and militias. Doctors, lawyers, writers,
journalists, and countless others have already been singled out for exter-

mination for choosing democracy and civil society over politics by bullets and car bombs. The terror that plagued Pol Pot's Cambodia in the 1970s and Algeria in the 1990s now stalks every decent person in the center and south of Iraq.

When American troops leave, they can't (or, more accurately, won't) bring all these people home with them. Fortunately, the Kurdish autonomous region already admits some of them as refugees. Iraqi Kurdistan is about twice the size of Switzerland: Not big enough to absorb every moderate person in Iraq who wants to live in a normal country, but with room enough to shelter those who are exposed by name. Securing Kurdistan with American forces, on the condition that Erbil admits a certain number of refugees, could demonstrate that the United States at least tries to keep its word—not only with its Kurdish allies, but with its Arab ones as well.

It may also serve as a lesson on what happens to those who don't cooperate with the United States. After all, the Sunni Triangle and Iraq's Shia south could have followed Kurdistan's lead; the choice was theirs alone to make. Sadly, both the innocent and the guilty alike will likely suffer the terrible consequences of that decision. Let Middle Easterners beyond Iraq's borders pay heed: If they wish to experience a less convulsive transition of power when their tyrants are deposed, Kurdistan will stand as the model to emulate. Arab Iraq will be the anti-model, the warning: If you prefer bullets to ballots, you will be left to your fate.

Fifteen million Kurds live in eastern Turkey, and the separatist war between the government and the PKK has raged there, at varying degrees of intensity, for decades. In the all but impassable mountains on Iraq's northeastern border with Turkey, the PKK has dug in its heels. Its guerillas launch hit-and-run-attacks against soldiers—and sometimes civilians—in Turkey, then retreat into their Iraqi valleys and caves. The Turkish military shells the redoubt from its side of the border, crosses the frontier in hot pursuit of the terrorists, and threatens to launch a major invasion if the Kurdistan Regional Government won't militarily shove the PKK back into Turkey.

Why won't the Kurds of Iraq evict the PKK? Why do they give Turkey an excuse to invade? Colonel Mudhafer was tired of that question. He impatiently unscrolled a map when I met with him in his office. "That's where we lived when we fought against Saddam Hussein. We chose that place for a reason. It was impossible for Saddam to flush us out there, and it's impossible for us to flush out the PKK now."

If only it were that simple. The Kurdistan Regional Government could work with the Turks to prevent this from exploding into a larger, international struggle. But the Kurds are torn. Kurds in every country have a terrible history of fractious, internecine war. After Saddam was ejected from Iraqi Kurdistan, and before he was removed from power in Baghdad, Iraq's Kurds fought a pointless civil war over resources and power. The results were devastating, but at least they learned an important lesson from the experience: When surrounded by enemies, don't go fighting each other.

As their inaction in dealing with the PKK shows, however, the Kurds may have learned that lesson too well. Like both Hamas in Gaza and Fatah in the West Bank, the PKK arguably harms Kurds and their interests far more than their enemies do: It brings increasingly destructive reprisals down on their heads and makes a diplomatic solution to their problems all but impossible.

"Fighting is not a solution," one Kurd told me. Nor do the Iraqi Kurds want to fight, he continued, because the reason for the PKK's terrorist activity is that the Kurdish people in Turkey don't have rights.

Apologists for Palestinian terror say much the same thing. The analysis is partly persuasive because it isn't entirely wrong. Kurds in Turkey really do have legitimate grievances, just as stateless Palestinians do. But those grievances can't be addressed by exploding bombs in Tel Aviv and Istanbul.

Iraq's Kurds know better, but they are locked in a holding pattern. They are pulled in one direction by their political morality, and in another by ethnic solidarity. They'll need help if they are to avoid an all-out war with Ankara.

And make no mistake: The Turks may say their problem is the PKK, but they have also threatened to launch a full-scale invasion of Iraqi Kurdistan should the people there dare to declare independence. After all,

Turkey fears a Turkish Kurdish unraveling of its own—not to mention an emboldened PKK—should an independent Kurdish state exist anywhere.

Certainly these are legitimate fears, not to be dismissed. But they don't change the fact that nations inconvenient to Turkey have a right to exist. The United Nations can't—or won't—act as an honest broker between the two sides: It's too weak and uninterested. But the United States can. Indeed, Americans are the only people in the world who consider both Turkey and Kurdistan allies. The Turkish-American alliance is strained, to be sure, but it is still an alliance. American soldiers could flush out Iraq's PKK terrorists on the condition that Turkey's relationship with its Kurdish minority is properly liberalized.

On the matter of Iran and Syria, however, the United States should make no such deals. Both these countries have restive Kurdish populations of their own—and both also sponsor insurgencies against the United States, Lebanon, Israel, and Iraq. Surely, they don't deserve insurance against insurrections of their own.

The Americans are learning that violent insurgencies against conventional state forces work. And the Iraqi insurgency's sponsors— Tehran and Damascus—are learning it, too.

The Kurds of Iran and Syria would like nothing more than American assistance in launching anti-regime insurgencies of their own. An American-guaranteed Kurdish state in Iraq would serve to make such insurgencies only more likely, even without American help. Of course, the United States should never sponsor, or threaten to sponsor, an insurgency that isn't morally just, or that's merely temporarily useful. The Kurds of Iraq were used this way once before, with terrible and shameful results. Yet a Kurdish insurgency in Iran and Syria could be both a useful weapon and a just cause, so long as the moral corruption from the likes of the PKK can be neutralized.

Some critics would no doubt accuse Americans of imperialism were they to support Kurdish resistance in these countries. Yet it can more plausibly be argued that such support demonstrates the very opposite. Take the case of Iran: Almost half the country isn't even Persian. That's because Iranian territory is, in fact, what remains of the Persian Empire, which includes not only Persia but also Kurdistan, Western Azerbaijan, Balochistan, and the Arab region of Khuzestan. If Palestinians, Tibetans, and Chechens (to name just three examples) should have the right to self-determination, so should Kurds, Azeris, Balochis, and Iranian Arabs. Sure, there may be a case for the preservation of what's left of the Persian Empire. But so long as Tehran is ruled by clerical tyrants, the case for American-supported Kurdish resistance may be the stronger one. Therefore a large presence of American troops between Turks and Kurds may be the only military force in the world that can prevent a bloodbath.

Terrorism works. Up to a point. That is the tragic lesson of recent history in the Middle East. The Palestinians aren't the only people in the world who seek a homeland of their own, but the squeaky wheel gets the grease. The Kurds do not receive billions of dollars in aid. The Kurds don't even receive much media attention. There are no rallies on Western campuses demanding their freedom, nor does the United Nations Security Council require that a state be created for them, although—unlike the Palestinians—they fought honorably against their enemies and have already carved out a functional de-facto state of their own. They are America's allies, but most Americans know nothing about them.

One could argue—and thank God the Kurds of Iraq don't—that waves of suicide bombers would surely attract world attention and garner sympathy for their cause. After all, the international community has long acted as an enabler of violent national liberation movements, not because terrorism is acceptable but because appeasing it is the path of least resistance for the conflict-averse. Meanwhile, liberal and moderate groups that seek the same goal but do not employ terrorism are shunted aside. The way of reason and morality, it would seem, is bound to go unrewarded.

If the Kurds of Iraq get their state before the terrorists in Turkey and Palestine get theirs, it will be the great reversal the Middle East desperately needs. Terrorism will have proven to be the less effective tactic. And who knows? Perhaps others who seek independence will take note. Palestinian terror groups like Hamas won't, of course, but Kurdish terrorists in Turkey just might. And the Kurds of Iran and Syria are even more likely to do so.

But the real moral case for an American-guaranteed Kurdistan is simpler than that: They've earned it. They fought alongside the United States in Iraq and built a decent society there. They don't start wars, they don't terrorize people, and they don't deserve to be bullied and lorded over by others. America owes them. Everyone owes them.

"I ask Americans not to leave us," Colonel Ameen said to me at the Ministry of Peshmerga. "From 1920 until now, we have been frustrated and disappointed by their pledges and promises. Eight times we have been disappointed. I ask the American people, do not make it nine."

Azure
Autumn 2007

Four

Where Kurdistan Meets the Red Zone

Just south of the Kurdish autonomous region in Iraq's northernmost provinces lies the violence-stricken city of Kirkuk, the bleeding edge of Iraq's "greater" Kurdistan, and the upper-most limit of the asymmetric battleground known as the Red Zone. Kirkuk is claimed and counterclaimed by Iraq's warring factions and is a lightning rod for foreign powers—namely Turkey—that fear a violent ethnic unraveling of their own that could be triggered by any change in Kirkuk's convulsive status quo.

I spent a day there with Member of Parliament and Peshmerga General "Mam" Rostam, Kirkuk's Chief of Police Major Sherzad, my colleague Patrick Lasswell, and our driver Hamid Shkak. You could stay a month in Kirkuk hunkered down in a compound or a house and not see or hear signs of war, but violence erupts somewhere in Kirkuk several times every day. If you go there with a Kurdish army general, as we did, and spend your day with the city's chief of police, as we also did, you will see violence or at least the aftermath of some violence. This isn't a maybe.

From the safety of Sulaymaniyah, Kirkuk looks like the mouth of Hell. It's outside the safe fortress of the Kurdistan mountains and down in the hot and violent plains. The city doesn't look much better up close, and you can feel the tension rise with the temperature in the car on the way down there.

Patrick and I woke Mam ("Uncle") Rostam first thing in the morning at his house in Sulaymaniyah. He told us we could follow him to Kirkuk, where he works every day, so we hired a world class driver to do the job.

Hamid Shkak spent years driving foreigners around war zones in south and central Iraq. He has more experience than anyone I know steering clear of improvised explosive devices (IEDs), barreling through ambush sites at 120 miles an hour, and veering around spontaneous firefights. He was perfect for the job, and we had little choice but to trust him and Mam Rostam with our lives.

Hamid told us more than I really wanted to know about the limits of armored cars in a war zone. (Our car did not even *have* any armor.) "B7 and B8 cars are armored in the factory," he said. "They put armor on top and below for IEDs. It provides a cage around the passengers. The whole car could explode, but you'll be safe inside the cage. The only problem is the cage might get locked and sealed from the heat. Also, if four bullets strike the same place, the fourth will go through the armor. The companies will not tell you this."

We followed Rostam's car through a Kurdish police checkpoint on our way outside Sulaymaniyah. He got big smiles and waves all around from the police as they recognized the famous general and member of parliament on his way to work in the morning

Rostam is a genuine bad ass, and he's either famous or infamous depending on whom you ask.

"He's a nutter!" said an academic friend of mine in Washington who knows him well.

"He's a show-off," said another friend in Erbil. "He took some journalists to see the oil fields in Kirkuk and purposely drove down a street where he knew they would be shot at with mortars. The journalists screamed and cowered in the back while Mam Rostam laughed in the front seat. Tell him to roll up his pants and show you the scars on his leg."

A few nights earlier Patrick and I had dinner at Judge Rizgar Mohammad Ameen's house. Rizgar was the first of many judges in Saddam Hussein's trial. He told us that when he flew with Mam Rostam in a plane from Sulaymaniyah to Baghdad, they were forced by the airport control tower to circle for an hour and twenty minutes before they received permission to land. "They knew Mam Rostam was on the plane," the judge joked. "They did not want him landing in their city."

Thirty minutes or so outside Sulaymaniyah the mountains began to get smaller. Jagged snow-capped peaks were replaced with surreal rugged hills.

We were on our way out of Kurdistan. I could see it. Hamid hurtled us down the road at 90 miles an hour. The air pressure and temperature climbed, along with the tension in the car, as the sky became hazy and dusty. Cows mooed and lumbered along the side of the road.

"Up ahead is a ridge," Hamid said, "above Cham Chamal. Saddam's Iraqi army was perched on that ridge over the city until 2003 when the Americans came. Near there was the last Iraqi army checkpoint before the first Peshmerga checkpoint."

You could have fooled me. Nothing indicated the area was recently a line of death imposed by the Baath. I saw only hills, trees, and fields of flowers where children ran and played. I hadn't yet seen the hell of Kirkuk, but I knew that what lay ahead beyond the control of the Kurdistan Regional Government would not look like this.

"In between that ridge and the city was a no-man's land," Hamid continued. "Cham Chamal belonged to Kirkuk Province before 2003. But it's entirely Kurdish, so it was added to Sulaymaniyah Province after the war."

When we entered territory that was recently controlled by Saddam Hussein, I felt we had crossed an invisible barrier or through a ripple in the dimension. Everything looked and felt heavier and much more unstable. Kurdistan was behind us. We were surrounded by eerie rolling plains, vanishingly empty of people. The horizon was swallowed up by the hills. I could no longer see the mountains of Kurdistan.

A Kurdish friend in Erbil emailed me that day: "Kirkuk lacks major services and is extremely ugly," he wrote. "The reason for that is that Saddam Hussein never considered it part of his country. He knew one day it will be taken from him. I will not go to Kirkuk, especially not to the Arab parts at night. It is *full* of terrorists."

There is no formal boundary, no road sign that says *Welcome to War*. There is no line, visible or otherwise, where you're safe on one side and in peril on the other. Rather, each mile on the hour-long drive from Sulaymaniyah to Kirkuk is incrementally more dangerous than the last. When you reach the Arab parts of Kirkuk—if you make it that far—you'll be in extreme and immediate danger if you're a Westerner.

War-blasted rubble lined the side of the road. The skeletal remains of shelled concrete houses could have been props in a World War II movie. Which wave of destruction wiped out this village, I couldn't say. It could have been Saddam's genocidal Anfal Campaign in the late 1980s, or any number of other violent catastrophes since.

Black smoke rose in a plume on the horizon. I've seen smoke plenty of times in the northern Kurdistan governates, and I never assume it's from anything other than a smoke stack at a cement factory, a pile of burning trash, or burn-off from a newly discovered oil well. This new plume of smoke was in the Red Zone, though, and it could be anything.

My ears popped from the increase in pressure as we finished our descent from the mountains of Kurdistan toward the vast muddy plains of Mesopotamia. The city appeared on the horizon. The road in was smooth at even 90 miles an hour, but we had left the fortress of the Kurdish autonomous region and entered the war.

"Kirkuk is the richest city in the world," Hamid said, "and also the poorest."

Indeed. Kirkuk, with all its resources, if properly managed, should be as prosperous as Kuwait and Dubai. Glittering skyscrapers should make up the city center. Instead it is a sprawling disaster ground down by decades of fascism and war.

We drove to, and through, the Kurdish side of the city, which is less dangerous than the Arab side. The Iraqi police at the checkpoints wore body armor, though, something I never once saw up north in the Kurdish autonomous region.

Kirkuk's cars are old and beat up. Its buildings are shabby. Houses are made of grey cinder blocks. Residents live behind walls. Dirt, pulverized rocks, and garbage are strewn where sidewalks should be. Every street is utterly bereft of beauty and grace. There are no trees to walk underneath, no social places to hang out in, no sights worth sighing at, and nothing to take pictures of. Kirkuk induces agoraphobia and a powerful urge to get inside and hunker down somewhere safe. It is the most broken city I have ever seen.

A few people have told me I'm brave because I went to Kirkuk. I appreciate what is meant as a compliment, but I don't feel brave. Old men live there. Young mothers with infants live there. They don't feel brave for being there, and when I see them walking the streets, I feel no braver. They go about their lives as best they can in this shattered environment, and somehow they manage.

The city is divided between Kurds, Turkmen, and Arabs. The Arab quarter is extraordinarily violent. The Turkmen and Kurdish areas are much less so, though random acts of terrorism and mass murder can erupt anywhere at any time.

People in areas where the Baath Arabs live help terrorists plant bombs, Hamid explained as he drove. The Baathists have no support whatsoever in Kurdish and Turkmen neighborhoods. Terrorists have a much harder time operating in those places, so they don't bother trying as often. The available methods of killing are limited without local logistic support. Everyone knows everyone else. Strangers are instantly suspected, often searched, and apprehended if necessary.

Kirkuk's terrorists are, my Kurdish hosts explained, mostly Baathists, not Islamists. Their racist ideology casts Kurds and Turkmen as the enemy. They're boxed in on all sides, though, and in their impotent rage murder fellow Arabs by the dozens and hundreds. They have, in effect, strapped suicide belts around their entire community while their more peaceful Kurdish and Turkmen neighbors shudder and fight to keep the Baath in its box.

Not every Arab in Iraq is a terrorist, of course. Arabs make up most of the *victims* of terrorism in Iraq, living, as they tragically do, in a place that has been poisoned, as the Lebanese-American scholar Fouad Ajami put it, by Saddam Hussein's legacy of iron and fire and bigotry.

Mam Rostam is a gruff man with a thin moustache and a thick forest of chest hair who does not wear a uniform. He has two official jobs; member of parliament and general in the Iraqi Kurdish Peshmerga. Unofficially, he describes his job in Kirkuk as "the wild card." He's a jack-of-all-trades, a Mr. Fix It. He's the guy you call when your forces are overwhelmed, when you don't know what to do, and when somebody needs a swift kick in the ass.

Patrick, Hamid, and I met up with him at a house that he keeps as a base in what was recently an Arab neighborhood, a part of the city that looks *much* better than most of the others. He sat in the sun in a plastic chair on the porch, chain smoking, slamming cups of Arabic coffee, and constantly answering his phone while Patrick and I interviewed him.

"This place, where we are now," he said, "was emptied of people, of residents. The government of Iraq brought Arab people to settle here. Those houses," he said as he gestured across the street, "were built for them. The majority are Kurds now. Many of the Arabs sold their houses and Kurds bought them."

Kirkuk is historically a Kurdish and Turkmen city, but Saddam Hussein tried to Arabize it. He forced out as many Kurds and Turkmen as he could and resettled the neighborhoods with Arabs from the south. He hoped to use the Arabization campaign to solve two of his ethnic and sectarian problems at once. Most of the Arabs he placed in Kirkuk were undesirable Shias from Karbala and Najaf he wished to be rid of. The city is now torn, then, along racial and sectarian lines. The legacy of Stalinist politics will take a long time to die.

"Can you explain the main reasons why Saddam Hussein changed the makeup of this city?" I said. "Was it for the resources, because of the Baath ideology, or both?"

I heard a loud thump somewhere off in the distance and wrote "possible explosion" in my notebook.

"It was for ethnic reasons," Rostam said. "The proof of this is that not only Kirkuk was involved. Sulaymaniyah and Erbil were also involved. They wanted to remove all the Kurds from everywhere in Iraq. They just destroyed whole villages and provinces and moved people into collective towns and concentration camps. Some of the Turkmen villages around here were demolished for the same reason. The point was to make it an Arab area, and no other. Saddam Hussein intended to be the leader of the Arab nation, the whole Arab world. He didn't want anyone other than Arabs to exist around him. That was his policy."

Saddam Hussein wasn't content merely to force Kurds and Turkmen out of their homes so he could move Arabs in. He also smashed their villages and neighborhoods with air strikes, artillery, chemical weapons, and napalm.

"The Arabs use Islam as a cover for their aims," Rostam said. I hear this time and again from Kurds in Iraq who are just as Islamic—but much more moderate and democratic—as the residents of Fallujah.

"The Ottomans didn't do this," Patrick said. "They didn't try to make everyone Turks."

"Even when people gave birth here it was forbidden to give them Kurdish names," Rostam said. "They were only allowed to give their children Arabic names. If a Kurd wanted to purchase real estate he had to have it purchased in an Arab's name. Otherwise he could not have it. During the Anfal operations they took young women and used them as sex slaves. Even when the Mongols invaded they didn't do this. They just don't like people who are not Arabs. Whoever is not an Arab is an enemy, and they use religion as an excuse for their evil goals."

"What exactly are the people who bomb the Arab parts of the city trying to do?" I said. "Why are Arabs bombing other Arabs?"

"Most, if not all, the terrorists are the old Baath Party members," Rostam said. "They changed their names and became an Islamist party, but they are the same guys. They have unified with some Sunnis around the southwest of Kirkuk because they are living in this area. They are making these attacks to make this democratic experiment after Saddam fail."

I had heard much the same from Kurdistan Regional Government officials in Sulaymaniyah. What frustrates them most about the U.S. military strategy is the American prioritization of Al Qaeda. The vast majority of the violence in this particular area, according to my Kurdish sources, is committed by Baathists and old Baathists under new names.

"So their goals are not local to Kirkuk," I said. "They are for the whole of Iraq."

"They want all of Iraq to fail," Rostam said. "They want the Americans to feel that they are not able to succeed in this area. They want to force the Americans to negotiate with the Baath Party."

"So they aren't necessarily targeting you or us," I said.

"They are targeting anyone just to achieve instability," Rostam said.

"So there's no plan other than violence," Patrick said.

"There is no plan," Rostam said. "Sometimes they bomb a kindergarten in their own neighborhood. Or a university. Or the civil office. Or a municipality. Or wherever. In these offices there are people of every nationality and religion. There is no way to say there are only Sunnis or whatever in these places. This is a multicultural country. Everyone is everywhere."

Most Americans have soured on the war and want out. I was once optimistic myself, long ago, but I no longer am.

"The central government intends to send an army here, about 6,000 soldiers," Rostam said. "Those 6,000 soldiers will be working in Kirkuk to achieve stability in this city. We're expecting after this, which is going to happen in a very short time, for the terrorism to be reduced 80 or 90 percent."

"This is what you hope or expect?" I said.

"This is what we expect," Rostam said.

American military vehicles rumbled past the front of the house with their guns up.

"This is a big city," he continued. "The police can't control it by themselves. The police are not so many in number and they're not that good in quality. There are some people who work with the terrorists who then apply to work with the police. So they go to the police stations, and instead of faithfully working with the police and the government they just transfer information—especially the sensitive information—to the terrorists. Nobody is managing this in some places. On the Kurdish side, we have taken care of it and we're stressing they do the same."

"If we go outside this city," I said, "are there more Arabs in the countryside in this province? Or are most of them in the city?"

"Around 100 years ago there were no Arabs around Kirkuk," he said. "There are a few villages southeast of Kirkuk where there are Arabs, but the majority inside and outside the city are Kurds. If you take a ride around outside the city of Kirkuk you will notice that the names of all the places are Kurdish. It has been a Kurdish area for a long time, from the beginning. Even *Kirkuk* is a Kurdish name. The name of the place where they found oil for the first name came from a kid who was accompanying his father in the area. He noticed something was coming out of the ground. He tried to figure out what it was and found fire. He said *Daddy, Daddy, fire, fire.* And that became its name. But the governments and regimes that came from the beginning time until now wanted to change the city and the names. Sometimes for sheep, sometimes for salt, but always because the area is important and they wanted to remove the Kurds from here.

"If there was a wise leader in this country," he continued, "it would be the greatest country in the world. Because of our natural fortunes, not only the oil but also the other things. But the government has spent all the fortune on weapons and bombs. I know some countries that don't have any resources at all, but when you go to the cities they look like crystals. You see now what Kirkuk looks like."

I asked about Kurdish and Turkmen relations.

"As Kurds we don't have any problem with the Turkmen," Rostam said. "If you come back I will show you some villages where the Turkmen live and you will see how much they like us."

As if on cue, two Turkmen came to the house and joined us on the front porch. They enthusiastically shook hands with Patrick and me, as if they were meeting rock stars. This kind of treatment always embarrasses me. Rostam kissed both of them on their cheeks.

After exchanging pleasantries with his guests, Rostam steered back to the subject. Neither objected to what he said next.

"The Turkish government created a party here that makes problems for us and the Turkmen," he said. "The Turkmen got their rights as soon as we started managing the area here, more than before when they were under the Baath Party authority. If Turkey is honest and is actually helping the Turkmen, why didn't they defend the Turkmen when the Baath Party demolished their villages? They are not interested in the Turkmen here. They are afraid of the Kurds living in Turkey. We have about 400,000 or 500,000 Turkmen here in Iraq. There are millions in Iran. Why doesn't Turkey defend *them*?"

"What does Turkey do here to cause problems?" I said.

"In general the Turkmen are on our side," Rostam said. The two Turkmen who sat on the porch nodded in agreement. "The problem with this Turkish party is that they demonstrate against everything we ask for.

They bring in Turkmen who are loyal to *them* and who don't agree with the Turkmen here."

The Iraqi Turkmen backed by Turkey insist Kirkuk is not a Kurdish-majority city and that it should not be formally attached to Iraqi Kurdistan and administered by the Kurdistan Regional Government. The residents of the city—Kurdish, Turkmen, and Arab—may be asked later this year in a referendum whether or not Kirkuk should be administered from Kurdistan's capital of Erbil or from Baghdad.

What Turkey really fears is that Kirkuk, which sits on top of as much of half the oil in Iraq, will be added to an independent and wealthy Kurdish state that will embolden the Kurds in Turkey to break from Ankara and attach themselves to Erbil and Kirkuk.

"In Hamburg, Germany, there was a restaurant opposite the Turkish Embassy," Rostam said. "That restaurant was named Kurdistan, and they flew the Kurdistan flag. The Turkish government sent a notification to the German government that said *If you don't remove that sign and that flag and that name from that restaurant, we are going to pull our embassy out of Germany.* And they did it. The Germans removed it. If the Turkish government was smart they would know Kurdish rights is a good thing for them. They have to know this can be useful and beneficial for them. But they aren't wise enough. They aren't smart enough to understand this."

"They're afraid of losing the Kurdish portion of Turkey," I said.

"When I was a member of the Kurdistan parliament, a guest from Turkey came," he said. "He said they don't have problems with the Arab nations, that only the Kurds are their enemies. I said to him, frankly, 'You're an idiot. If we become a country, what harm are we going to cause you?' All the Turkmen here are going to get good jobs. For sure. And they're going to get most of their rights, if not all. Okay? And the other thing, we're going to manage ourselves and sell our oil to Turkey. And they can set up some refineries that will be useful for them and for us. The Turkish government promised not to understand. They don't understand today, and they won't understand in the future."

Just then Kirkuk's chief of police arrived and introduced himself as Major Sherzad. He wore traditional Kurdish men's clothes and carried a squawking walkie-talkie. I asked if I could take and publish his picture.

Many Iraqi police officers don't want to be photographed for security reasons.

"Yes, take my picture," he said. "I am not afraid of terrorists."

Rostam invited all of us, including the major and the visiting Turkmen, into the house for lunch. We ate chicken, rice, cucumbers, tomatoes, and soup. Liquid yogurt was served in tall drinking glasses.

"I am sorry for the quality of food for my guests," Rostam said. "This is what we had in the house."

A portrait of a younger, less grizzled, Mam Rostam hung on the wall over the table.

"The American troops based here refuse to eat outside their compounds," Major Sherzad said, "unless they are invited to Mam Rostam's. Here they will eat."

Patrick and I were in good hands, then. Rostam may be a high value target for the Baathists and other troublemakers, but they have an exceptionally difficult time getting a bead on him.

After lunch we moved into the living room and sprawled on the couches. Piping hot tea with sugar was served.

Rostam upended his glass, poured the tea into the saucer, blew on it for two seconds, and downed it all in one gulp. Showoff. My glass was still too hot to even pick up.

Everyone but Patrick and me spoke to each other in Kurdish. I did not interrupt or ask for translation. Kirkuk's security elite need not revolve around me. Instead I watched the TV. The channel was turned to Kurdsat, a highly professional Kurdish satellite station out of Sulaymaniyah.

The news was on, and I saw pictures of the war in Iraq. It felt so strange to watch the war in Iraq on TV from inside Iraq. It felt the same as when I watch the war in Iraq on TV in my house in the U.S. The violence and mayhem on the screen had nothing to do with me. I was in Iraq's Red Zone, but sunlight slanted in through the windows. The grass outside was green. Flowers bloomed in the yard. Birds chirped. The neighborhood was peaceful and quiet.

Iraq is a big place, roughly the size of California. If a car bomb goes off in San Diego, it won't disturb people who live in San Francisco. They would learn about it from the television just as I watched scenes of carnage from safety at Mam Rostam's in Kirkuk. The war was far away. That's what I told myself, anyway. The war at least was around a couple of corners. It wasn't outside in the yard, at least not at that moment.

But then the chief's walkie-talkie urgently squawked and he had to answer. The room was silent as he listened grimly.

"There has been a shooting," he said. "Two men on a motorcycle rode down the street and fired a gun at people walking on the sidewalk. One of the men was apprehended. They are bringing him here."

For some reason I assumed when the chief said "here" he meant the police station. He did not. He meant Mam Rostam's.

"They will be here in two minutes," he said.

"Here?" I said. "They're bringing him *here*? To the house?"

"They will bring him here before taking him down to the station," the chief said. "I'll interrogate him here. I'm not going to feel good until I slap him."

An Iraqi police truck pulled up in front of the house and slammed on the brakes.

"Here he is," the chief said.

I grabbed my video camera, flipped the switch to *on*, and ran out the door.

Five Iraqi police officers pulled a young man in hand-cuffs out of the truck and presented him before the chief. Sherzad slapped the kid on the cheek, punched him above his ear, then slapped him again on the back of his head. The kid tried and failed to duck his head out of the way. Sherzad then grabbed the kid by his hair and yanked him up.

The police officers had brought the motorcycle to the house with them.

"Whose bike is this?" the chief said.

"Mine," the kid said.

Rostam inspected the bike.

"Who was with you?" Sherzad said.

"Ismail," the kid said, as though nothing more than a first name was necessary.

"Why were you shooting?" Sherzad said.

"I don't know," the kid said. "I swear I don't know."

"This one was riding, the other was shooting," said one of the officers.

"I will stick the bike up your ass if you don't get your friend here now!" Sherzad said.

"Okay, sir," the kid said.

"Call Ismail now," Sherzad said. "Open his cuffs," he then said to one of his officers.

"No," the officer said. "Let him call like that, the son of a dog."

"I will pull out your soul for shooting at people!" Sherzad said.

Just then the kid's cell phone rang. "It's Ismail," he said.

"Tell him to come here," Sherzad said.

"Hello," he said into the phone. "Ismail, come and turn yourself in. They have arrested me. Why should you shoot and I get arrested? Here is Kak Sherzad, speak to him."

The kid then handed the phone to chief Sherzad.

"Come to the police station now!" Sherzad said into the phone.

Rostam rifled through the kid's bag for his ID card.

"I was on my way home," he said to Rostam. "He said to give him a lift, so I did. We came out of the alley and he started shooting."

"Why?" Rostam said.

"He was messing around with his friends."

"Messing around by *shooting*?" Rostam said and smacked the kid upside the head.

"I am innocent," the kid said. "I swear, he did the shooting."

Chief Sherzad turned off the cell phone. "Ismail said he is coming now," he said.

"I swear in my whole life," the kid said, "I haven't done anything wrong. As God is my witness, I haven't even stepped on an ant."

Sherzad ignored him. "Bring the witnesses," he said to his officers, "so we can record their testimonies. And take him and throw him in a room."

The officers stuffed the kid, still cuffed, into the back seat of the truck and took him away.

"Kak Sherzad," Rostam said. "We arrested someone once...what was his name? Zula! He reminds me of Zula."

Sherzad laughed, as did his officers. Everyone remembered Zula, whoever he was.

Sherzad took a separate car to the station to interrogate the shooter—assuming the shooter actually turned himself in. Rostam, Patrick, Hamid, and I returned to the porch and sat again in our plastic chairs.

"Where were we?" Rostam said, as though nothing important had happened and we could return to our interview now. What else was there to talk about, though, aside from what we had just seen?

"You knew exactly how hard to hit him," Patrick said. "His face wasn't damaged. I would have broken his nose."

Rostam laughed. "He still seems like a teenager," he said. "We have to fight them a little bit, to teach them not to do dangerous things, just to stop them where they are. They need to be adjusted more than they need to be punished. So we're trying this stage with them first. If it doesn't work, then there is another issue."

"His teeth were still intact," Patrick said.

Rostam laughed again. "Those slaps were advice," he said. "Because the city is unstable, we have to be a little bit violent with people to stop them. Otherwise they won't be afraid to do many other evil actions. We have to be a little bit severe."

He was concerned that the U.S. would withdraw from Iraq before the fighting was finished.

"If America pulls out of Iraq, they will fail in Afghanistan," Rostam said.

Few in Congress seem to consider that the Taliban insurgency in Afghanistan might become much more severe if similar tactics are proven effective in Iraq.

"And they will fail with Iran," he continued. "They will fail everywhere with all Eastern countries. The war between America and the terrorists will move from Iraq and Afghanistan to America itself. Do you think America will do that? The terrorists gather their agents in Afghanistan and Iraq and fight the Americans here. If you pull back, the terrorists will follow you there. They will try, at least. Then Iran will be the power in the Middle East. Iran is the biggest supporter of terrorism. They support Hezbollah, Hamas, Islamic Jihad, and Ansar Al-Islam. You *know* what Iran will do with those elements if America goes away."

I seriously doubt Iran would actually nuke Israel, as many fear, if the regime acquires nuclear weapons—although I'll admit I'm a bit less certain of that than I am of, say, Britain and France not nuking Israel. The Iranian regime, most likely, wants an insurance policy against invasion and regime change. The ayatollahs will then be able to ramp up their imperial projects in Lebanon, Iraq, and the Gulf with impunity.

Most of the violent troublemakers in Kirkuk are Arabs. Most of the victims of violence are Arabs, as well. While sitting a kilometer or so from Kirkuk's Arab quarter I felt physically repulsed from the area. Going there without serious weapons and armor would be near-suicidal. What about average Arabs, though, in Kirkuk? They can't all support the Baathists and Islamists.

"What do the Arabs who live here think of you?" I said to Rostam. "And I mean the civilians, not the terrorist groups."

General Rostam is well-known in Iraq as a formidable military leader. His body is covered with battle scars, but he's damn near invincible. He's the *last* guy you want on your case if you work with Al Qaeda or the remnants of Saddam Hussein's Baath regime.

"I have good relations with them," Rostam said. "They come over to the house. Last time some of the Arab tribal leaders came over I took them to our headquarters in Sulaymaniyah. We enjoy our relations with them. We have no difficulties with them and no differences in our opinions."

Don't be surprised by his statement. Obviously he's exaggerating to an extent. *Somebody* in the Arab quarter doesn't agree with his opinions or there wouldn't be car bombs. But it's only logical that everyday Arabs in Kirkuk wish to see an end to the insurgency and the terror campaign. Why wouldn't they? Most of the bombs explode in their neighborhoods. Some of them kill hundreds of people. If the Kurds of Kirkuk live in fear of the bombs, the more-endangered Arabs must feel especially vulnerable and desperate for change.

That's what General David Petraeus is betting on, anyway.

April 2007

PART TWO

BAGHDAD

Five

Welcome to Baghdad

Never again will I complain about the inconvenience and discomfort of airports and civilian airline travel delays. You won't either if you hitch a ride with the United States Army from Kuwait to Baghdad in July during a war.

Military planes leave Kuwait every couple of hours for Baghdad International Airport (or BIAP, pronounced *BIE-op*), and the Army's media liaison in Kuwait dropped me off at the airfield so I could take a flight "up."

I waited twelve hours in a metal folding chair in a room full of soldiers who had priority over me for available seats.

At least I had a meal. On the other side of the base a McDonald's and Pizza Hut were tucked inside trailers supplied by Kellogg, Brown, and Root (KBR). KBR seems to have built almost everything here that the military uses for housing and storage. Out of plywood, plastic, and sheet metal, and for exorbitant fees, they construct instant yet aesthetically brutal outposts of America.

I ordered a pizza from a Pakistani employee at the Pizza Hut trailer and paid with American dollars. They don't use coins on the base. They don't even have coins on the base. If your food costs $5.75 and you pay with six dollars you'll get a small round cardboard disk or chit that says "25 cent gift certificate" on it as change.

All night I waited for a flight and was bumped again and again by soldiers on their way to places with names like War Eagle, Victory, and Fallujah. Finally my name was placed on a manifest, and I gathered around a gruff barking sergeant with everyone else.

"I want you all back here in 20 minutes," he bellowed. "First I want you all to go to the bathroom. Then I want to see you standing in front of me with a bottle of water."

Everyone lined up with their gear and marched single file into the plane. I was the only civilian on board, and I felt terribly awkward and out of place. I also strangely felt a little like I was in the army myself.

The plane was windowless and as loud as 100 lawn mowers. I crammed pink foam plugs into my ears, strapped on my body armor, and seat-belted myself into the side of the plane like everyone else.

"Hang your bags on the hooks!" barked the sergeant. "Hang them all the way up!"

"Don't fall asleep!" the soldier next to me shouted over the roar. "When you see the rest of us grab our helmets, put yours on, too! We'll be beginning the spiral dive into Baghdad!"

"To avoid flying low over hostiles?" I said.

"Something like that!" he shouted.

This was not United Airlines.

The funny thing about the steep corkscrew dive is that I couldn't feel it. Anyone who says that dive is scary, as some journalists do, is talking b.s. You can't feel the turn, nor are there any windows to see out of. It's impossible to tell, as a passenger, if the plane is flying level or banking. I'm not sure how the soldiers knew when to put on their helmets. Perhaps someone signaled. No one could hear anything over the clattering machine roar of the plane through their ear plugs. All the same, though, everyone put their helmets on at the same time, so I did, as well.

The landing was smooth and felt no different from an American Airlines touch down in Los Angeles. When the back of the plane opened up onto the tarmac, light like a hundred suns blinded my darkness-adjusted and dilated eyes. I could barely make out the hazy shape of military aircraft in front of us amidst the pure stunning brilliance.

We dismounted the plane and I stepped into blazing sunshine with my fingers over my eyes.

You know how it feels when you get into a black car on a hot afternoon in July? It's an inferno outside, but inside the car it's even hotter? That's how Iraq feels in the shade. Direct sunlight burns like a blowtorch. If you don't wear a helmet or soft cap the sun will cook your brain. You'll just get headaches at first, but then you'll end up in the hospital.

Getting from BIAP to the IZ (the International Zone, aka the Green Zone) is an adventure all by itself. First you haul your gear to a bus stop that feels like the inside of a broiler. Then you get on the bus and ride for 45 minutes to an army base. Then you get off that bus and wait an hour to catch another bus. Then you get off that bus and wait for an hour to catch yet another bus to yet *another* base. Then you wait in the sun yet again—and by this time you're totally fragged from the heat—and take another damn bus to a helipad.

All this takes hours. You will be no closer to the center of Baghdad than you were when you started, and there are no short cuts, not even for colonels.

Once you make your way to the helipad you will sit in the heat and wait. A Blackhawk will eventually pick your ass up, but if you're a civilian like me, you will fly last.

I waited for my helicopter flight with two other civilians—Willie from Texas and Larry from Florida.

Willie and Larry do construction work for private companies in harsh places like Iraq and Afghanistan. They are both small town individuals with Red State tastes and political views, yet they have a certain worldliness that surpasses that of most people I know. They've seen parts of the world that most in the well-traveled jet set would never dream of setting foot. They aren't allowed to tell me how much money they make, but I know it is many hundreds of thousands of dollars per year.

"You get hooked on making money," Willie said. "You think you can do it for one year or two, then quit, but it's like a drug. Or like when you get one tattoo—all of a sudden you want two tattoos. My wife keeps saying, come on, you can do it for just one more year."

"My wife would hate it if I was out here for years," I said.

"You get vacation," Larry said. "You get more vacation than French people. Twenty one days every four months. And you don't have to pay taxes if you take your vacation outside the U.S. Your wife can meet you in the Bahamas."

A KBR employee who coordinates the Blackhawk flights called our names on the manifest.

"Get your gear, let's go, let's go, let's go!"

Military rules require all Blackhawk passengers to wear long-sleeved shirts in case there's a fire on board. This was the first I'd heard of it, and I hadn't brought anything warm with me to Iraq. Why would I want to do that? It's 120 degrees.

Willie let me borrow an extra sweatshirt. I put that on along with my body armor, my helmet, and my sunglasses. Then I hauled my 100 pounds of gear out to the landing zone and lined up with a dozen or so soldiers. We were ordered to stand there in line while we cooked in the sun. We waited. And waited. And waited. My clothes were drenched as though I had fallen into a pool. That's the army for you. Comfort just isn't a factor. None of the soldiers complain about the heat. I didn't either, at least not in front of them.

Our Blackhawk helicopter was ready.

"Move out!" bellowed the KBR flight coordinator.

Larry, Willie, and I ran behind a line of soldiers toward the Blackhawk.

"Hold up!" said the coordinator.

The Blackhawk pilot lifted off without picking up anyone up.

"Man," said the coordinator as he shook his head. The roar of the chopper rotors quickly receded. "No one was mission critical so they didn't want to give anybody a ride. I do not know what to tell you."

"Fuck!" Willie screamed.

We hauled our gear back to the waiting area and sat. I drank a bottle of water in seconds. The whole thing disappeared inside me as though I hadn't drank anything.

"Last year in Afghanistan," Larry said, "I waited a week for a flight. Choppers flew in and out all day every day. I showed up on the LZ for every flight, had my gear ready, and kept getting bumped. A whole week, just to fly one from place to another. At least I was on the clock. We might be here a while."

We could have walked to the Green Zone in just a couple of hours, but we weren't allowed to.

And we did wait for a while. Not for a week, but for 12 hours. We kept getting bumped by new soldiers who showed up with places to go.

Another pilot took off without picking anyone up. I couldn't figure out why he even bothered to land. Dozens of people needed a ride. On another occasion Larry, Willie, and I made it all the way to the helicopter itself before we got kicked for some reason.

I tried to embrace the suck. Willie became increasingly agitated.

"Good thing I don't have my Glock with me!" he yelled when we got bumped the sixth time. "I ought to pour a bottle of water on that electrical board over there and short out the whole frigging place."

After the sun went down the air mercifully cooled to 100 degrees or so. That's a lovely temperature after 120, especially when the sun is no longer shining. Bats flew overhead from a reedy lake a few hundred yards away. There were no bugs. They can't survive the heat in July.

I watched helicopters fly over the city in the distance and launch burning white countermeasure flares to confuse surface-to-air heat-seeking missiles as the pilots flew over hostile parts of the city.

"I read on the Internet that the war costs 60 billion dollars a year," Larry said.

"Well, if it's on the Internet it *must* be true," I said jokingly.

A soldier heard me and swiveled his head.

"Did you just say that?" he said incredulously. "You're with the *media* and you just said that? Man, we ought to throw your ass right out of here."

I laughed, but he was barely just kidding.

Most Americans soldiers and officers I've met in Iraq are not hostile, however. Most ignore me unless I say hello to them first. A few say hello or good morning first and call me "sir." Some are eager to chat. Those who do talk seem to want to know where I'm from. Many of them are from Georgia and Texas.

Larry, Willie, and I finally got on a Blackhawk at two o'clock in the morning (oh-two-hundred in milspeak.) We strapped ourselves into our seats. There was little room on the floor for our gear, so I piled mine up in my lap.

Blackhawk helicopters don't have windows. The sides are open to the air. Fierce hot blasts of wind distorted the shape of my face as we flew fast and low over the rooftops and street lights and palm trees and backyards of the city.

Baghdad is gigantic and sprawling, and it looks much less ramshackle from the air than I expected. Neighborhoods the size of cities-within-a-city are home to millions of people all by themselves. The sheer enormity of the place puts the daily car bomb attacks into perspective. Over time the bombs and IEDs have ravaged the city, but the odds that anyone in particular will be hit by one are pretty small.

Just a few minutes after takeoff we landed on a runway in the Green Zone. The soldiers left in Humvees. Willie, Larry, and I were left at the airbase alone. My two traveling buddies had rides picking them up, but no one was waiting for me, nor would someone show up. I was expected to make my way to CPIC, the press credentialing center, but I didn't know how to do that at 2:30 in the morning. I did not have a phone number to call, nor were they any taxis or busses to take.

"You can sleep tonight at our compound," Larry said, "and find your way to the press office tomorrow when it opens."

I would have been in bad shape if I hadn't met these guys. Wandering around loose on my own in Baghdad, in the middle of the night, hauling 100 pounds of luggage, sleep-deprived, in extreme heat, and with nowhere to sleep, does not put me in my happy place, even if it is in the Green Zone.

A man named Mike Woodley showed up in an SUV to give Larry a ride. He said he could get me a bed at their compound before he realized I did not yet have a military-issued ID badge.

"They won't let you in," he said.

"Can't we just tell them I'm on my way to CPIC to pick up a badge?" I said.

"Doesn't matter," he said. "If you don't have it, the guards will not let you in."

"Is there a hotel I can check into?" I said. "What about the Al Rashid?"

"Al Rashid is in the Red Zone," he said. "And you can't get in there without a badge either."

Actually, the Red Zone is on the other side of the Al-Rashid's security wall, but Mike was right about the hotel guards not letting me in without a security badge. And I needed to get to the press office during business hours to get it.

"What should I do?" I said. I'd be damned if I was going to sleep on the sidewalk in Baghdad.

Mike pondered my options. And he came up with a great one.

"I can get into the embassy with my badge," he said, "and I can get you a temporary badge and a bed."

And that's exactly what he did. He secured me a temporary badge for the embassy annex, and he got me a bed with a pillow and fresh linens. I was one lucky bastard. The embassy annex, and the bed I got to sleep in, was at Saddam Hussein's grand downtown palace. The tyrant is dead. And I got to sleep at his house my first night in his capital. What better welcome to Baghdad could anyone possibly ask for?

July 2007

Six

In the Wake of the Surge

Eighty Second Airborne's Lieutenant William H. Lord prepared his company for a dismounted foot patrol in the Graya'at neighborhood of Northern Baghdad's predominantly Sunni Arab district of Adhamiyah.

"While we're out here saying hi to the locals and everyone seems to be getting along great," he said, "remember to keep up your military bearing. Someone could try to kill you at any moment."

I donned my helmet and vest, hopped into the backseat of a Humvee, and headed into the streets of the city with two dozen of the first infantry soldiers deployed to Iraq for the surge. The 82nd Airborne Division is famous for being ready to roll within 24 hours of call up, so they were sent first.

General David Petraeus' "surge" of additional counterinsurgency troops to Iraq started with these guys. Its progress here is therefore more measurable than it is anywhere else.

Darkness fell almost immediately after sunset. Microscopic dust particles hung in the air like a fog and trapped the day's savage heat in the atmosphere.

Our convoy of Humvees passed through a dense jungular grove of palm and deciduous trees between Forward Operating Base War Eagle and the market district of Graya'at. The drivers switched off their headlights so no one could see us coming. They drove using night vision goggles as eyes.

I sat in the back. Just to the right of my knees were the feet of the gunner. He stood in the middle of the Humvee and manned a machine gun in a turret sticking out of the top. I heard a loud clack-clack-clack sound as he swiveled it from side to side and pointed it into the trees as we approached the urban sector in their area of operations.

A car approached our Humvee with its lights on.

"I can't see, I can't see," said the driver. Bright lights will blind you if you're wearing night vision. "Flash him with the laser," he said to the gunner. "Flash him with the laser!"

A green laser beam shot out from the gunner's turret toward the windshield of the oncoming car. The headlights went out.

"What was that about?" I said.

"It's part of our rules of engagement," the driver said. "They all know that. The green laser is a warning, and it's a little bit scary because it looks like a weapon is being pointed at them."

We slowly rolled into the market area. Smiling children ran up to and alongside the convoy and excitedly waved hello. What was this? I had heard stories of Iraqi children throwing rocks at American soldiers, but the kids in this neighborhood treated the 82nd Airborne like a liberating army.

Graya'at' strangely does not look or feel like war zone. American soldiers just a few miles away are still engaged in almost daily firefights with insurgents and terrorists, but this part of the city has been cleared. Before the surge started, the neighborhood was much more dangerous than it is now.

"We were on base at Camp Taji [north of the city] and commuting to work," Major Jazdyk told me earlier. "The problem with that was that the only space we dominated was inside our Humvees. So we moved into the neighborhoods and live there now with the locals. We know them and they know us."

Lieutenant Lawrence Pitts elaborated. "We patrol the streets of this neighborhood 24/7," he said. "We knock on doors, ask people what they need help with. We really do what we can to help them out. We let them know that we're here to work with them to make their city safe in the hopes that they'll give us the intel we need on the bad guys. And it worked."

The area of Baghdad just to the south of us, Adhamiyah, is surrounded by a wall recently built by the Army. It is not like the wall that divides

Jerusalem from the West Bank. Pedestrians can cross it at will. Only the roads are blocked off. Vehicles are routed through two very strict checkpoints. Weapons transporters and car bombers can't get in or out.

The area inside the wall is mostly Sunni. The areas outside the wall are mostly Shia. Violence has been drastically reduced on both sides because Sunni militias—including Al Qaeda—are kept in, and Shia militias—including Moqtada al Sadr's Mahdi Army—are kept out.

Graya'at is the mixed Sunni-Shia neighborhood immediately to the north of that wall.

We stepped out of the Humvees. The soldiers set up a vehicle checkpoint on the far side of the market area. Curfew was going into effect. Anyone trying to drive into the area would be searched.

Dozens of Iraqi civilians milled about on the streets.

"Salam aleikum," the soldiers and I said as we walked past.

"Aleikum as salam," said each in return.

They really did seem happy to see us. It was not what I was expecting. Children ran up to me.

"Mister, mister, mister!" they said and pantomimed the snapping of photos. I lifted my camera to my face and they nodded excitedly.

A large group of men gathered around a juice vendor and greeted us warmly as we approached. A large man in a flowing dishdasha spoke English and, judging by the deference showed him by others, seemed to be a community leader of some sort.

Kids pulled on my shirt as Lieutenant Lord spoke to the group about a gas station the Army is helping set up in the neighborhood. Gasoline is more important to Iraqis than it is to even Americans. Baghdad is as much an automobile-based city as Los Angeles. They also need fuel for electric generators. Baghdad's electrical grid only supplies one hour of electricity every day. It is ancient, overloaded, in severe disrepair, and is sabotaged by insurgents. The outside temperature rarely drops below 100 degrees in the summer, even at night. Air conditioners aren't luxuries here. They are requirements. No gasoline? No air conditioner.

"The gas station on the corner should be opening soon," the lieutenant said to the group of men. "Do you think the prices are fair?"

The fat man understood the question. Our interpreter, a young woman from Beirut who calls herself "Shine," translated for everyone else.

Most gasoline in Iraq has to be purchased on the black market for four times the commercial and government rate partly because there is an acute lack of proper places to sell it. A new gas station in this country, then, is a big deal.

The men thought the price of gasoline at the station was reasonable. The conversation continued mundanely and I quickly grew bored.

Everybody was friendly. Nobody shot at us or even looked at us funny. Infrastructure problems, not security, were the biggest concerns at the moment. I felt more like I was in Kurdistan than in Baghdad.

It was an edgy "Kurdistan," though. Every now and then someone drove down the street in a vehicle. If any military-aged males (MAMs as the Army guys call them) were in the car, the soldiers stopped it and made everybody get out. The vehicle and the men were then searched.

"What are you guys doing out after curfew?" said Sergeant Lizanne to a group of young men.

"I'm sorry, sorry," one of them said.

"There is no *sorry*," said Sergeant Lizanne. "I don't give a shit. The curfew is at the same time every night. I don't want to have to start arresting you."

"Why are you stopping these guys," I said to Lieutenant Lord, "when there are so many other people milling around on the streets?"

"Because they're MAMs who are driving," he said. "We're going easy on everyone else. We've already oppressed these people enough. They have a night culture in the summer, so if they aren't military aged males driving cars we leave them alone. We were very heavy-handed in 2003. Now we're trying to move forward together. At least 90 percent of them are normal fun-loving people."

"Do they ever get pissed off when you search them?" I said.

"Not very often," he said. "They understand we're trying to protect them."

"This is not what I expected in Baghdad," I said.

"Most of what we're doing doesn't get reported in the media," he said. "We're not fighting a war here anymore, not in this area. We've moved way beyond that stage. We built a soccer field for the kids, bought all kinds of equipment, bought them school books and even chalk. Soon we're install-ing 1,500 solar street lamps so they have light at night and can take some of the load off the power grid. The media only covers the gruesome stuff."

Not everything they do is humanitarian work unless you consider counter-terrorism humanitarian work—and maybe you should. Hardly any Westerners associate personal security with human rights, but they might if they've been to Baghdad. Political rights don't mean very much if you have to barricade yourself in your house to stay clear of death squads and car bombs.

In another part of Graya'at is an area called the Fish Market. Gates were installed at each entrance so terrorists can't drive cars rigged with explosives inside. The people here are extraordinarily grateful for this. Businesses, not cars, are booming at the market now that residents feel safe and free enough to go out.

"The kids here do seem to like you," I said to Lieutenant Lord.

"They do," he said. "In Sadr City, though, they still throw rocks and flip us off."

The American military is staying out of Sadr City for now. The surge hasn't even begun there, and I don't know if it ever will.

I wandered over to the man selling juice at a stand. An American soldier bought a glass from him.

"Have you tried this juice?" the soldier said to me. "It's really good stuff. Here have a sip."

He handed me the glass. It was an excellent mixture of freshly squeezed orange juice and something else. Pineapple, I think.

The kids kept pulling my shirt.

"Mister, mister!" they said, still wanting me to take their picture.

I knew before I got there that not everyone in Baghdad was hostile, but I was still surprised to see that entire areas in the Red Zone are not hostile. Perhaps many of the people on the street were just pretending to like Americans and being friendly for form's sake, but at least no one was shooting at us. Something clearly had changed.

"When we first got here," one soldier said and laughed, "shit hit the fan."

Anything can happen in Baghdad, even so. The convulsive, violent, and overtly hostile Sadr City is only a few minutes drive to the southeast.

"Want to walk past your favorite house?" Lieutenant Lord said to Sergeant Lizanne.

"Let's do it," said Sergeant Lizanne.

"What's your favorite house?" I said.

"It's a house we walked past one night," said Sergeant Lizanne. "Some guys on the roof locked and loaded on us."

Gun shots rang out in the far distance. None of the Iraqis paid much attention, but the soldiers perked up and stiffened their posture like hunting dogs.

"Gun shots," Lieutenant Lord said to me.

"I heard," I said. "You going to do anything about it?"

"Nah," he said and shrugged. "They were far away and could be anything, even shots fired in the air at a wedding. A lot of these guys are stereotypical Arabs."

Gun shots in Baghdad are a part of the general ambience.

We walked on a narrow path along the Tigris River in darkness. "The house," as they called it, where someone locked and loaded a rifle, was a quarter mile or so up ahead.

"What will you do when you get to the house?" I asked Lieutenant Lord.

"We'll do a soft-knock," he said. "We're not going to be dicks about it."

I couldn't see well, but I could see. Much of Iraq is a desert, but the banks of the river look and feel almost like jungles in some places. The heat was unspeakable.

The soldiers had night vision goggles. They could see perfectly, if everything rendered in green and black counts as perfect. One let me borrow his for a few minutes. Putting on the goggles was like stepping into another dimension.

The soldiers' rifles are mounted with an infrared light that shoots a beam like a laser that's only visible to those wearing the goggles. It helps soldiers zero in on their target. It also lets them "point" at things in the terrain when they talk to each other. Some used the green beam to point out locations in the area the way a professor points at a chalk board with a stick.

I gave the soldier his night vision back and I returned to the dark world where Iraqis lived. We walked in silence. I could just barely make out the silhouettes of the soldiers' helmets and rifles and body armor in front of me.

"Where should I be when this goes down?" I quietly said to the lieutenant.

"Just stay next to me," he whispered back.

We stopped in front of the house. It was shrouded in total darkness on the bank of the river. I heard water gently lapping the shore and sticks softly snapping under soldiers' boots.

Lieutenant Lord quietly signaled for half his platoon to go around to the other side of the house. I scanned the roof looking for snipers or gunmen, but didn't see anyone. Still, I decided to step up to the outer wall of the house so no one could shoot me from the roof.

We waited in silence for ten minutes. The area was absolutely quiet and still. The curfew was in effect. We were away from the main market area where pedestrians were allowed out after dark.

Feeling more relaxed, I stepped away from the house and toward the river. Once again I checked the roof for snipers or gunmen. This time I saw the black outlines of two soldiers standing up there and motioning to us below. I didn't hear them go up there, and I doubt anyone inside did either.

It was time to walk around to the front door and go in. I stayed close to the lieutenant.

The other side of the house, the front side of the house, was lit by street lights. Children laughed and kicked around a soccer ball.

Gun shots rang out, closer this time.

"Take a knee," Lieutenant Lord said to one of his men.

The soldier got down on one padded knee and pointed his weapon down the street in the direction of the gunfire. The children kept playing soccer as though nothing had happened. I casually leaned against the wall of the house in case something nasty came down the street.

We heard no more shots. It could have been anything.

A soldier pushed open the gate leading into the front courtyard and moved up the stairs toward the door. I followed cautiously behind the lieutenant to make sure I wouldn't get hit if anything happened.

We found an open area in the house that hadn't yet been finished by the construction workers. I quietly took a few photographs and found that Lieutenant Lord had gotten far ahead of me. I found him speaking to an old man and his family. He, his military age son, his wife, and some children were herded into a single small room where everyone could be watched at the same time.

"We're not going to be dicks about it," he had said, and he lived up to his promise. The family was treated respectfully. The old woman blew kisses at us. The children smiled. This was not a raid.

I stepped into the room and noticed a picture of the moderate Shia cleric Ayatollah Sistani on the wall. It suddenly seemed unlikely that this family was hostile. I wouldn't have thought so if they had Mahdi Army leader Moqtada al Sadr's face on the wall. Still, someone in the house had locked and loaded on patrolling American soldiers.

The man handed Lieutenant Lord an AK-47. The lieutenant pulled out the magazine.

"Do you have any more guns?" he said. Our Lebanese interpreter translated.

"I have only one gun," he said. "I am an old man."

"I have a pistol," said the man's son.

"If you go down into Adhamiyah do you take your pistol with you?" the lieutenant said. This was a serious question. Adhamiyah is a Sunni-majority area, and this family is Shia.

"No," he said. "Of course not."

"Someone here locked and loaded on me when we did a foot patrol along the river a while ago," Lieutenant Lord said. "Who was it?"

The old man laughed. "It was me!" he said and laughed again. He couldn't stop laughing. He even seemed slightly relieved. "I thought it might have been insurgents! It was dark. I couldn't see who it was. All Americans are my sons."

Lieutenant Lord looked at him dubiously.

"What did you see?" he said. "Tell me the story of what you saw."

"I heard people walking," said the old man. "I did not see Americans.

I looked over the roof and heard who I guess was your interpreter speaking Arabic."

"Sergeant Miller," Lieutenant Lord said.

"Sir," Sergeant Miller said.

"Does that sound right to you?"

"Sounds right to me, LT," he said.

"If this is a nice neighborhood," Lieutenant Lord said, "why did you lock and load?"

"I thought maybe there were insurgents down there," the old man said.

"*Are* there insurgents here?"

"Maybe. I don't know. I don't think here, no."

"Then why lock and load?"

The old man mumbled something.

"Sergeant Miller, I want to separate the old man from his family," Lieutenant Lord said. "Keep an eye on them."

The lieutenant walked the old man to the roof. I followed.

"I'm very concerned about what you're telling me," he said. "Who is making you live in fear?"

"I'm a good guy," said the old man.

"I'm not saying you aren't," said the lieutenant. "I'm just very concerned that you are afraid of somebody here."

"It was the first time. It was dark. I couldn't see. I'm very sorry."

"It's okay," said the lieutenant. "You don't need to be sorry. You have the right to defend yourself and your home. Just be sure if you have to shoot someone that you know who you're shooting at. Thank you for your help, and I am sorry for waking you up."

The old man hugged the lieutenant and kissed him on his both cheeks.

The family waved goodbye.

"Ma Salema," I said and felt slightly guilty for being there.

We walked back to the Humvees.

"Do you believe him?" I said to the lieutenant.

"I do," he said. "I think he's a good guy. His story matched what happened."

"He didn't want to answer your question, though," I said, "about who he is afraid of."

There are terrible stories around here about the masked men of the death squads. Sometimes they break into people's houses and ask the children who they're afraid of. If they name the right enemy, they are spared. If they have the wrong answer—if they say they're afraid of the very men who have broken into the house—they and their families are killed. It's a wicked interrogation because it cannot be beaten—the children don't know which squad has broken into the house.

"He didn't want to say who he's afraid of *because* he's afraid," Lieutenant Lord said. "If the insurgents find out he gave information to us, or that he helped us, he's dead."

July 2007

Seven

Raid Night

W e want to use you as bait," Sergeant Eduardo Ojeda told me when I embedded with his unit on what was shaping up to be a night raid.

"Excellent," I said. "That's why I'm here."

This is what passes for black army humor in Baghdad.

"Our TST [time-sensitive target] blew up a vehicle and killed four soldiers and an interpreter in the next AO [area of operations]," he said. "He's somewhere in our AO now."

He could tell by the frozen and dubious look on my face that I wasn't sure I wanted to go.

"Don't worry," he said. "These guys hardly ever fight back when we nail them. And they *always* lose when they do. Come on. Let's go fuck 'em up."

I donned my armor and helmet, slung my Nikon around my neck, and jumped in the back of one of the Humvees.

"I need your full name and blood type," First Sergeant Ray Fisher said. "In case something happens."

"Stay close to me," said Sergeant Ojeda as he plugged his mouth with tobacco. "In the dark just look for the short guy. And call me Eddie."

The military intelligence officers at the War Eagle outpost knew the target was somewhere in their area, but they didn't know precisely where or how long he'd be there. My unit's job was to go out and patrol the neighborhood known as Tunis until they could pinpoint his location.

We drove in the dark. The soldiers used night vision goggles. I had to rely on my eyes.

"How long are you in Iraq, sir?" Sergeant Fisher asked me.

"As long as I feel like it," I said. "A month and a half maybe."

"You're lucky, sir" he said. "We're here for 18. I just got back from leave and missed the birth of my baby boy by two days. At least I got to see him."

"You don't have to call me sir," I said.

"Ok, sir," he said and laughed.

"What's the situation in Tunis?" I said.

"It's not too bad anymore," said Lieutenant Evan Wolf. "It's a rich neighborhood. Lots of educated and cultured people live there, doctors and lawyers, people like that. It was infested with Al Qaeda a while ago, so the neighborhood formed a protectionist militia. They set up road blocks, gates around the mosque, and they drove Al Qaeda out. But now the militia harasses and extorts the residents. They follow us from house to house and intimidate whoever we talk to."

Our convoy of Humvees crossed an overpass and stopped on a dark road among trees just outside the neighborhood. Half the soldiers dismounted the vehicles and set out to patrol the streets on foot. The other half stayed with the Humvees.

I joined those who went out on foot.

"How long will we be out?" I said to Eddie.

"Could be a while," he said and plugged his mouth with more smoke-less tobacco. "Last time we had a raid night we were we out for more than twelve hours." He spit on the sidewalk. "We chased a guy from house to house to house. Didn't catch him that night, but he was caught somewhere else three days later."

Baghdad gets only one hour of electricity each day. Some parts of the city at night are almost as dark as wilderness. The soldiers I was with could see everything, but I could barely see anything. It was next to impossible to tell who was who in the dark.

Eddie was obvious, though. He was the short guy. He told me to stay next to him, so I did.

It was a hundred degrees outside even at midnight. My shirt felt disgustingly hot and close under my body armor. I heard choppers roaming low in the sky over the city.

"This country would be beautiful if it were not for the invention of the plastic bag," somebody said. "That bag is everywhere—in the trees, stuck in barbed wire, on the sidewalks, crammed in every corner. Man, when this war is over I'm coming back to open a recycling factory. I'll be raking it in."

The area did appear to be nice, billowing plastic bags notwithstanding. I couldn't make out many details, but I could see the shapes of the houses. Most were considerably larger than the average American home.

"I suppose I shouldn't smoke," I said to Eddie.

"You got that right," Eddie said. "Snipers wearing night vision can see the tip of your cigarette from a mile away. They'll watch as you lift the cigarette to your mouth and figure out where your head is. Then BLAMMO. They're really good shots."

I kept the cigarettes in my pocket.

"We're being followed," said Sergeant Fisher.

Eddie, the rest of the soldiers, and I turned around.

"Four of 'em," Eddie said.

Without night vision I couldn't see anyone but the soldiers standing right next to me.

"Where are they?" I said.

"In the shadows two blocks behind us," Eddie said. "There weren't there a minute ago."

Curfew enforcement in Tunis was total. In some areas of Baghdad only military aged males driving cars are stopped after 10:00 p.m. Tunis, though, is infested with a militia. No one is allowed on the streets after dark except licensed generator repairmen.

We kept walking. Half the soldiers walked backwards so they could keep an eye on the men following us.

Some of the soldiers stood in the light from a storefront lit by generator power. I tried to stick to the shadows. Presumably the men following us were militia. If they didn't have night vision goggles—and they probably didn't—they wouldn't be able to see me any better than I could see them. And I couldn't see them.

"Five of 'em now," somebody said. "They're still following."

The soldiers took up positions, crouched on one knee, and pointed their rifles down the street in the direction of our stalkers. I ducked behind a wall separating two driveways and checked the windows and the roofs of the houses to make sure nobody saw me.

"Why don't you send the Humvees after them?" I said to the nearest soldier.

"We're sending them now," he said.

"More are out now," said another. "Seven or eight of them."

No one knew how many were coming out of their houses on side streets. No one knew who they were, either. They could be local militia. They could be the Al Qaeda cell the Army was hunting. Perhaps they found us before we found them. I no longer thought "we want to use you as bait" sounded funny.

An old man speaking on a cell phone walked toward us.

"Turn that phone off right now!" yelled one of the soldiers. "Right now!" He ran toward the man. "You turn it off *now!*" The man kept talking in Arabic.

Our interpreter told him to shut it off. He shut it off. Perhaps he was giving information to the militia. Perhaps he was talking to his wife. Nobody knew. Either way he was violating the curfew.

"Go home," somebody told him.

Suddenly the soldiers started walking back in the direction we came from—toward the men who were following us and who hid in the shadows.

"We're walking toward them?" I said to the soldier next to me. I still couldn't tell who was who. "Are they still there?" I still couldn't see them. I could hardly see anything.

"They're still there," he said. "We're pushing back to see what they do."

For the first time since I arrived in Iraq, I wished I had a weapon myself. When I couldn't stay in the shadows, I zigzagged at random to make myself a more difficult target.

Eddie sidled up beside me.

"Stay right next to me," he said. "If there's shooting I'll get you in the safest possible place." The safest possible place, I thought, was *outside* Iraq. "If it escalates..." He trailed off.

"If it escalates...what?" I said.

"We'll deal with it," he said.

"Four more to west," said a soldier. "They're running."

This time I could see them—four men rounding a corner and running away down a street. They were more afraid of us than we were of them.

"Does this kind of thing happen around here a lot?" I said to Eddie.

"It happens," he said.

The Humvees finally pulled up to the area where the hidden men lurked. When our foot patrol caught up with them I saw that two had been caught.

The rule for properly building suspense in horror movies is based on how fear works in real life. Faceless and invisible enemies are scary. Real human beings with faces and fears of their own aren't so much.

Our two busted stalkers looked a lot less intimidating in person. They seemed rather pathetic, actually, and they were not armed.

"My air conditioner's broken," said the first through our interpreter. "I was just going to a friend's house to get another one. I can show you the broken one now."

I've been on patrol with soldiers after curfew a number of times. Most Iraqis out after dark don't appear to be threatening or up to no good. This guy stood out, though. I didn't believe he was only trying to borrow an air conditioner. He was twitchy and much more nervous than anyone I had seen questioned before.

And anyway, aside from the twitchiness, why was he following soldiers around in the dark?

Our Iraqi interpreter wore a mask over his face to avoid being recognized by the locals. He checked the suspect's identification.

The man did live in the area. ID cards, though, don't say "militia man" on them.

Two soldiers guarded the second suspect while the rest of us walked to the first suspect's house and knocked hard on the door.

No one came to the door. A soldier banged on the door again with his fist. "Open up!" he yelled.

The residents of the house finally stirred. Faint shadows darkened the windows.

"There are lots of people in there," someone said.

I stepped back, having no idea what to expect.

A large man wearing shorts and no shirt opened the door. An old man in a dishdasha stood behind him. They weren't armed and didn't seem threatening.

"Salam aleikum," said the shirtless man.

"Can we come in?" said the soldier who knocked.

The shirtless beckoned us in, and so we went in.

Soldiers dispersed throughout the house and rounded up everyone— four men, three women, and two children—into one room. Everybody, soldiers and Iraqis alike, were mellow and cool. No one seemed to be angry at anyone. Our shirtless host seemed to be the head of the household, so the soldiers spoke mainly to him instead of to the suspect they had captured outside.

"You're right, he was bad," the man said.

"The curfew is for your safety," said a soldier through the interpreter. "We're hot, too, okay? Finding an air conditioner isn't a good enough reason to go outside after dark."

"Sorry," the man said. "Please forgive us. Anything you want, we are with you."

"There are bad guys out after dark."

"I understand, very sorry."

We said good night and left the house. There was no interrogation. All the soldiers did was drop the guy off at home to get him off the street. Whether he really was trying to borrow an air conditioner, or whether he belonged to the neighborhood militia, I'll never know.

The second man was still being detained.

"I work at the mosque," he said through our masked interpreter. "I work there at night. I was just out getting some dinner."

We had walked past the neighborhood mosque earlier and there were no lights on inside. It didn't look like anyone worked there at night, at least not in any normal capacity.

All of us walked toward the mosque.

"What are you going to do with him?" I said to Eddie.

"We're going to take him to the mosque and see if he really works there," he said.

When we arrived outside the mosque, some of the soldiers squatted in driveways across the street and scanned the roof. I joined them as Eddie and the others took the suspect to the gate.

"There are four men on the roof," a soldier said. "You can't see them anymore. They just ducked away as we got here." I crouched near the ground. "They have a little bunker up there. You can't see it from here, but it has sand bags and sniper netting around it."

"What are you going to do?" I said.

"Nothing," he said. "It's a mosque."

"They're violating curfew," I said, "and stalking us in the dark from a militarized mosque. And you aren't going to do anything?"

"Our rules of engagement say we can't interfere in any way with a mosque unless they're shooting at us," he said.

So we dropped off our stalker with his "co-workers" and left.

We walked the streets of Baghdad at midnight while waiting for the call from intelligence officers back at the outpost. If they could determine which exact house the Al Qaeda target was in, the soldiers I patrolled with would be first on the scene. All he had to do was make one more call on his cell phone and he'd be located. Then he'd be quietly surrounded by two dozen infantry soldiers, along with myself with my note pad and camera, before he had any idea what was happening.

In the meantime we chased shadows and silhouettes and dark vehicles on blacked out streets without any headlights.

We chased a car so far from our starting point I wondered if anybody still even knew where we were. We sure as hell weren't in Tunis anymore. Eventually the driver pulled over and stopped. I got out of my Humvee and followed Eddie to the driver's side door. Vicious dogs snarled at us from behind a gate.

Three men were inside. All were told to get out of the vehicle and were questioned and patted down.

It's possible the three young men in the car didn't even know we were trying to catch them. Humvees are driven in Iraq in the dark without headlights. They're almost invisible. And they don't go very fast.

None of the young men were armed. Soldiers searched the vehicle, didn't find anything, and sent everyone home.

This is what it is like most nights during counter-insurgency warfare.

"It's like we're Baghdad P.D.," as one soldier put it. It's not open war and constant explosions and bang-bang. Much of it entails patient police work and the chasing of ghosts.

We never did get the call from the intelligence officers. The insurgent commander, whose name I know but was asked not to reveal, was almost, but not quite, captured that night. His capture would have saved lives, and it would have been something to see.

This isn't the movies, however. The Iraqi counterinsurgency would be a hard war to film accurately. Most of the time it's so quiet. But it's the quiet of an Alfred Hitchcock movie, not of rural Middle America. Explosions, mortars, bullets, rockets...these things can come flying at you at any time.

We drove. I watched the dark city through bullet-proof glass. Most homes were blacked out. Very few families stayed up late and ran their generators past midnight. Most Iraqis—and I knew this even though I could not see it—slept on the roofs of their houses where it's cooler at night.

The dark shapes of palm trees somehow looked menacing and benign at the same time. They looked slightly more ominous we drove into a dense grove bathed in an eerie glow from starlight shining through dust.

Anything could have been waiting for us on the road up ahead. Anyone could have been watching and waiting, perhaps even with the same night vision goggles the soldiers themselves wore.

Suddenly the trees were gone and the sky opened up. I couldn't see anything.

"We're in the slum now," Lieutenant Evan Wolf said. "It's a nasty one, too. Some houses are literally made out of cardboard. I would kill myself before I lived here."

I have no idea how these people survive without air conditioning and clean water. The environment here in the summer is unrelentingly hostile.

"How did you get into this job?" Eddie said.

"I needed to get out of the office," I said.

"You're way out now," Eddie said and laughed.

"I can't wait to get *in* the office," Lieutenant Wolf said.

"Do you like your job?" Eddie said.

"I love my job," I said. "It's the best I've ever had. Do you like yours?"

"I wouldn't say it's the worst decision I ever made," he said. "It's hard for soldiers. We all want to go home, of course. But we also want to stay and make sure our buddies did not die for nothing."

There were no street lights. All I could see was absolute darkness and the faint outlines of hovels against a backdrop of stars.

"It's always interesting, though," Eddie said. "No one gets to see places like this. Only Iraqis. And you. And us."

July 2007

Eight

An Iraqi Interpreter's Story

"Please, sir, can you help me? I must work with Americans because my psychology is demolished by Saddam Hussein. Not just me. All Iraqis. Psychological demolition." — Iraqi woman to reporter George Packer.

Iraqis who are not American citizens and who work as interpreters for the American military cover their faces when they work outside the wire. Terrorists and militiamen accuse of them of collaboration. They and their families are targetted for destruction.

Here is the story of one such interpreter who works with the 82nd Airborne Division in Baghdad. He calls himself "Hammer."

MJT: Why do you work with Americans?

Hammer: When I was 14 years old all I liked was American cars and American movies. America was my dream. It was a dream come true when the United States Army came to Iraq. It was a nightmare in 1991 when they left again.

Maybe someone will think I'm lying, that I'm just saying this. If my friends say something like Russian weapons are the best or German cars are the best I say, no, Americans are. Everyone who knows me knows this about me.

If anyone says Arabs will win against the U.S. they are wrong. The leaders don't want to be like Saddam. But if the U.S. leaves Iraq it will be a big failure, especially for me. I don't want to see this. Never.

MJT: Do you like working with Americans?

Hammer: A lot. Especially when I go outside the wire. I feel like a stranger here. When I go back inside, I'm home. I have no friends outside, only family. When I go home I stay in my house. I don't go out on the streets.

MJT: Why don't you have any friends?

Hammer: I don't feel like I belong to this society. They think like each other, but they don't think like me. I can't continue with them.

I like to know something about everything, to learn as much as I can. In Iraq if you know too much they will laugh and call you a liar.

When I was 20 I liked American music. They don't like it. (Laughs.) I don't like Saddam. I hate his family.

MJT: Why do you have to cover your face?

Hammer: To protect my family. My family lives in Iraq. If they go to the U.S. I won't have to do it. But I don't want anyone to know me, to follow me and see where I live and kill my wife and son.

MJT: How did you feel when the U.S. invaded Iraq?

Hammer: Happy. It was like I was living in a jail and somebody set me free. I don't want Saddam ruling me. Never. I was just waiting and waiting for this moment.

MJT: What do you think about the possibility of Americans leaving?

Hammer: It is like a bad dream. Very bad dream. A nightmare. Worse than that. Like sending me back to jail. Like they set me free for four years then sent me back to jail or gave me a death sentence.

MJT: Tell us about living under Saddam Hussein.

Hammer: It was crazy life, like feeling safe inside a jail. If they sent you to an actual jail nothing changed. They arrested everyone, literally everyone, for no reason and sent them to jail for two weeks just so they could see the jail.

I went there three times, the first time because I worked for a movie company. They sent all of us to jail. It had nothing to do with me.

I was given a three year sentence. My family has money, so I paid the judge 50,000 dollars. I gave it directly to the judge, plus four new tires for his car and a satellite TV. He gave me a three month sentence instead of a three year sentence. He scratched "3 years" off my sentence and wrote "3 months" in by hand.

They sent me to Abu Ghraib. I saw so many things. If you want me to talk about that I would need a whole newspaper.

MJT: Tell us a little about Abu Ghraib.

Hammer: On the bus to the jail I didn't have handcuffs. I asked why. The guard said "Look behind you."

The first guy behind me got a 600 year sentence.

The next guy got six hanging sentences.

The third guy was sentenced to be thrown blindfolded out of a second story window. Twice.

Another guy fucked his mother and sisters three times. He was freed on Saddam's birthday.

Another guy had his hand cut off.

There was this last guy. He went to the market with his wife. She waited in the car when he went to buy something. When he came back to the car his wife was screaming. Two guys were in the car with her. One held her arms and the other was raping her. He grabbed his AK-47 and chased them away. They ran to their car and he shot them. Their car blew up. They were *mukhabarat* [Saddam's secret police]. He got a death sentence. On his second day in Abu Ghraib they killed him and sent the mother- and sister-fucker free for the fourth time.

The guards who ran Abu Ghraib sold hallucinagenic drugs to prisoners for money. They forced me to take them.

You need protection in there. You find someone and give him drugs and cigarettes. You pay off the guards to just punch you in the face or move you to a different cell instead of kill you.

I was freed 26 days after I arrived, on Saddam's birthday, before I finished the three months.

I can't live with this nightmare anymore.

MJT: What's it like out there now for the average Iraqi?

Hammer: If you give average Iraqis electricity right now it will be enough. This is the most important thing. Give them power for seven days in a row and there will be no fights.

After the U.S. came and Saddam fell they earned 3 dollars a month. Now they earn between 100 and 700 dollars a month.

Giving them electricity would reduce violence. If you don't believe me, ask yourself what would happen to this army base if the power was cut off forever and the soldiers had to spend the rest of their lives in Iraq. Do think think these soldiers would still behave normally?

Iraqis are paid to set up IEDs. They do it so they can buy gas for their generator and cool off their house or leave the country. Their hands do this, not their minds.

TV is the most interesting thing to Iraqis. They learn everything from the TV. Right now they only have one hour of electricity every day. Do you know what they watch? Al Jazeera. Al Jazeera pushes them to fight. If they got TV the whole day they would watch many things. Their minds would be influenced by something other than terrorist propaganda.

Right now they have no electricity. They have no dreams. Nothing. And Saddam messed with their minds. For more than 30 years he poisoned their minds.

You can't understand Iraqis because you can't get inside their mind. When you get inside their mind…it is a crazy mind.

MJT: Why is Iraq such a mess? Is it the Americans' fault?

Hammer: No. You can't blame it on the Americans. Iraqis are number one at fault for this mess. They are greedy and will do anything for money. They are like people who were in jail for 30 years, were suddenly set free, were given money, then had their money taken away. What will they do next? They will kill for money. They are selfish.

They got selfish from Saddam. Iraqi people used to be different. I am the same person I always was, but most Iraqi people are different now. They feel that no one will help them so they help themselves.

MJT: Is there a solution to the problems in this country?

Hammer: Nuke Iraq.

MJT: Be serious.

Hammer: I am serious. If you screen all Iraqis, 5 million of them would be good people. Clear them out, then kill everyone else. Syria and Iran would surrender. [Laughs.]

Right now they see 100 corpses every day in the streets. It's not okay to kill the bad people who do that?

Ok, if you want a serious solution try this: Charge money to the families of insurgents. Fine them huge amounts of money if anyone in their family is captured or killed and identified as an insurgent. Make them pay. You can put it into law. Within one week they won't do anything wrong because they want money. Their familes will make them stop.

The militias pay them 100 dollars to set up IEDs. Fine them thousands of dollars if they are caught and their families will make them stop. Give them that law. Go ahead. Try it.

MJT: What will happen if the Americans leave next year?

Hammer: Rivers of blood everywhere. Syria and Iran will take pieces of Iraq. Anti-American governments will laugh. You will be a joke of a country that no one will take seriously.

I will kill myself if it happens. I am completely serious. The militias will hunt down and kill me and my family. I will beat them to it by killing myself.

I worked for the U.S. government for four years. Everyone who works as an interpreter for four years and gets a signature from a general or a senator gets a Green Card. My hope is to get this somehow. I will do anything for this.

I am doing this for my son. Everything for my son. I don't want my son living here getting into religion and militias and Al Qaeda. I want my son to be free, to have a girlfriend, to get married, and to be a good citizen.

MJT: How often do you get to see him?

Hammer: Two days a month. Sometimes two days every two months. I leave this base without my uniform and dress like them, wearing filthy jeans and a t-shirt, so they don't know I work here. Then I drive to my house and hug my wife and son.

MJT: What does he want to do when he grows up?

Hammer: He wants to be an American soldier. He has his chair in his room with an American flag on it. Has a toy M-4. He has a little uniform that I got at the P/X.

When he sees Saddam he curses Saddam. I never told him to do that. He does this himself. When he holds his toy gun he says he will kill the insurgents. He wants to go to Disneyland. His hero is Arnold Schwartznegger—not the Terminator, but Arnold Schwartznegger. He has all his movies.

Bill Gates is my hero. [Laughs.]

MJT: Do you ever get death threats?

Hammer: Seven times. Once I had to sell my car because of it. Some come from Shia militias, others from Al Qaeda. I had two IEDs in front of my car and was shot at with an RPG when I was working in Kirkuk for Bechtel at an oil plant.

MJT: Why is there peace in Kurdistan but not in this part of Iraq?

Hammer: The Kurds got rid of Saddam earlier. They fought against Saddam just like the Shia fought against Saddam, but the Kurds won their war and the Shia lost. In 1991 the Americans were heroes to the Kurds, but they disappointed the Shia and left them to Saddam. They were not reliable. So the next time, in 2003, some Shia thought they should get help from Iran. They know Iran is not going anywhere. Iran is a more reliable ally than the Americans.

The Shia never forgot being abandoned by the Americans. They talk about this all the time, still. They know the U.S. will leave Iraq and they will face Al Qaeda alone.

Shia people here are very simple, very easy. They are easy to control. They don't need too many things. Just electricity, rights, a decent life, a good opportunity to get a job.

MJT: Would it be possible to flip the Shia supporters of Moqtada al Sadr into supporting Americans instead?

Hammer: Yeah, it's easy. Just give them those things. You will push away all the reasons for this trouble. Sixteen percent of the Shia support Moqtada al Sadr. They have no education. They don't know what to do. I know how these people think. Give them a good reason to join your side and they will do it.

MJT: What is the worst thing you have ever seen in this country?

Hammer: 60 guys from Al Qaeda kidnapped an interpreter's sister. She had a baby boy, six months old. They raped her, all 60 guys. Then they cut her to pieces and threw her in the river. They left the six month baby boy to sleep in her blood.

We found him on a big farm south of Baghdad. All that was left was his legs and his shoes. The dogs ate him.

I don't want this for my family.

These people are like animals who came from another planet.

MJT: What is the most beautiful thing you have ever seen in this country?

Hammer: In all my life? When I was seven years old I heard the sound of wild pigeons every morning. Then something happened and I never heard them again. Then, on the morning of the U.S. invasion of Iraq, I heard the pigeons again.

Really, I am not joking. I can see you don't believe me, but I am not faking it.

MJT: What is the most important thing about Iraq that the Americans don't understand?

Hammer: Don't just open the jail after 25 years. Let people out step by step. Iraqis need rehab. Give them instant direct freedom and they are going to go crazy. That's what the U.S. did.

MJT: Will the Americans win this war?

Hammer: I hope it's going to happen. But it's not going to happen if the Americans keep doing what they are doing unless they are a lot more patient.

MJT: Anything you want to say that I didn't ask you about?

Hammer: Because of the few bad Iraqis who work as interpreters for the U.S., no one trusts us. But if you give me a gun I will fight harder than the Americans. You can go home. I can't. I have to live in this country. If the Americans don't give a Green Card to me and my family, I have to stay in this prison.

At Camp Taji the First Cavalry Division thinks interpreters are the enemy. They decided that interpreters who aren't American citizens have to take the American flag off their uniforms before they are allowed to enter the dining facility.

I cried that day.

I wasn't supposed to, but I complained. I said, "It's okay for me to die outside wearing the American flag, but I can't eat wearing the American flag with Americans?" That was the worst day of my life with the American army.

I'll tell you what I tell my family. If I die here, wrap me in the American flag when you bury me. I don't want to be wrapped in the flag of Iraq.

August 2007

Nine

Balance of Terror

The American soldier sitting next to me flipped open his Zippo lighter and gloomily lit a cigarette. "Do you know why this base isn't attacked by insurgents?" he said.

I assumed it was because his area of operations in Graya'at, in northern Baghdad out of the War Eagle outpost, had been cleared. Many American military bases and outposts in Iraq are attacked by Al Qaeda terrorists and Mahdi Army militiamen with mortars and rockets, but War Eagle was quiet and had not been bombarded for months.

"We aren't being attacked because the Mahdi Army is in the next building," he said. "They don't want to hit their own people."

American soldiers from the 82nd Airborne Division shared the small outpost with Iraqi army soldiers who lived, worked, and slept in the building next door.

"The Iraqi army unit here has been infiltrated?" I said.

He nodded grimly and took a pull from his cigarette.

"That's a bad reason for us not to be mortared," I said.

"Yeah," he said and laughed. It was obvious, though, that he did not think it was funny.

"How do you know this?" I said.

"Heard it from intel," he said. "Getting information out of them is like pulling teeth, but sometimes they say stuff."

I went inside the Tactical Operations Center and spoke to the public affairs officer. "What can I help you with, Mike?" he said.

"I want an on-the-record interview with military intelligence," I said.

"Why?" he said.

I told him what I had heard. "I can print rumor or fact," I said.

He got me the interview.

Master Sergeant Jeffrey K. Tyler met with me privately.

"It's true," he said. "Many of the Iraqi army soldiers here are supporters of JAM." JAM is military shorthand for *Jaysh al Mahdi*, Moqtada al Sadr's radical Shia Mahdi Army militia. "They aren't in JAM cells necessarily, but they are sympathizers. They may let JAM guys through checkpoints, for example. They aren't out kidnapping Sunnis or anything like that. They are sympathizers, not direct actors. Almost all the Iraqi army soldiers here are Shias."

"Is their presence here the reason we aren't getting mortared?" I said. "Because the Mahdi Army doesn't want to blow up their own people?"

"We think that's probably so," he said and nodded with confidence.

I didn't hear *that* in the briefing when I first got there.

The Graya'at neighborhood really has been cleared of active insurgents, however. You might even say it's safer than the Green Zone, which is still attacked with incoming rockets and mortars.

"If someone sets up a mortar," said Lieutenant Colonel Wilson A. Shoffner, "we get phone calls from the locals before it is fired. We reached a tipping point here where we have more friends than the insurgents."

Major Michael Jazdyk concurred. "We were a target at first," he said. "Insurgents shot at us with rockets and mortars. But most of the time they killed local civilians. The locals want us here now because we pushed the insurgents out and are keeping them out."

"How do the local civilians help?" I asked.

"We go on foot patrols and joint patrols with the Iraqi army," he said. "We give people tip cards with a phone number on it that they can call and give us intel. An Arabic speaker answers the phone."

The peace, though, isn't stable. Many areas of Baghdad have been cleared—even the notoriously violent Haifa Street area—but insurgents and terrorists need only drive a few minutes to get from one of their strongholds to another part of the city. Gunmen and car bombers from other sectors of Baghdad can and do pass through War Eagle's area.

Until recently the biggest threat was from the adjacent neighborhood just on the other side of the Tigris. It *hasn't* been cleared of insurgents. When the outpost was still struck by mortars, they were fired over the water from there. It is the insurgents in *that* sector who apparently have decided to stop attacking the outpost so they won't hurt their comrades who infiltrated the base.

American soldiers at War Eagle are therefore training Iraqi army infiltrators every day as part of their job.

"They act like our friends," said Master Sergeant Tyler. "It is a façade to an extent, yes. They get benefits from having a good relationship with us and will do and say anything to keep us on their side."

I heard rumors that the Iraqi army colonel in charge of his side of War Eagle is himself a supporter of Moqtada al Sadr. I could not, however, confirm that. Maybe it's true and maybe it isn't. American soldiers there believe it is.

The Mahdi Army is Iran's major proxy in Iraq. In some ways it's like an Iraqi branch of Hezbollah, though Iran has less control over Sadr than it has over Hezbollah in Lebanon. The Iranians know what they're doing. Lebanon was their proving ground. The Revolutionary Guards built Hezbollah from scratch in the Bekaa Valley during the chaos of civil war and Israeli occupation. In Iraq they're trying to repeat the formula.

Most of Lebanon's Shias were moderately pro-Israel before Iran barged onto the scene and before the Israelis overstayed their welcome after evicting Yasser Arafat's Palestine Liberation Organization in 1982. Twenty five years later, and more than 15 years after Lebanon's civil war ended, Hezbollah is still a menace to Israel and the elected government in Beirut. Hezbollah still has its own foreign policy. Hezbollah can unilaterally ignite hot wars with foreign countries whether the rest of Lebanon wants war or not. The level of precarious "stability" Lebanon enjoys may be the best Iraqis can hope for in this generation if the Mahdi Army and its supporters are not somehow purged from the government, the military, and the police.

If some of the Iraqi army soldiers at War Eagle only pretend to be friends with Americans, what about the civilians in the area? Are they faking it, too?

Who knows?

On a typical patrol at dawn the soldiers I embedded with did only two things: they kept up a visible presence in the area and tossed boxes of Girl Scout cookies to children.

As the morning progressed and more people woke up, entire families came out of their houses to greet us and wave. Private Goings, the gunner in the Humvee I rode in, threw one box of cookies after another. Kids and their parents received them ecstatically. We did this all morning, for four hours. Aside from a 20 minute dismounted patrol near a palm grove, we didn't do anything but drive around and throw cookies.

"Right now," said Sergeant Daniel Lizanne, "all we're doing is waiting for somebody stupid to shoot at us. A lot of the people around here are Sadr supporters. But they're also pro-coalition. I don't really understand how that works."

Don't ask me to explain it. Iraq is a bewildering country. I can tell you what I see and what I hear, but I can't unravel and explain with confidence the contradictions in the hearts and minds of its people. The Kurds are fairly straightforward and easy to read. Baghdad, though, is all but impenetrable. I don't suggest you trust any Westerner who hasn't spent years there who says he or she understands the alleyways and secrets of the city.

"Do you think the civilians here are genuinely friendly or just faking it?" I asked Sergeant Lizanne as Private Goings tossed more boxes of cookies.

"I wouldn't want to be out here by myself at night, I'll tell you that much."

I have a story for *you*," said an interpreter named Feris. He moved from Damascus, Syria, to Cedar Rapids, Iowa, in 1967. Now he's in Baghdad with the U.S. Army. "There's someone you need to meet around the back of the building."

I grabbed my camera and note pad. Feris took me to the far edge of the outpost into an area concealed in camouflage netting and roped off with razor wire.

"Are we allowed to be back here?" I said.

"Doesn't matter," he said. "Come on, so the others can't see."

An Iraqi civilian waited for us. He panicked when he saw my camera and hurriedly covered his face and turned his back.

"No pictures, no pictures," Feris said.

"Okay," I said. "No problem. Tell him I won't take his picture."

Feris put his hand over the lens. I pointed the camera at the ground and said "No picture, no picture."

The Iraqi who waited turned and looked me in the eye.

"*Jaysh al Mahdi* took me," he said. "They kidnapped me and dragged me off to the mosque where they beat me."

"Where?" I said. He didn't speak any English. Feris translated.

"To the Ahl al Bayt mosque in Sadr City," he said. "It is next to Muzaffer Square and the Fire Department in Area 55. It is loaded with weapons. Every mosque in Sadr City is full of weapons. At every mosque in Sadr City they beat people. I can take you right to the spot where they beat me."

He took off his shirt and turned around. More than a dozen horizontal red and blue bruises crisscrossed his back like blunt lash marks.

"They beat me with iron sticks," he said, "and fired a gun in the air next to my head."

Then they shaved his head. The Mahdi Army does this to people they kidnap, to mark them, perhaps, or to humiliate them.

"Why?" I said. "Why did they do this to you?"

"Because I work here," I said.

He works at the outpost as a civilian, not for the Americans but for the Iraqis.

"They say I work with Americans," he said. "It's not true. I told them I don't even speak English. How can I work with Americans? I want to work with Americans, but I'm afraid. If I could I would kill them and stay on this base forever."

"Where did they kidnap you?" I said. "From here?"

"They took me from the street in Sadr City," he said. "They know where I live."

"How do they know you work here?" I said.

He gestured toward the building where Iraqi army soldiers live and sleep. *Of course.*

"The Iraqi army told them," he said.

"How do you know?" I said. "How do you know it was them?"

"*No one* else knows I work here," he said. "Only them."

If the young man is right, the Mahdi Army sympathizers who infiltrated the Iraqi army barracks may be a little bit more than the mere passive sympathizers Master Sergeant Tyler suggested.

He lit another cigarette from what remained of his first.

"I smoke so much because I'm upset," he said.

He took out his cell phone and pointed at the screen.

"They found a video of girls dancing on my phone," he said. "They deleted it and put a picture of Moqtada al Sadr on it instead. If you have a Sadr picture on your phone, that's okay, that's good. If you have a picture of anything else on your phone they will beat you. I don't like the sonofabitch. Why would I want his picture on my phone?"

I kept looking behind me to make sure no one in the Iraqi army saw us talking. It probably wouldn't make any difference, but it seemed like something I should do.

Feris shifted his weight from one foot to the other and kept sighing deeply. He was clearly upset. He grew up in Syria under the brutal regime of Hafez al-Assad, but has lived in Iowa longer than I've been alive. He is hardly more accustomed to hearing these kinds of stories than I am.

"Is there anything you can do to protect yourself?" I asked the young Iraqi.

"What can I do?" he said. "No one can stop *Jaysh al Mahdi*. They live in the 16th century. Everyone I know in Sadr City hates Moqtada al Sadr, but they can do nothing. Many people want the Americans to invade."

I did not need to ask questions. He just kept on talking.

"*Jaysh al Mahdi* has a special car they use to pack people in, take them away, and shoot them," he said. "They have people on street corners watching out for American soldiers. They watch the city at night with night vision goggles. If anyone is out after midnight they think you're a spy."

He was on a roll now, telling me everything unprompted because I was a safe person to talk to and because I stood there and listened.

"Sadr is getting rich from Iranian money. They offered me money to join them. Three million dinars [slightly less than 2,500 dollars]. They wanted me as a fighter. But I said no. I won't do that. I hate *Jaysh al Mahdi*."

I heard the low sharp boom of outgoing artillery somewhere off in the distance, perhaps from Camp Taji just north of the city.

"They tied my hands behind my back," he continued. "They kicked my knees backwards." His lifted up the legs of his pants. Feris looked away. "They made me lay on my stomach and put heavy iron on my back. I had to sleep like that for five nights. My back is all screwed up now."

"But you still have this job," I said, "even though they beat you for having it."

"I have to support my family. My mom and dad don't work. Everyone in Sadr City is very poor. My whole family lives there, except my brother. He went to Lebanon. So many terrorists and criminals live there. If we had money we would all move tomorrow, but I only make 300 dollars a month. We have no TV, nothing, at my house. No one else from my family works. My dad is too old and has a bad back. My mom is too old. I want to get married. I'm engaged, but I have no money to get married."

Neighborhoods all over Baghdad are being cleared of terrorists and insurgents as part of the surge. American soldiers are pushing them out of the city and moving into small houses and stations themselves in the neighborhoods where they can maintain security 24 hours a day. But Sadr City is still a no-go zone for American troops. I asked several high-ranking officers why, but they either don't know or they don't want to tell me.

"What if the U.S. assaults Sadr City?" I said.

"We would all love that," he said. "Everyone except the Mahdi Army would love that. Every single person I know hates Moqtada al Sadr."

But some people do like Moqtada al Sadr. Someone in Graya'at put up a billboard with his face on it.

Lieutenant William H. Lord told me earlier that when American soldiers have gone into Sadr City in the past, children flipped them off and threw rocks. Children in our area of Baghdad, by contrast, treat the American soldiers like heroes. General Petraeus has his work cut out for him if and when he decides to surge into Sadr's domain.

"Even Saddam was better than *Jaysh al Mahdi*," he said. "They treat everyone bad. Americans treat us good. Sadr does not. They say Americans rape our women. They lie. It is just propaganda. Americans have plenty of women. *Jaysh al Mahdi* rapes our women for real. They are animals. But soon enough their day is coming."

He got antsy and seemed to feel he had spent too much time talking to me. He had to get back to work before someone noticed him missing.

"I cry all the time," he said just before he set off. "I wish I was outside Iraq where I would not have to be afraid."

I shook his hand. He returned to his post. And I felt useless. What could I do for this man? There are so many with stories like his in Iraq.

"What kind of country is this," Feris said to me in a trembling voice, "where people do this sort of thing to their own people?"

Meanwhile, or at least so it appeared, I was *safer* at that outpost because Mahdi Army sympathizers had infiltrated. They did not want to hurt their own people with rockets and mortars. Iraq is a dark place. It is also a strange place. Where else can American civilians like me be protected by terrorists who voluntarily function as human shields?

August 2007

Ten

The Road Up IED Alley

A l Qaeda terrifies the locals," said Major Mike Garcia before he put me in a convoy of Humvees with 18 American military police on their way to the small town of Mushadah just north of Baghdad. "The only people Iraqis may be more afraid of is their mothers. When we arrest or detain people and threaten to call up their mom, they completely freak out. 'Please, no, don't tell my mother,' they say. Women are quiet outside the house, but they severely smack down their bad kids inside the house. When your Iraqi mother tells you to knock something off, you knock it off."

The American military has slowly figured out how to leverage Iraq's culture to its advantage, but only to an extent. Locating, killing, capturing, and interrogating terrorists and insurgents is the easy part. The hard part is training Iraqis to do it themselves.

Our destination in Mushadah was the local police station where American military police officers train and equip Iraqi police officers, and where it's still too dangerous for either Iraqis or Americans to walk on the streets.

"I am not trying to scare you," said Captain Maryanne Naro. "But don't get out of your vehicle unless something catastrophic has happened to it."

I walked the streets of Baghdad every day with soldiers from the 82nd Airborne Division, but that clearly wasn't going to happen in Mushadah.

"It's pretty bad up there," she added. "AQI [Al Qaeda in Iraq] is all over the area because they've been pushed out of Baghdad, Ramadi, and Fallujah."

Just driving to Mushadah from the base at Camp Taji was dangerous in a weird sort of way.

"Our convoys are hit with IEDs every day on the road," she said.

I swallowed hard. "Should I really be going up there?" I said.

"Oh, don't worry," she said. "It's fine."

I laughed. *It's fine*? How is that fine? Nothing, except perhaps for the kidnappers, is scarier in Iraq than IEDs, especially now that Iranian-manufactured armor-piercing EFPs—Explosively Formed Penetrators—are deployed by Shia militias.

"None of us have been hurt," she said. "They're just small harassment attacks. Most of the IEDs are mortar rounds, and the Humvees are armored. They usually just pop tires and blow off our mirrors. They do it to piss us off."

"The route clearance team is out there right now," mission leader Sergeant James Babcock said as he showed me which of the five Humvees I was to ride in.

Mine was in the middle of the convoy. The Humvee behind mine was recently hit with an IED.

"That shrapnel can't go through the armor," Sergeant Babcock said when he saw me taking a photograph of the damage. "The doors are armored and the windows are bulletproof. All that shrapnel did was tear holes in the trunk and rip through cases of Gatorade. It was kind of annoying."

"No one fires off EFPs in the area?" I said, referring to the unstoppable molten copper penetrators.

"Nah," he said. "It's just Al Qaeda here."

We saddled up, left the base, and drove north. Everyone locked and loaded their weapons on the way out the gate.

"Hopefully we won't have any fireworks for you today," my driver said.

Well, I thought, it certainly would be *interesting* if there are some fireworks for me today. Not every Humvee in Iraq is up-armored, and not every IED-laced road in Iraq is free of those terrifying EFPs. And so, I figured, if I'm ever going to be hit with an IED, this would be the best day.

It was a strange feeling, a bit like being in a shark cage—inches away from mortal peril, but kinda sorta okay…as long as an IED didn't explode *under* the vehicle.

"AQI always puts the IEDs in the same places on this road, in culverts and holes they already dug," Captain Naro said. "We just swerve around them."

"Are they stupid?" I said.

She gave me a look, as if the question was a little too cocky, as if it was dangerous to dismiss Al Qaeda as stupid. I agree, of course, in general, but I can't help but think putting IEDs in the same places over and over again isn't too bright.

Getting into a Humvee with the army in a war zone all by itself can be a little bit stressful. The ranking officer inside often reminds everyone else of the safety procedures—which are not at all like the safety procedures you'll hear from a stewardess on United Airlines just before take off.

"Combat lock!" he might yell, which means everyone must lock their door so no one can open it from the outside and shoot anyone inside.

"Everybody remember what to do if someone throws a grenade in the truck?"

No, I did not remember. It is not something anyone ever taught me.

"Yell *grenade grenade grenade* and get the hell out as quickly as possible. If you don't have time to get out, turn your back to the blast and hope for the best."

Fast moving targets are harder to hit. And because the IEDs don't explode on their own, the odds of any Humvee in particular being hit were no greater or less than the odds of any other Humvee being hit. Riding in the front of the convoy was no more dangerous than riding anywhere else. And riding in the middle or in the rear wasn't safer. Of course that didn't stop me from trying to convince myself that I rode in the lucky Humvee that wouldn't be hit for some reason.

There weren't any fireworks that day, at least not against my convoy. But we still weren't safe once we reached the police station.

"Get inside," Sergeant Anthony Doucet said to me when we stepped out of the Humvees. "This place is a mortar magnet."

Every place in Iraq is hot during the summer, but the Mushadah police station was merciless. Only two rooms had air conditioning. The rest were miserable sweat boxes.

Captain Maryanne Naro was supposed to join us, but she had to remain at Camp Taji. That was too bad. I was hoping to see how Iraqi police officers interacted in person with an American woman who outranked almost all of them.

"The police won't leave the station," Major Garcia had told me, "unless Americans are there to protect them. They wouldn't leave under any circumstances until Captain Naro showed up and was willing to go out on patrol. They were ashamed that a woman had more guts than they did."

"They will go out alone now for something real basic," she had told me. "Otherwise if Americans aren't with them they'll hide in the station. They're hard to work with at times, like they're kids."

Incompetence, though, is the least of their problems.

"About half of them are corrupted," she said, "and it's hard to get the bad ones out. Some of the higher ups are corrupted too, but it's hard to prove. They help Al Qaeda, they set up illegal checkpoints, and they raid civilian houses so they can steal stuff."

Not surprisingly then, local civilians are just as afraid of the police as the uncorrupted police are afraid of the neighborhood.

"Locals come in here all the time and talk to Americans," she told me. "They're afraid to give intel to the Iraqi police."

Mushadah is a bad area with bad police officers and a bad police station. The building itself is filthy and ramshackle. The stairs to the second floor are murderously uneven, not because they've been damaged but because they were built by incompetents. I've seen dodgy construction in Iraq—even at Saddam's palaces, believe it or not—but this station was the worst. I'll spare you a description of the bathroom, but I was warned in no uncertain terms not to touch anything in there.

A high wall surrounded and protected the station, but one side had recently been destroyed by a mortar round. A spring wind storm had blown down the wall on the south side.

The whole place was almost destroyed not long ago. An Al Qaeda suicide bomber filled a dump truck with explosives and tried to ram it into the building, but the whole thing tipped over when he drove too fast around a corner. He would have killed everyone inside had he succeeded.

Sergeant Doucet led me to the front door from the inside so I could photograph some of the Iraqi police standing at attention outside.

"How many of these guys do you suppose are Al Qaeda infiltrators?" I said. I just couldn't look at them without wondering.

"I don't know," he said. "We speculate about it. We don't investigate them or anything like that."

"You *don't?*" I said. "Why not?"

"We aren't passive about it," he said. "If we suspect someone has gone over the edge, he'll raise a red flag and we'll deal with it."

"How much support do you get from local civilians?" I said.

"Locals bring in tips against bad guys all the time," he said. "Several times a week. What they tell us is not very tangible though. Sometimes it's useless. Someone will come in here and scream, 'There's bad guys out there!' We'll ask where. 'To the west!' they'll say. Well, no crap.

"Residents are still afraid to give intel on bad guys," he continued. "Insurgents will kill them if they do. The area is totally unsecured. Even if we question people who live right in front of an IED trigger point they won't say anything. But, look, forget what you see on the news. People in this community are just like people in any other community. This guy is pissed off at that guy, and you have to deal with it."

I've been in parts of Iraq where local civilians cooperate with the army and police and where they do not. Civilians cooperate as much as security on the streets will permit them. The dynamic here isn't all that hard to understand or even that foreign. If you want to see how this has played out in America, watch Elia Kazan's *On the Waterfront*, the classic film from 1954 starring Marlon Brando about the mafia's infiltration of a longshoreman's union. No one in that story wanted to cooperate with the police department's murder investigations against the mob because they were terrified they would be "next" if they did.

"We have a medical facility here," Sergeant Doucet said. "Local civilians can come here and use it, and they do."

They did while I was there. A three year old boy was badly burned at his house—how, I don't know—and he was brought in to be treated by a medic.

I didn't want to get in the medic's way, so I stepped into the Tactical

Operations Center, one of only two rooms in the station that had air conditioning.

"Hello again, sir," Sergeant Babcock said and pulled up a chair for me. He then gave me more background and asked me not to take pictures of anything in that room.

"Lots of Iraqi police here had orders to work in Baghdad," he said, "but they refused. They are Sunnis. This is a Sunni area. Baghdad, as you know, is mostly Shia. Their names and license plates mark them for death. They work here but are counted as AWOL and are not being paid."

Some of the Iraqi police are honorable men. (And they are all men.) I don't want to leave you with the impression that all of them are terrorist infiltrators. They aren't.

"Because of logistics problems we have to go to Baghdad for fuel," Sergeant Babcock said, "and we have to go to a Shia area. It's very dangerous for them and they ask us to go with them. They have problems getting ammo as well. There are always problems with ammo."

And there are severe problems with other stations.

"The Taramiyah station was hit by insurgents earlier this spring," he said. "It was completely destroyed. Only six officers from that station are brave enough to come to work here."

A poster on the wall caught my eye. It showed a grainy photograph of an AK-47 and a masked man who looked like a terrorist. "Citizens of Iraq," the poster read. "Effective immediately: Any weapons carried or displayed in public will be confiscated by Security Forces. This weapons confiscation plan has been endorsed by the Prime Minister. This is for the safety of you, your family, and the citizens of Iraq."

Sergeant Babcock introduced me to the man in charge of the station, Captain J. Dow Covey from New York City.

"Do you know the *Weekly Standard* magazine?" Captain Covey asked me.

"Of course," I said.

"My buddy Tom Cotton was just written up there," he said. "It was pretty cool seeing him in that magazine."

"What did he do to get in the magazine?" I said.

"He's like me," he said. "He's a Harvard Law grad who joined the army after 9/11. I'm an attorney."

"You're an *attorney*?" I said. "What are you doing out here in Iraq?"

"I practiced law for three years," he said, "then got into investment banking. When 9/11 happened I just had to sign up with the army. Investment banking is a lot more stressful than this."

"You're kidding, right?" I said.

"No," he said and laughed. "I am totally serious."

If he was deployed in, say, Kurdistan I could see it. But Mushadah was stressful. Less stressful than investment banking? Investment banking in New York must really be something.

Not much happened the first half of my day at the station, so I lounged with the MPs in their broiling quarters. None had anything positive to say about the Iraqi police they were training.

"What can you really ask for in a lazy society? You go in their houses and the floors are covered in pillows."

"You can tell who is corrupt because their convoys *never* get hit."

"This place wouldn't be so bad if it wasn't so fucking hot. I can deal with being shot at and blown up, but 150 degrees is a bit much."

"Some Iraqi police recently left the station, we got hit with a bunch of mortars, then they came right back inside. This sort of thing happens a lot. It makes us suspicious."

"We're giving them 50,000 dollar Chevy trucks and it's like a junk yard out back. It's like *Sanford and Son* out there. They drive stuff better than we can afford, and they don't even take care of it."

"I miss Baghdad. One day we'd be walking out on the street buying sandwiches and playing soccer with kids. The next day we'd get in a firefight with burning tires and RPGs and shit. The next day we'd be hanging out and chilling like normal again. It's a weird place, and really keeps you on your toes."

"It's not like Germany or Japan where people wanted a change. The Kurds up north wanted a change, so they got one. The Arabs don't, so they aren't. They hardly change even with *us* here."

The Iraqi army in the area isn't faring much better.

"They are severely infiltrated by Al Qaeda and the Mahdi Army,"

Colonel John Steele told me back at Camp Taji.

The Iraqi army soldiers who aren't double agents are still nowhere near ready to defend their own country.

"Their logistics are very immature," he said. "They are always short on ammo. And we have to hold their hands and make sure they don't kill themselves and others. We still do some unilateral U.S. actions even though we want to become partnered with the Iraqi army in all our operations. But we first want to make sure they have all the skills they need to survive in combat."

Most American soldiers I spoke to about the Iraqi army and Iraqi police, not just in Mushadah but also in Baghdad, have a dim view of their local counterparts. I wanted to know what the colonel thought.

"Do you trust them?" I said.

He paused for a long time and answered very carefully.

"We won't tell them about sensitive operations until the last second," he said. "I trust some individuals, though, because I know them. I'd share a foxhole with them as far as ideology goes, but I'm not sure how good their skills are when they are shot."

Pride is much more important in Arab culture than it is in the West. Humiliation is therefore more painful. I wondered if this created problems when Americans train Iraqi soldiers and police officers. What must it feel like for local men to be yelled at by foreigners who showed up uninvited and knew their job better than they did?

Colonel Steele insists it isn't a problem.

"They don't want to be babied," he said. "They want to be treated as equals and adults. Their shame culture actually helps. Our new recruits recently complained about having sore feet during a march. When they noticed our female soldiers are in better shape than they are, they never complained again. Also, when we first had them try on our body armor, it nearly broke their spines. They want to be physically capable of wearing it, too."

It's at least possible that some infiltrators might switch sides later. Some former insurgents elsewhere in Iraq are now openly siding with the Americans.

There's also this: "We give them rudimentary skills and a work ethic," he told me. "They attend the same classes on character and honor and professional conduct becoming a soldier that our own people attend."

Is he optimistic?

"I am optimistic," he said. "But only for one single reason. Because I talk to the average Joe in Iraq. I meet the children and parents. Iraqi parents love their children as much as I love mine."

Sergeant Babcock invited me to a meeting with Iraqi police Colonel Hameed, the man responsible for the station on the Iraqi side. Sergeant Babcock, Sergeant Doucet, an interpreter, the colonel, and I sat together in the only other room at the station that had air conditioning.

"You are most welcome," the colonel said to me in an obviously insincere tone of voice. Some of the MPs think he's corrupt. I don't know if that means they think he works with Al Qaeda.

"Thank you," I said. "May I take your picture?"

"No," he said, "please don't." It didn't sound like he actually cared though, as if he was only pretending to need protection from terrorists.

He and the American MPs discussed fuel logistics.

"The only reason the Iraqi police got fuel on the last mission," he said, "is because you were with us. Otherwise they wouldn't have given us anything."

Suddenly Captain Covey, the New York City attorney, nearly broke down the door as he barged into the room.

"Hey!" he screamed at the colonel. "I'm tired of you motherfuckers stealing our fuel cans. I'm going to kick *all* you motherfuckers out of here. I'm sorry for interrupting your little meeting, but at noon I want every single one of you people *off* this post." He stared at the interpreter. "Translate that!" he said.

He slammed the door behind him. Everyone looked at each other. A horrified expression washed over the colonel's face when he saw me taking notes.

The meeting was over, obviously. I stepped into the hallway and asked the nearest MP what was going on.

"Sixty one fuel cans have been stolen over the last week by Iraqi police officers here," he said. "Three more were stolen today. These are fuel cans that Iraqis and Americans risk their lives to go get."

The tension in the hallway was palpable. None of the Iraqis could look me in the eye.

"Can the captain really kick the Iraqis out of here?" I asked Sergeant Babcock.

"Actually, he can," he said. He sounded mortified by the idea.

Colonel Hameed walked up to Sergeant Babcock. He was furious.

"Your captain offended us by coming in here and yelling like that," he said. "I need you to find a solution."

"I'm a staff sergeant," Sergeant Babcock said. "He's a captain. I'm also an MP and he's infantry. I have to obey him whether I like it or not."

"This station does not belong to his family," the colonel said curtly. "This is unacceptable. The building is ours, and he is our guest. A guest cannot fire the owner of the house."

"We'll go talk to him and come back," Sergeant Babcock said.

As it turned out, the whole thing was a screw up. Somebody forgot to update the board and account for three fuel cans that were taken legitimately.

Captain Covey was embarrassed.

"Would you really have kicked them all out of here?" I said.

"In the state of mind I was in then, yes," he said. "I was ready to do it. But I calmed down and would have gotten in trouble anyway. So no, I wouldn't have actually done it."

Sixty one fuel cans really had been stolen earlier in the week, however. The Iraqi police were in serious trouble.

Another Iraqi police colonel, whose name I did not catch and who no one thinks is corrupt, arrived on the scene and yelled himself hoarse at his deputies.

"Coalition forces are screaming at us!" he hollered. "Screaming at us because *you* keep stealing fuel!"

He kicked an empty metal garbage can and knocked it clanging to the floor. The Iraqi police officers glowered at him as if they wanted to scream back and were trying mightily to restrain themselves.

An American MP walked past me. "That's the first time I've seen those guys yelled at," he said and grinned with satisfaction.

Shortly after noon an international police advisor from Michigan named Paul taught an hour-long class to the Iraqis about how to take weapons from potentially dangerous people who are under arrest. The officers seemed to learn as much sitting through that course as I did. Apparently they had never gone over the procedures before.

I couldn't help wondering as I watched the Iraqis...which of you work for Al Qaeda?

Maybe none of them did. I don't have a sense of how many infiltrators there actually are, although Captain Naro thinks the number could be as high as 50 percent.

"Please don't publish my picture," Paul said to me after the class. "And use only my first name. Only my wife knows I'm in Iraq."

I wanted to know what he thought of the trainees. He has trained police officers not only in Iraq and the United States, but all over the world. He could, perhaps, see them through more worldly eyes than the American MPs who had a narrower range of experience.

"They've made leaps and bounds in the past two months," he said. "Every day they make progress. Today they made progress."

"Are you optimistic about them?" I said.

"Oh, absolutely," he said. "The Iraqi police are like sponges. It's all new to them."

"Lots of American soldiers I've talked to about the Iraqi army and Iraqi police don't think very highly of them," I said.

"Look," he said. "The other contractors I know who train the police are also optimistic. Many file extensions to stay longer because they feel like they're making a difference. I never hear anything negative from any of them. We watch the Iraqis progress over time because we work with them daily. Most American soldiers don't see the progress because they observe the Iraqis from more of a distance. You yourself are only seeing a snapshot in time. If you think it looks bad now, you should have been here two months ago."

It was time to head back to Camp Taji. The MPs and I saddled up in our Humvees while, in front of us, Iraqi police officers piled into their trucks. We would escort them out of the station, then they would be on their own. They were going out alone, apparently for something "real basic," as Captain Naro had told me.

The Iraqi police truck in front of my Humvee had an office swivel chair crazily bolted into the flatbed. A policeman strapped himself into that and manned a mounted machine gun.

"Is he really going out all exposed like that?" I said.

"He is," Sergeant Babcock said. "I can't quite decide if that's pathetic or if it's a testament to the human spirit. Maybe it's a little of both."

We drove back down IED Alley to Camp Taji. It was four in the afternoon and so unbearably hot. The air conditioner in the Humvee hardly did anything. I desperately wanted a shower so I could wash Iraq off my skin.

Nothing exploded on our way back.

Major Garcia wanted to know what I thought. I didn't know what to say.

"Whether we like it or not," he said, "and whether we like them or not, they are the future of this country."

August 2007

PART THREE

ANBAR AWAKENS

Eleven

The Battle of Ramadi

After spending some time in and around Baghdad with the United States military I visited the city of Ramadi, the capital of Iraq's notoriously convulsive and violent Anbar Province, which only a few months ago was one of the most dangerous cities in the world. It was another "Fallujah," and certainly the most dangerous place in Iraq.

In August 2006 officers in the Marine Corps, arguably the least defeatist institution in all of America, wrote off Ramadi as irretrievably lost. They weren't crazy for thinking it. Abu Musab al Zarqawi's Al Qaeda in Iraq had moved in to fight the Americans, and they were welcomed as liberators by a substantial portion of the local population.

I wrote recently that Baghdad, while dangerous and mind-bogglingly dysfunctional, isn't as bad as it looks on TV. Almost everywhere I have been in the Middle East is more "normal" than it appears in the media. Nowhere is this more true than in Beirut, but it is true to a lesser extent in Baghdad, as well. Baghdad is in horrendous condition, but it appears normalish in most places most of the time. Ramadi, in my experience, is the great exception. Ramadi was in worse shape than you'd have any idea from the media.

Baghdad suffers from political paralysis, an infrastructure collapse, a low-grade counterinsurgency, and a slow-motion civil war. It doesn't look or feel like a war zone most of the time, although it does sometimes. What recently went down in Ramadi wasn't like that. The city didn't suffer the surreal sort of war-lite that still simmers in Baghdad. No. Two American colonels in charge of the area compared the battle of Ramadi to Stalingrad.

"We were engaged in hours-long full-contact kinetic warfare with enemies in fixed positions," said army Major Lee Peters.

"There were areas where our odds of being attacked were 100 percent," Captain Jay McGee told me. "Literally hundreds of IEDs created virtual minefields."

"The whole area was enemy controlled," said Lieutenant Jonathan Welch with the Marine Corps. "If we went out for even a half-hour we were shot at, and we were shot at accurately. Sometimes we took casualties and were not able to *inflict* casualties. We didn't know where they were shooting from."

Anbar Province is the heart of Iraq's so-called Sunni Triangle, and Ramadi is its capital. Iraq has 18 provinces, but until recently almost a third of all U.S. casualties were in Anbar alone. More than a million people live there, mostly along the Euphrates River, and roughly a third live in Ramadi. Most of the rest live in the also notorious and now largely secured cities of Haditha, Hit, and Fallujah.

I haven't visited the other cities yet because I wanted to begin in the province's largest and most important city. Ramadi isn't the most important solely because it's the capital or because it's the largest. It is also the most important because Al Qaeda declared it "The capital of the Islamic State of Iraq."

"You have to understand what every side's end state is in Iraq to really understand what's going on," said Captain McGee in his military intelligence headquarters at the Blue Diamond base just north of the city. An enormous satellite photo map of Ramadi and the surrounding area took up a whole wall. Local streets were relabeled by the military and given very American names: White Sox Road, Eisenhower Road, and Pool Hall Street for example.

"The ideology of AQI is to establish the Islamic Caliphate in Iraq," he said. "In order for them to be successful they must control the Iraqi population through either support or coercion."

I briefly met Army Reserve Lieutenant Colonel Eric Holmes from Dallas, Texas, while he was on his way home after volunteering to serve in Ramadi for six months. "I didn't realize until I got here that the problem in Anbar Province was 100 percent Al Qaeda," he said. "The old Baath Party insurgency here is completely finished. That war was won and

Americans, including me, had no idea it even happened."

Al Qaeda fighters were initially welcomed by many Iraqis in Ramadi because they said they were there to resist the Americans. The spirit of resistance against foreign occupiers was strong, but the Iraqis got a lot more in the bargain than simply resistance.

"Al Qaeda came in and just seized people's houses," said Captain Phil Messer. "They said, 'we're taking your house to use it against the Americans. Get out.'"

"Every mosque in the city was anti-American," Captain McGee said. "They were against us, but Al Qaeda made it even worse by ordering them to broadcast anti-American propaganda at gunpoint."

"Market Street [the main street downtown] was completely controlled by Al Qaeda," Lieutenant Welch said. "They rolled down the streets, pointed guns at people, and said, 'we are in charge.' They had crazy requirements for the locals. They weren't allowed to cut their hair. Girls were banned from going to school. They couldn't shave or smoke. One guy defiantly lit a cigarette and they shot him four times."

Sergeant Kenneth Hicks took me on my first foot patrol in the city. We dismounted our Humvees near Market Street in the center of one of Al Qaeda's old strongholds.

"This is an infamous sniper corner," he said before we had even walked twenty feet.

"A few months ago we would be dead standing here," he said. "But there were so many IEDs on this street, and so much piled up garbage, that we could *only* go out on foot."

After Al Qaeda took over Ramadi, the local government was replaced with terrorists who only cared about fighting Americans and violently suppressing Iraqis. Al Qaeda was in charge, but it wouldn't be accurate to say they were the new government. None of the basic city government services functioned. There was no electricity, no running water, no telephone service, and no garbage collection. Every single local business closed down. The city could not have been any more broken.

"Ramadi didn't even have a city government until April," said Colonel Charlton. "They couldn't come to work because of security. And the city was down to zero electricity just three months ago."

"I'm sure it looks to you like there's lots of trash all over the place," Sergeant Hicks said. It certainly did. I don't recall ever seeing so much garbage outside a dump. It was so thick in places I could not walk around it. I had to walk through it and on it. "But there is massive cleanup going on. There really is a lot less of it now than there was a few months ago."

We walked a block or so and came to a series of concrete barriers blocking vehicle traffic.

"We put up those walls to keep the rat line [enemy logistics route] out in the open desert from coming into the city," he said.

Kids saw us and scattered. Nobody needed to tell me that was bad.

"Look out," Sergeant Hicks said. "It's not a good sign when kids run."

Children who run at the sight of American soldiers often know something the soldiers do not. They may know an explosion or an insurgent attack of some other kind is imminent.

The same is true in Afghanistan. Soldiers know they can gauge the friendliness of an area by the response to their presence of its children. When kids run up and greet them, the area is friendly. When children just stand there and watch, the area is neutral or possibly hostile. When kids run away it usually means the area is violently hostile and that something is about to explode.

Sergeant Hicks raised his weapon and pointed it across the street.

I suspect he was more worried than I was. Ramadi is a friendly city that has been cleared and pacified. The children were most likely running out of sheer habit. They lived right in the heart of what was recently Al Qaeda's main stronghold.

Nothing exploded and nobody shot at us. The first kids I ever saw in Ramadi ran from us, but it never happened again. Only two or three minutes later, children excitedly greeted us as they did every other time I stepped out into the streets of the city and the surrounding countryside.

"Three months ago people turned their backs to us," Sergeant Hicks said. "They refused to even smile. They were like beaten dogs."

We walked down Market Street.

Small shops had re-opened since the war ended, but there was still a substantial amount of visible damage. Shattered buildings were everywhere. Most were pocked with bullet holes. Others looked as though they had been brought down by a megathrust quake.

"People are giving us information," he said. "And, you know, these people really open up to you, automatically, when you're in their houses. They'll just start telling you what it was like living under Saddam—the most unbelievable things." And this is a part of Iraq that was favored by Saddam Hussein. It was much worse in the Shia and Kurdish parts of the country.

I also went on patrol with Captain Phil Messer. He was the most hospitable officer I met in Iraq. He and his men lived in a large rented house about the size of a university co-op in the Hay al-Adel neighborhood. He gave me his private room next to the Tactical Operations Center and slept in a crowded room with some of the other soldiers so I would be comfortable. "I've been immersed in this culture a long time," he said. "The Arab code of hospitality is starting to wear off on me." I don't think he was sucking up for good press. He is just a nice guy.

"What do you want to see in Ramadi?" he said.

"Destruction," I said. "I need to photograph what the war did to this place."

So he took me out to see the destruction. He did not ask me why or what I would do with the pictures.

We drove out to "Route Michigan."

"When we first started using this road," he said, "we thought it was a dirt road. Then we cleaned it up and, sure enough, there was asphalt under it. Route Michigan was hit by IEDs and gunfire every single time a convoy went down it. There was a foot and a half of water on it because the IEDs shattered so many water mains. Our vehicles were not allowed to travel on it unless they were specifically on a combat mission."

Most of the city's buildings and houses are more or less intact, but some areas have been completely destroyed. Whole pieces of the city have been simply erased. There is literally nothing left. The buildings have been destroyed, the rubble has been carted away, and all that remains is the pavement. Whole swaths of the city look like gigantic parking lots outside a mall, as if they had been deliberately paved over. I never saw anything even remotely like it in Baghdad, yet it went on for miles along main streets in Ramadi.

"We took the gloves off," Captain Dennison told me. "We had to."

I spent the next day at a Joint Security Station (JSS), a tiny outpost in a rented house where American soldiers and Marines live with Iraqi soldiers in the heart of the city.

Army Lieutenant Markham met me first thing in the morning at Camp Corregidor and drove me over there.

"What's the plan today?" I said.

"There's this thing—I don't know if you've heard of it—called the GWOT," he said. "The Global War on Terrorism. We have to win it."

"And what about me?" I said.

"I'll be taking you over to the JSS and leaving you with Lieutenant Hightower," he said. "Think of it as me dropping you off at school."

"Ok, Dad," I said. "Which truck am I riding in?"

Living conditions at the JSS were unspeakable. The building had sustained battle damage from the war. Everything was hot and filthy. The stairs were broken. The bathroom was covered in spider webs and dried mud left over from the last time it had rained. Aside from a few select rooms, there was no air conditioning. It's hard to describe how awful that is in Iraq in August. Somebody told me it was 138 degrees that day in the sun. It's hotter in Ramadi than even in Baghdad, and it's made worse by the fact that the JSS didn't have showers. "I once went three months without a shower," a soldier told me outside. Amazingly, the place didn't smell bad.

The toilets didn't work and there were no porta-johns, so everyone had to use plastic bags and wash up with bottled water. "If you let the water from the sink get on your skin," a soldier told me, "there's a ten percent chance you'll get a horrible rash."

American and Iraqi soldiers live in this place. "Most Americans have no idea how bad we have it here," someone told me, and I'm certain he's right. Most, though, didn't complain. Life is a *lot* better in Ramadi now that the fighting is over, regardless of the heat and living conditions.

"Can I take pictures of this place?" I said to Sergeant Hicks. Only in the rarest of circumstances does the military object to journalists taking pictures, and even then only when the photographs might help the other side plan attacks.

"Hmm," Sergeant Hicks said.

"Uh," Lieutenant Markham said.

"It's not that important," I said.

"Just make sure there aren't any full-page spreads showing the layout of this place so suicide bombers would know how to hit us," Sergeant Hicks said.

"Yeah, Mike," Lieutenant Markham said. "What are you trying to pull here?" He didn't sound like he was joking, but he probably was. He's just a dead-pan kind of guy.

He introduced me to Marine Lieutenant Andrew Hightower, a man who had recently returned from three months on medical leave.

"What happened?" I said.

"I got blown up," he said.

"You don't look blown up," I said.

"I got hit with a 120 mortar round IED," he said. "Near Market Street. I got shrapnel all in my leg."

"How did *that* feel?" I said. Some people don't feel pain even when they get shot, so I didn't know.

"It felt like someone was pushing a hot iron onto my skin," he said. "Then I felt the blood running down my leg." The doctors gave him the pieces of shrapnel which he now keeps in a jar.

"Lieutenant Hightower is a terrific Marine officer," said Lieutenant Markham, who was in the Army. "He gives me hope for the future of the Marine Corps."

He said that so seriously I thought he might not be joking this time.

"Did you actually worry about the future of the Marine Corps *before* you met him?" I said.

"Well, yes, kind of," he said. "The Marines are just...really different from the Army." He said it with such gravity and disappointment and concern and shook his head.

I couldn't possibly care less about the rivalry between the Army and the Marines, although I was occasionally asked by members of each which branch I preferred.

One Marine tried to get an Iraqi soldier to take sides.

"Which do you think is better?" he said. "Army or Marines?"

"The Navy is best," said the Iraqi.

The Marine was taken aback. "The *Navy*?" he said.

"Yes, Navy," said the Iraqi.

The Marine looked slightly annoyed when I laughed.

Lieutenant Markham handed me over to Lieutenant Hightower who was supposed to take me out on a patrol, but a dust storm blew in from the desert and we were grounded. Soldiers and Marines aren't allowed to go on patrols when the air is "condition red" because medevac helicopters have a hard time evacuating the wounded. So I was stranded and spent as much of the day as I could talking to those who fought and survived the battle of Ramadi.

"We have genuinely good relations with the Iraqi army here," Lieutenant Hightower said. "We live in the same rooms. They are almost like my own soldiers. We go to their funerals."

Every soldier and Marine I met in Anbar Province spoke highly of and with great admiration for their Iraqi counterparts. It was a completely different world from the Baghdad area where so many Americans hold the Iraqis in contempt as corrupt incompetents who let themselves be infiltrated by terrorists and insurgents.

"What are you doing here anyway?" he said. "Not much happens in Ramadi anymore. Nothing blows up anymore. There's no blood and guts here."

There certainly had been blood and guts, though. Just a few blocks from the station is a soccer stadium that was used during the war as a mass grave site.

"We found bodies buried in the middle of the soccer field by insurgents," he said. "After the war ended the Iraqis had to unearth the bodies. They called it Operation Graveyard. Now there's a soccer game there every night at 5:00. There was another soccer field north of the city in the Sofia area, a kids' soccer field. It was also used as a dump site. AQI killed civilians by castrating them, stuffing their genitals in their mouths, and cutting off their heads. Al Qaeda killed a lot more civilians than they ever killed soldiers."

Captain Jay McGee concurred. "Suicide car bombers rarely attacked the coalition," he said, meaning Americans. "They almost always attacked Iraqi security forces and civilians. They know the U.S. will leave eventually, but AQI ultimately *must* fight Iraqis and destroy Iraqi institutions in order to prevail."

They did kill Americans, though, certainly. And they paid willing local Iraqis to help them.

"To get paid by AQI for killing Americans," Lieutenant Hightower said, "the attack must be videotaped. They often used tracer rounds so they could prove it was real. We found whole piles of these tapes when we cleaned the city out. We found and killed a sniper just northeast of the city. He had all kinds of video tapes of himself shooting and killing American soldiers."

Snipers were everywhere in Ramadi. Some were committed Al Qaeda fighters, and others were just paid to help out.

"One of my soldiers was shot in the head through his helmet by a sniper," he said. High powered bullets will pierce helmets if they hit at a head-on angle. "The sniper was shooting from behind a curtain in a van. He was a teacher at a women's vocational school by day and a sniper for extra money at night. AQI just recruits people who need money and hires them as insurgents as if it were a regular job."

Conveniently for Al Qaeda, the economy in Ramadi utterly disintegrated during the war. Almost everybody needed money, and even those who did have money had a hard time buying anything since all the stores had closed down.

Mortars were a big problem, too, and they came from random directions.

"AQI would launch three mortars from a truck," Lieutenant Hightower said, "then drive off. We usually couldn't shoot back fast enough before they had scurried off somewhere else."

The worst, though, were the IEDs. It's the same everywhere in Iraq.

"They used acid to liquefy the asphalt and bury the IEDs under the road," he said. "Then they would push the liquid asphalt back into the hole. Their work looked almost perfect. You could tell where they had buried the IEDs if you looked closely enough, but the roads are filthy and the evidence was barely detectable when we were driving. We found a lot of them with slow-moving road clearance vehicles that use metal detector arms."

He had to take a phone call, so I walked around the station and noticed that the filthy place was suddenly cleaner than it was when I had arrived just a few hours before. The Iraqis were hard at work fixing the place up since they couldn't go on patrols while the dusty air was still at condition red. Cases of MREs and bottled water were more organized. The floors had been swept clear of dust. Soon the station might actually be suitable for people to live in.

"Al Qaeda hit a six month-old baby with a mortar when they were trying to hit us," Lieutenant Hightower said when he got off the phone. "They also hit a six year-old girl. *We* went in and medevacced the victims, and we made lots of friends that day. It was a clarifying experience for the Iraqis."

It was a clarifying experience for the Iraqis because they had been raised on virulent anti-American conspiracy theories and propaganda from Saddam Hussein and the Baath Party. They truly believed the army and Marines were there to steal their oil and women. Americans saving the lives of children wounded by fellow Sunni Arabs who passed themselves off as liberators was not what many Iraqis ever expected.

"The six month baby had shrapnel in his head," Lieutenant Hightower said. "The six year-old girl had shrapnel in her leg. It was the most disturbing thing I've seen since I got here." This from a man who saw one of his own men shot in the head.

Ramadi is in terrible shape even now. If it were an American city it would be declared in a state of emergency. Months of accumulated garbage is still piled up everywhere. The electricity still isn't on for even twelve hours a day, although the eight hours the city does get—because, as Colonel Charlton says, Al Qaeda no longer blows up the electrical towers—certainly beats the *one* hour of electricity they get each day in Baghdad. Sewage flows in the street. The economy has a pulse, but four months ago it was at zero.

"The city completely bottomed out," Colonel Holmes told me. "It hit absolute rock bottom."

Ramadi was in worse shape even than Gaza. And Ramadi was once one of the loveliest cities in all of Iraq.

Nineteen Arab tribes led by sheikhs live in Anbar Province. In June of 2006, nine of those tribal sheikhs cooperated with the Americans, three were neutral, and seven were hostile.

In October of last year the tribal leaders in the province, including some who previously were against the Americans, formed a movement to reject the savagery Al Qaeda had brought to their region. Some were supremely unhappy with the American presence since fighting exploded in the province's second largest city of Fallujah, but Al Qaeda proved to be even more sinister from their point of view. Al Qaeda did not come as advertised. It was militarily incapable of expelling the U.S. Army and Marines. And it was a worse oppressor than even Saddam Hussein. The leaders of Anbar Province saw little choice but to openly declare them enemies and do whatever it took to expunge them. They called their new movement *Sahawa al Anbar*, or the Anbar Awakening.

Sheikh Sattar is its leader. Al Qaeda assassins murdered his father and three of his brothers, and he was not going to put up with them any longer. None of the sheikhs were willing to put up with them any longer. By April of 2007 every single tribal leader in all of Anbar was cooperating with the Americans.

"AQI announced the Islamic State of Iraq in a parade downtown on October 15, 2006," said Captain McGee. "This was their response to *Sahawa al Anbar*. They were threatened by the tribal movement so they accelerated their attacks against tribal leaders. They ramped up the murder and intimidation. It was basically a hostile fascist takeover of the city."

Sheikh Jassim's experience was typical.

"Jassim was pissed off because American artillery fire was landing in his area," Colonel Holmes said. "But he wasn't pissed off at us. He was pissed off at Al Qaeda because he knew they always shot first and we were just shooting back."

"He said he would prevent Al Qaeda from firing mortars from his area if we would help him," Lieutenant Hightower said. "Al Qaeda said they would mess him up if he got in their way. He called their bluff and they seriously fucked him up. They launched a massive attack on his area. All hell broke loose. They set houses on fire. They dragged people through the streets behind pickup trucks. A kid from his area went into town and Al Qaeda kidnapped him, tortured him, and delivered his head to the outpost in a box. The dead kid was only sixteen years old. The Iraqis then sent out even nine year old kids to act as neighborhood watchmen. They painted their faces and everything."

"Sheikh Jassim came to us after that," Colonel Holmes told me, "and said *I need your help.*"

"One night," Lieutenant Markham said, "after several young people were beheaded by Al Qaeda, the mosques in the city went crazy. The imams screamed jihad from the loudspeakers. We went to the roof of the outpost and braced for a major assault. Our interpreter joined us. *Hold on,* he said. *They aren't screaming jihad against us. They are screaming jihad against the insurgents.*"

A massive anti-Al Qaeda convulsion ripped through the city," said Captain McGee. "The locals rose up and began killing the terrorists on their own. They reached the tipping point where they just could not take any more. They told us where the weapon caches were. They pointed out IEDs under the road."

"In mid-March," Lieutenant Hightower said, "a sniper operating out of a house was shooting Americans and Iraqis. Civilians broke into his house, beat the hell out of him, and turned him over to us."

"There were IEDs all over this area," Lieutenant Welch said. "On every single street corner, buried under the road. They were so big they could take out tanks. When we came through we cleared the whole area on foot. The civilians told us where the IEDs were. I was with one group where a guy opened his gate just a crack and pointed out where one was. It was right in front of his house. Later we went back and had tea. He was so happy to see us."

"One day," Lieutenant Hightower said, "some Al Qaeda guys on a bike showed up and asked where they could plant an IED against Americans.

They asked a random civilian because they just assumed the city was still friendly to them. They had no idea what was happening. The random civilian held him at gunpoint and called us to come get him."

"People here tacitly supported Al Qaeda," Captain McGee said, "because Al Qaeda was attacking us. But they took control of the city. They forced girls to stay home from school. They dragged people outside the city and shot them in the head. They broke people's fingers if they were seen smoking a cigarette. They forced men to grow beards. Once they started acting like that they could only establish a safe haven by using terrorism against the local civilians."

"Al Qaeda struck out three times," said Major Peters. "Strike one: They killed a sheikh and held his body for four days. Strike two: They executed young people in public. Strike three: They attacked the compound of another sheikh. The people here said *enough*. They aligned with us because they realized Al Qaeda was the real enemy. They didn't like Al Qaeda's version of Islam at all."

Credit for purging Ramadi of Al Qaeda must go to Iraqis themselves at least as much as to the American military. The Americans wouldn't have been able to do it without the cooperation of the people who live there, and the Iraqis wouldn't have been able to do it, at least not so easily, without help from the American military.

"Al Qaeda had dug in the northeastern and southern parts of the city," Captain McGee told me. "The coalition walled off areas and fought block to block, house to house. Then the Provincial Security Forces went in and recleared it. There was an immediate decrease in attacks."

He was referring Operation Murfreesboro, which brought about a dramatic change in offensive tactics.

"For a long time," Colonel Holmes said, "they were driving away from the base in Humvees down a street that was infested with Al Qaeda forces. The gunners spun their turrets in circles and just shot at everything, thinking they could provide cover for themselves so they could drive without being shot at."

"Didn't that violate the rules of engagement?" I said.

He froze for a second and answered that question very carefully.

"That was the wrong way to do it," he said. "And they knew it. So they slowly cleared one block at a time, house by house, and kept the supply lines open to the base in the area that was already cleared. Everything behind them got cleared and stayed cleared, so their safe area got gradually larger. We don't want to hurt civilians. Our job here is to *protect* Iraqi civilians."

He's right. It *is* the job of the United States military to protect the people of Iraq even before protecting themselves. It is always the job of (American) soldiers to protect civilians before protecting themselves. In doing so they protect themselves better than if they did not. It may be counter intuitive, but it's straight-forward, by-the-book counterinsurgency.

"Ultimate success in COIN [counterinsurgency] is gained by protecting the populace, not the COIN force," according to the Petraeus counterinsurgency manual. "If military forces remain in their compounds, they lose touch with the people, appear to be running scared, and cede the initiative to the insurgents. Aggressive saturation patrolling, ambushes, and listening post operations must be conducted, risk shared with the populace, and contact maintained. . . . These practices ensure access to the intelligence needed to drive operations. Following them reinforces the connections with the populace that help establish real legitimacy."

"As soon as we were on Easy Street running through the Malaab area every day, 24/7, it got quiet," said Private First Class Baringhouse. "We sealed off the entire area with barricades and blocked all vehicle traffic. Then they couldn't get weapons and IEDs in. It calmed the place down fast."

Vehicle traffic is still banned in most of Ramadi. The streets are dead quiet. No one drives but the American military, the Iraqi army and police, and a few select taxis.

How well is *that* going over, I asked Lieutenant Welch.

"Civilians complain about lots of things," he said. "But they never complain about this. They are so terrified of car bombs they don't want any car traffic in this city at all. If we could shut down all vehicle traffic everywhere in Iraq, the war would be practically over."

There were more than just IEDs and car bombs. There also were house bombs.

"The house across the street was rigged to blow," he said. "Four Syrians were living in it. Now it's a pile of rubble. This building," meaning the Joint Security Station, "was rigged to blow, too, but they hadn't quite finished the rigging. They hadn't put the detonator equipment in yet."

Some of the blown-up buildings in Ramadi can be partially blamed on American screw ups.

"Did you see that flattened parking lot looking area out front?" Lieutenant Welch said.

I had.

"It was a bunch of shops in the last area we cleared," he said. "We busted the locks and opened the doors. Everyone had to stay in their houses then. We found tons of weapons and IEDs. Just as we were finishing up, some of the military dogs refused to sit on the flour bags. We opened up the bags and it felt like soap. We tested it. We didn't think it was an explosive, but an accelerant. We took everything, put it into piles, and blew it up without warning anybody. It was a *much* bigger explosion than we expected. Urea-nitrate was in the bags. It's an explosive made from fertilizer. That blast was so big that people at Camp Ramadi, all the way on the other side of the city and *outside* the city, thought it was a nearby car bomb. People at Camp Corregidor thought they were being mortared. Windows blew out for blocks and blocks in every direction. It destroyed the whole block. Civil affairs officers paid compensation to locals for injuries and property damage. Thank God no one was killed. The media reported it as a car bomb at the soccer stadium. Reporters in the Green Zone have no idea what goes on out here."

"There was no head to cut off," Major Lee Peters said. "It was like a hydra. We didn't win by killing their leaders. We won by eroding their support base. These people *hate* Al Qaeda much more than they ever hated us."

The tribes of Anbar are turning their *Sahawa al Anbar* movement into a formal political party that will run in elections. They also hope to spread it to the rest of Iraq under the name *Sahawa al Iraq*. It is already taking root in the provinces of Diyala and Salah a Din.

Captain McGee provided me with the eleven points of their political platform, for the record.

1. Election of new Provincial Congress.

2. Formation of Anbar Province Sheikhs Congress, with the condition that none was or will be a terrorist supporter or collaborator.

3. Begin an open dialogue with Baath Party members, except those involved in criminal/terrorist acts in order to quell all insurgent activities with all popular groups.

4. Review the formation of the Iraqi Security Forces and the Iraqi army, with tribal sheikhs vouching for those recruited

5. Provide security for highway travelers in Anbar Province.

6. Stand against terrorism wherever and whenever it occurs, condemn attacks against coalition forces, and maintain presence of coalition forces as long as needed or until stability and security are established in Anbar Province.

7. No one shall bear arms except government-authorized Iraqi Security Forces and the Iraqi army.

8. Condemn all actions taken by individuals, families, and tribes that give safe haven to terrorists and foreign fighters, and commend immediate legal and/or military remedies to rectify such acts.

9. Recommend measures to rebuild the economy, to entice industrial prosperity, and bolster the agricultural economy. Also find funds and resources to reopen existing manufacturing facilities. The main objective is to fight for welfare and deny the insurgents any grounds for recruitment.

10. Strengthen sheikhdom authorities, help tribal leaders adjust to democratic changes in social behavior, and maintain sheikhs financially and ideologically so they can continue this drive.

11. Respect the law and Constitution of the land, and support justice and its magistrates so no power will be above the law.

Ramadi isn't completely safe yet. Al Qaeda wants to take back their "capital of the Islamic State of Iraq," and they have tried unsuccessfully to attack it from outside on a couple of occasions since they lost it. (They also tried to move their capital to Baqubah in Diyala Province, but they lost that too in Operation Arrowhead Ripper this summer.) Also, Colonel Charlton said, "there may still be one small cell remnant here." But the war in Ramadi is effectively over. "It's boring here now," Private First Class Baringhouse said. "It's like we're babysitting the Iraqis. But it's weird and amazing to be bored here."

This now "boring" city, which is just barely beginning to recover from utter catastrophe, is a different cultural and political environment than it once was.

"The mosques in Ramadi all have pro-coalition messages now," Captain McGee said.

"How do you know this?" I said. "Do you actually attend Friday services?"

"We have relationships with the imams," he said. "We have very good relations with all of them."

"The Abdullah Mosque next to our outpost was hit by insurgent fire," Captain Messer said. "The Marines are giving them money to fix it."

Another mosque, just north of the city in the area known as Jazeera, wasn't hit by Al Qaeda. It was used as a terrorist base by Al Qaeda.

"It's blackened," Captain Dennison told me, "and abandoned. Insurgents used it, so the locals consider it desecrated. No one is willing to set foot in it now."

September 2007

Twelve

Hell is Over

Combat operations are finished in Ramadi. The American military now acts as a peacekeeping force to protect the city from those who recently lost it and wish to return.

It is not, however, completely secured yet.

"Al Qaeda lost their capital," Major Lee Peters said, "and the one city that was called the worst in the world. It was their Stalingrad. And they want to come back."

In July and again in August they did try to retake it and lost pitched battles on the shores of Lake Habbaniya and Donkey Island just on the outskirts. They destroyed a bridge over the Euphrates River leading into the city with a dump truck bomb. Four other bridges in Anbar Province were also destroyed in acts of revenge in the countryside by those who no longer have refuge in cities. And just last week Sheikh Sattar Abu Risha, the leader of the indigenous Anbar Salvation Council that declared Al Qaeda the enemy, was assassinated by a roadside bomb near his house.

That murder can't undo the changes in the hearts and minds of the locals. If anything, assassinating a well-respected leader who is widely seen as a savior will only further harden people here against the rough men who would rule them.

"All the tribes agreed to fight al Qaeda until the last child in Anbar," the sheikh's brother Ahmed told a Reuters reporter.

Whether Anbar Province is freshly christened pro-American ground or whether the newly founded Iraqi-American alliance is merely temporary and tactical is hard to say. Whatever the case, the region is no longer a breeding ground for violent anti-American and anti-Iraqi forces.

"We've had only one attack in our area of operations in the past couple of months," said Captain Jay McGee at the Blue Diamond base. He was referring to the Jazeera area immediately north of the city and including the suburbs. "And we haven't had a single car bomb in our area since February."

Violence has declined so sharply in Ramadi that few journalists bother to visit. It's "boring," most say, and it's hard to get a story—especially for reporters who need fresh scoops every day.

When the soldiers at Blue Diamond took me along on their missions I could see why so many reporters write off Ramadi as a place where nothing happens: I was sent along in a convoy of Humvees to the outskirts of the city in a palm grove to attend an adult literacy class for women, the kind of event that's neither interesting to write about nor to read about.

The class was cancelled at the last minute, though, so our trip to the palm grove was actually pointless. But Iraqis descended on us from their countryside houses and kept us busy happily socializing for hours.

Experiences like this are now typical for the infantrymen of the United States military, but extraordinary for a civilian like me who isn't accustomed to casually hanging out with Arabs in Iraq's notorious Sunni Triangle.

I was greeted by friendly Iraqis in the streets of Baghdad every day, but the atmosphere in Ramadi was different. I am not exaggerating in the least when I describe their attitude toward Americans as euphoric.

Grown Iraqi men hugged American soldiers and Marines. Young men wanted me to take their pictures with their arms around Americans in uniform. The Americans seemed slightly bored with the idea, but the Iraqis were enthusiastic.

Ramadi has changed so drastically from the terrorist-infested pit that it was as recently as April 2007 that I could hardly believe what I saw was real. The sheer joy on the faces of these Iraqis was unmistakable. They weren't sullen in the least, and it was obvious that they were not just pretending to be friendly or going through the motions of culturally-mandated hospitality.

"It was nothing we did," said Marine Lieutenant Colonel Drew Crane who was visiting for the day from Fallujah. "The people here just couldn't take it anymore."

What he said next surprised me even more than what I was seeing.

"You know what I like most about this place?" he said.

"What's that?" I said.

"We don't need to wear body armor or helmets," he said.

I was poleaxed. Without even realizing it, I had taken off my body armor and helmet. I took my gear off as casually as I do when I take it off after returning to the safety of the base after patrolling. We were not in the safety of the base and the wire. We were safe because we were in Ramadi.

Only then did I notice that Lieutenant Colonel Crane was no longer wearing his helmet. Neither were most of the others.

I would *never* have taken off my body armor and helmet outside the wire in Baghdad. I certainly wouldn't have done it casually and unconsciously. If I had I would have been sternly upbraided for reckless behavior by every soldier anywhere near me.

But in Ramadi the Marines are seriously considering dropping the helmet and body armor requirements because the low level of danger makes the gear no longer worth it. Protective gear doesn't look intimidating, exactly, but it is hard to socialize properly with Iraqis while wearing it. It creates a feeling of distrust and distance.

When we got back in the Humvees I was required to don my helmet again in case we hit a bump in the road. So bumps in the road are now officially seen as more hazardous than insurgents and terrorists in Ramadi. (There is a lot of hard metal inside a Humvee that you can bang your head up against.) I have my doubts about the relative dangers of each in the real world. Ramadi isn't totally safe yet. But this kind of juxtaposition is absurdly unthinkable in Baghdad.

The Iraqis of Anbar Province turned against Al Qaeda and sided with the Americans in large part because Al Qaeda proved to be far more vicious than advertised. But it's also because sustained contact with the American military—even in an explosively violent combat zone—convinced these Iraqis that Americans are very different people from what they had been led to believe. They finally figured out that the Americans truly want to help and are not there to oppress or steal from them. And the Americans slowly learned how Iraqi culture works and how to blend in rather than barge in.

"We hand out care packages from the U.S. to Iraqis now that the area has been cleared of terrorists," one Marine told me. "When we tell them that some of these packages aren't from the military or the government, that they were donated by average American citizens in places like Kansas, people choke up and sometimes even cry. They just can't comprehend it. It is so different from the lies they were told about us and how we're supposed to be evil."

The literacy class for women and girls may have been cancelled, but the local would-be students wanted me to take pictures of them at their desks. So the classroom was opened and they sat in their seats for staged photos. We had no language in common. It was just obvious, from their beckoning hand gestures, what they wanted me to do. They seemed to be proud that they were learning to read, and that women and girls were allowed to be schooled again now that Al Qaeda is gone.

Earlier this year these very same people would have treated me as an enemy to my face had I shown up. Al Qaeda is gravely mistaken if they believe they can flip Ramadi back into their column by assassinating Sheikh Sattar Abu Risha.

Shortly before Sheikh Sattar was killed near his home he explained the Anbari point of view to Fouad Ajami, the Johns Hopkins University professor from South Lebanon.

"Our American friends had not understood us when they came," he said. "They were proud, stubborn people and so were we. They worked with the opportunists, now they have turned to the tribes, and this is as it should be. The tribes hate religious parties and religious fakers."

Old school methods defeat insurgencies," Captain McGee said, "not brute force or technology. The key is to kill existing terrorists and prevent additional recruitment. Al Qaeda *must* have a safe haven or they will barely be able to operate."

That doesn't mean they can't operate at all, but it does mean they can't control territory, work out in the open, or rule over others. They are hunted now and must spend an enormous amount of energy avoiding detection instead of stirring up trouble. The former would-be "liberators" have become hated fiends who lurk in the shadows and lash out in rage at the society that has rejected them. Victory for them, in this place, is all but impossible now.

"Having the Arabic press note that AQI is rejected by Sunni Arab Iraqis is better than any message we could ever put out," Major Lee Peters said.

It is not reasonable to expect violence in Ramadi to wind down to absolute zero before the rest of Iraq is secured, or perhaps even ever. But the city has been successfully transformed from a war zone to a place that, like Beirut and Jerusalem, suffers acts of terrorism of the kind the world is long used to. The hokey phrase "war on terrorism" simply fails to describe what happened before, when a city of 450,000 people was chewed to pieces by an army of hundreds of sadists and killers, where every single day was September 11. Surveying the destruction was distressing, especially after meeting some of the children who survived the experience.

Terrorism is emphatically *not* what it used to be. We all knew that, of course, when hijacked plans were used to destroy skyscrapers in New York. Previously, terrorism was what the Irish Republican Army did. Many innocents were murdered in Britain, but Northern Irish separatists never made a crater out of a city of nearly half a million people. Nor did they even want to. Hamas and Islamic Jihad have murdered hundreds of Israeli civilians in restaurants and coffee shops and probably *would* do to Tel Aviv what Al Qaeda did to Ramadi if they could, but they can't and likely never will be able to do so.

Al Qaeda may be a relatively small part of the "insurgency" in Iraq, but their destructive power nearly reached that of a state for a while, at least in this area. I don't know of any place in Iraq that has suffered as much violence since Saddam Hussein's genocidal Anfal Campaign against Kurds. Baghdad is nowhere near as torn up as Ramadi.

The city is still in terrible shape, but its regeneration is unmistakable.

"How safe is it here, really?" I asked Major Peters. "What if I rented a house here for a month and lived alone without any protection? What would happen to me?"

"You could rent a house here for a while," he said, "and be okay without bodyguards, but I wouldn't stay *too* long. Something might happen to you eventually. Remember AQI wants to retake the city. They might eventually find you."

I asked Captain McGee the same question. I have no plans to do this. The question is purely theoretical.

"You would probably be okay downtown," he said, "but you would *definitely* be fine just north of town. If you tried that in February you would not have lasted four hours."

"You trust the locals that much?" I said.

"I do," he said.

"The only people I trust with my life in this country are the Kurds," I said.

"I trust these people almost as much," he said. "Are they petty? Yes. Are they tribal? Yes. Are they Arabs?" He rolled his eyes. "Yes. Do they believe in conspiracy theories? Yes. But they have their act together now."

I patrolled Market Street downtown with Sergeant Hicks and Lieutenant Markham. Kids loudly cheered as we drove past. Some children ran all the way up to the Humvees and knocked on the doors, beckoning us to get out.

When we did dismount our Humvees, every civilian on the street except vendors dropped what they were doing and came forward to greet us.

I photographed a freshly painted cell phone store that looked new.

"That's when you know life is coming back to normal," Sergeant Hicks said, "when they open a cell phone shop."

"It's amazing for us to see people out on that street buying and selling things," Captain Phil Messer said to me later. "That *never* happened for the first months we were out here. Literally *zero* businesses were open. People were scared shitless of Al Qaeda. If you pissed them off they would show up at your house in the middle of the night, rape your women in front of you, kill your sons, and say you will *not* help the Americans. Huge numbers of these people just fled to Syria."

I saw young Iraqi men picking up trash that had been dumped all over the city when there was no garbage collection during the fighting.

"This cleanup operation is a big deal for counterinsurgency," Sergeant Hicks said. "We're helping them organize it, and it shows Al Qaeda that the people are with us now. They would have been killed if they tried this before."

Iraqi children may know only a handful of words in English, but *mister* and *picture* are two of them. Every kid in Iraq demands to be photographed. I heard "Mister, mister, picture, picture!" literally hundreds of times whenever I stepped into the streets of Ramadi.

Some of the soldiers started handing out candy to children. Mass pandemonium broke out. Iraqi kids will shove and even punch each other to get a piece of candy. The soldiers should probably hand this stuff out a little more orderly.

The kids are cute, but their aggressiveness is a little distressing.

"One thing these people really understand," a soldier sadly told me by way of explanation, "is pain."

Back at the Joint Security Station, the Iraqis teach Arabic to the Americans. The Americans teach English to the Iraqis. The Iraqis gently help the Americans with their Arabic accents and use basic books as learning tools where words are spelled out in both Arabic and Latin letters. The soldiers and Marines are learning basic Arabic, what you would expect to learn in an Arabic 101 class at most. The Iraqis are a little bit farther along in their English, but not much.

The Iraqis make tea for Americans. The Americans make coffee for Iraqis.

I could see that these men (and they are all men) feel genuine affection for each other. The soldiers and Marines clearly think of me, a fellow American, as more of an outsider than the Iraqi army soldiers who also are there. They ate, slept, worked, fought, bled, and died next to each other in the heat of battle against those who had earlier taken over the city. My status as a fellow American seems to count for less with the soldiers and Marines than the trauma they share with their Iraqi counterparts.

I do not hold it against them.

"We Americans and Iraqis have been through hell together here," said Captain McGee.

When I visited the police station in Mushadah just north of Baghdad, where American military police are training Iraqi police, most Americans saw the Iraqis as lazy, corrupt, and contemptible. In Mushadah the Americans seemed to relish the opportunity to complain about the Iraqis to me, a fellow American whom they clearly felt they had much more in common with. They were sure I would sympathize with their complaints, and they were right. It does not bode well for the future in Baghdad. Anbar Province really is different, and it's not just because Al Qaeda has been driven out.

The Iraqi army soldiers in Ramadi were also much nicer to me than their counterparts in Baghdad, who politely said hello but never, not once, said anything else.

I started to prepare an MRE (Meal Ready to Eat) for myself—Chicken Tetrazzini, which somehow tastes the least processed of all the MRE options—and flipped through an old issue of *Air and Space* magazine that Lieutenant Hightower had fished out of his desk for me.

"No, no, no, no, no, no, no," an Iraqi soldier said when he saw what I was doing. "You eat Iraqi food," he said. "MRE food no good."

"It's fine," I said. "I don't mind."

"No!" he said. "We give you Iraqi food. Come with me."

An Iraqi cook had prepared a delicious meal of barbecued chicken and rice with a spicy red sauce I had never eaten before. The Iraqi was right. It was much better than MRE food.

"We have one Iraqi lieutenant here who speaks pretty good English," Marine Lieutenant Jonathan Welch told me. "You should talk to him. He has a sarcastic sense of humor and a really interesting point of view."

"That would be terrific," I said. "Can you introduce me to him?"

He went to find the lieutenant, but came back with bad news.

"He won't talk to you," he said. "Apparently some reporters recently spent a few days with him and his men. They wrote an agenda-driven story with a few quotes yanked out of context. He said the story was a total lie and that he refuses to have anything to do with the media."

I heard complaints of that sort about the media every day from American soldiers and Marines, but this was the first time I had heard it, albeit indirectly, from an Arab Iraqi.

Lieutenant Welch didn't mind talking to me, though. None of the Americans refused to talk to me even if they were suspicious of journalists.

What did he think of the Iraqi army and police in Anbar Province? I hadn't heard any complaints yet, not from one single person.

"The Iraqi army here is very good," he said. "One of the best battalions in Iraq."

"Have they been infiltrated?" I said. "I went to a police station in the Baghdad area and was told that perhaps half of them work with Al Qaeda."

"They're not infiltrated here," he said. "Most of the Iraqi soldiers here are Shias." Al Qaeda is exclusively Sunni and views Shias as infidels worthy only of slaughter. "They are Muslims, but very secular in their outlook. They are no more religious than Sunday Catholics. The Shias in the army work very well with the Sunnis in the army here. There isn't any friction at all. It's sort of like when the U.S. Army integrated black and white Americans. It breaks down bigotry. The Shia soldiers helped rescue Sunni civilians from Sunni terrorists and reduced sectarian tensions on both sides."

"Why is the Iraqi army here in so much better shape than in Baghdad?" I said.

"One reason," he said, "is because most of these people have been in the army longer. They were among the first to sign up. They have more experience, and the bad ones have been weeded out."

"We're learning to use local conflict resolution strategies," said Colonel John Charlton. "Living with Iraqis every day helps us understand local culture. We've actually become attached to these people on a personal level. We feel responsible for their safety. We're concerned about what will happen to our Iraqi friends if we don't succeed in this country."

I heard quite a number of soldiers and Marines express the same sentiment. Whether it's true or it isn't, and whether it's supposed to be this way or not, sometimes I sensed they feel like they're fighting for Iraqis more than they feel they are fighting for Americans.

"We play soccer with the Iraqis," Captain McGee said. "They always win. We taught them American football, though, and we always beat them at that. They can't even throw the ball right."

"All the mosques have pro-U.S. messages now," Major Peters said.

"They used to be anti-American, in part because AQI barged in and told them to broadcast anti-Americanism or die."

"We have excellent relationships with every imam and every mosque in the city," Colonel Charlton said. "Terrific relations. There are no negative comments about the coalition in mosques whatsoever. Previously there was, partly because they hated us for a while, and also because AQI said to broadcast anti-American messages or they would be killed."

"We get positive atmospherics from the locals," Captain McGee said. "They say, 'We feel really safe with you out here.' We want to make sure they never think of us as an oppressor."

If that ever happens (again), the Americans in Ramadi will be in deep trouble. They should count themselves lucky so far.

"We still haven't seen a re-emergence of nationalist cells even four months after defeating Al Qaeda," he continued. "That's because we're helping with projects and humanitarian aid. They could have chosen to come back, but so far they haven't. Partly, I think, it's because personal contact with Iraqis over time has disproved the conspiracy theories about how we're supposedly here to steal oil and women."

Half the world seems to believe Americans invaded Iraq for the oil. I hadn't heard about Americans supposedly invading Iraq to steal women, but it makes sense now that I've heard it. Many Iraqis initially compared the American invasion of Iraq to the far nastier Mongol invasion in the 13th century. That was the chief point of reference for many of the nation's Arabs (but not Kurds) when the Americans first showed up.

Other strange conspiracy theories abound. I never saw an American wearing a red beret, but apparently some Iraqis believe red berets are dyed in human blood. Perhaps the most amusing theory, which I know many Iraqis believe to this day, is that American soldiers and Marines have what they call "cold pills" so they can't feel the blistering heat of the summer.

"I demand cold pills!" an Iraqi officer said when he let himself into Colonel John Steele's office at Camp Taji.

"Listen," the colonel said to the Iraqi and pointed at his own forehead. "You see these beads of sweat on my forehead that are running down toward my nose? That's because I feel *just* as hot as you do."

One American soldier told me about a time he was having tea in a friendly Iraqi civilian's house.

"It's hot today," said the Iraqi, "but at least you have your air conditioner on."

"What do you mean?" said the soldier.

"Your air conditioner," the Iraqi said and pointed at the soldier's bulky body armor.

The soldier laughed out loud.

"That's body armor," he said. "Not an air conditioner!"

"Come on," the Iraqi said. "We all know those are air conditioners."

The soldier took off his body armor and handed it to the Iraqi. "Here," he said. "Put it on and see for yourself."

The Iraqi donned the armor and suddenly felt even hotter.

"Hmm," he said. "It is pretty hot. But I'm sure it will get cold after a while."

Every couple of days now people come home," Captain Messer said, referring to the small part of the city he's responsible for. "They swing by the station and tell us they're moving back and ask if it's okay if they return to their houses. Of course it's okay. They don't have to ask that. But they don't know. We tell them, 'Welcome home, welcome back to the neighborhood.' And they always invite us over for dinner."

Ramadi, along with Anbar Province in general, still has serious problems.

"We still have to worry about potential destabilizing factors in the future," Colonel Charlton said. "Reconstruction delays, economic stagnation, the isolation of Anbar by the government. Any of these things could happen. The central government needs to come out here and create some good faith."

"They are pretty strongly against the government here," Captain McGee said. "But last I heard that wasn't any kind of a crime. Half of America opposes our own government, so...so what?"

The biggest problem, of course, is that Al Qaeda isn't dead yet. Last week's assassination of Anbar Awakening movement leader Sheikh Sattar Abu Risha is only the most recent grim reminder that Ramadi is still a part of Iraq.

"AQ will try to re-take the city," Colonel Charlton said. "I am certain of it. They've already tried. They came in from Samarra, swung around, and approached from the south through the desert." They did the same thing again even more recently. "It was an attack planned at the AQ national level and it erupted in a day-long fire fight. The whole province is a major failure and defeat for Al Qaeda. They need to 'fix' this, so to speak."

The city, and the rest of Anbar Province, will continue to suffer the tragic consequences of its geography even if it manages to repair its politics and its culture. Will another insurgency erupt? Will the Sunnis of Anbar declare war on the Shias in Baghdad? I don't know. This is Iraq. But whatever happens, and whether it's good news or bad, never again will Al Qaeda find a warm home here.

September 2007

Thirteen

Hope for Iraq's Meanest City

"Fallujah is strange, sullen, wild-eyed, badass, and just plain mean," writes Bing West in his 2005 war chronicle *No True Glory*. "Fallujans don't like strangers, which includes anyone not homebred. Wear lipstick or Western-style long hair, sip a beer or listen to an American CD, and you risk the whip or a beating." Fallujah has been Iraq's bad-boy city since at least the time of the British in Mesopotamia; even then, travelers were warned to stay out. More recently, Saddam Hussein recruited some of his regime's most ruthless officers from Fallujah. Even though it was a quieter city than most in Iraq after the American invasion in 2003, with less looting than in Baghdad and a staunchly pro-American mayor, the Americans should have known that Fallujah was trouble.

But they didn't, and so they were unprepared when a rogues' gallery of Islamists, Baathists, and garden-variety malcontents made the city the launching pad for an Iraqi insurgency. The Fallujans who embraced the insurgency were foolhardy, too: had they looked at what similarly-minded Islamist totalitarians had done to Afghanistan, they would have known what hell awaited them at the insurgents' hands. General David Petraeus's radical transformation of counterinsurgency tactics has come at just the right time: the overwhelming majority of Fallujans, deciding that America is the lesser of evils, have now aligned themselves with the Marines and the American-backed city government.

The insurgency arose in Fallujah before spreading to the rest of the country. Perhaps it is fitting, then, that the insurgents—now on the run elsewhere in Iraq—were first beaten here in the City of Mosques.

Fallujah's darkest period began with a lynching. Simmering resentment against the American presence exploded in an orgy of violence on March 31, 2004, when a Fallujah mob murdered four security contractors from the Blackwater corporation, mutilated them, and strung them up from a bridge. The following month, the U.S. Army and Marines stormed in. But concerned that their assault would provoke violent reactions across Iraq—as, in fact, it did—the Americans retreated, their mission unfinished, and insurgents seized power. Taliban-style rule had come to Iraq.

Some of the insurgents were just looking for work and shot at Americans because they were paid to do so. Many were born and raised in Fallujah, where the Saddam regime had fed them a steady diet of anti-American propaganda; they sprouted from the same supply of xenophobic fanatics that had given the city its cruel reputation for so many decades. But the fiercest insurgents were foreigners—freelance jihadists from the Persian Gulf states, North Africa, and the Levant, some of them veterans of battles in Chechnya and Afghanistan—who formed the Iraqi franchise of the same international terrorist group that had slammed hijacked jetliners into lower Manhattan skyscrapers. Abu Musab al-Zarqawi's Al Qaeda in Iraq made the two biggest cities in Anbar Province—Fallujah and nearby Ramadi, Anbar's capital—the heartland of its so-called Islamic State in Iraq.

Many Fallujans initially welcomed Zarqawi and his lieutenants as liberators from the hated American occupiers. But the jihadists did not fight for freedom. Instead, they enforced Islamic law at the point of a gun, establishing a brand of fascism even worse than Saddam's. They murdered sheikhs who opposed them. They butchered their enemies' families, burning women alive and slashing children's throats with kitchen knives, and massacred other families for accepting food from Marines. City officials, tribal authorities, police officers—anyone in charge of anything was targeted for destruction.

Though Al Qaeda in Iraq is Sunni, like most Fallujans, its totalitarian vision has little in common with Islam as traditionally practiced in this conservative city. It was even more at odds with local secular habits and conventions. The new order in the city under American occupation, the old order under Saddam Hussein, and the ancient tribal system that predated both—all had to be swept away.

Realizing that Fallujah had become the terror capital of Iraq, the U.S. began a second assault in November 2004, seven months after its initial failure to secure the city. Ordered out of the way by the American military, civilians abandoned Fallujah en masse, reducing a city of more than 400,000 people to a booby-trapped, explosives-laced ghost town inhabited only by the insurgents. Then the United States Army and Marine Corps crashed through the walls and fought the massive battle that today even Americans call *al-Fajr* ("Dawn"). The insurgents lost, but their loss wasn't decisive, and they continued to tear the city apart for almost three years, terrorizing the civilians who trickled back slowly after the battle.

By late 2006, Fallujans had had enough. Though they had little desire to be ruled, or even nurtured into self-rule, by Americans, the jihadist alternative was clearly worse. So Fallujah formed an alliance with its former enemies. The alliance is one of convenience, and possibly temporary, but it was forged in the crucible of the most wrenching catastrophe Fallujans have experienced in living memory.

"I feel the sincerity in the American support for the Iraqi civilians here," one Fallujah resident tells me. "I am not going to say any bad words about Americans. I can feel that they really are eager to accomplish that mission."

Another Fallujan, who works as a money changer, says, "It will be a shame on all of us if the terrorists ever come back."

"Security is good now because the coalition, Iraqi army, and Iraqi police all work together," says a third, the owner of a fruit stand. "One hand does not clap."

While the Americans were lucky, in a sense, that Al Qaeda so thoroughly disgusted the locals, Petraeus's strategy shift was crucial to beating the insurgents. Before the surge, American counterinsurgency had followed a "light footprint" model: soldiers and Marines lived on large protected bases and did everything they could to avoid casualties. The thinking was that this approach not only protected the military; it also would keep Iraqis from viewing Americans as oppressive occupiers. But the light footprint model prevented the Americans from providing security to Iraqis, who began to regard their occupiers as not merely oppressive but incompetent to boot.

Marines also took the vitally important step of surrounding Fallujah with concrete Jersey and Texas barriers, forcing all incoming traffic through checkpoints manned by Iraqi police. Visitors can no longer bring cars in—they must park outside the city limits and walk—and locals must affix resident stickers to their windshields. High-tech surveillance cameras monitor every inch of ground outside the city; sneaking in is impossible. Perhaps it's fitting that people as provincial and, yes, medieval-minded as these live in a place that's as fortified as a thirteenth-century walled city. (One Marine describes Fallujah as "the Dark Ages with TVs and cars"; Iraqis think of this city in much the same way.) The barriers were unattractive, so the Americans hired local artists to paint murals on them depicting ancient Iraqi and Babylonian architecture, idyllic scenes from greener countries than this, and messages of peace in Arabic calligraphy.

The barriers don't merely separate the city from the rest of Iraq; they separate neighborhoods from one another, too. Foot traffic isn't restricted, but no one can drive from one neighborhood to another without passing through a police checkpoint. Smuggling weapons is prohibitively difficult. Anyone who wants to set off a car bomb will have to content himself with blowing up his own neighborhood. The walls are a major hassle, but they work. Fallujah's most recent car bomb exploded last July.

The barriers also divide each section of the city into intimately patrollable precincts. Inside these precincts, U.S. Marines and Iraqi police have forged a straightforward agreement with civilians: we'll keep you safe if you identify insurgents and lead us to IEDs and weapons caches. Americans no longer patrol in Humvees, as they did at the peak of the insurgency. Instead, the Marines have embedded themselves, so to speak, in Fallujah's communities. They have transformed large rented houses into Joint Security Stations that look and feel like low-budget university co-ops, where they share sleeping quarters, eating areas, movie rooms, and makeshift gyms with Iraqi police. They live together, work together, study Arabic and English together, and, above all, patrol their own neighborhoods together.

This is community policing, Fallujah-style, and so far it has been even more effective than similar programs that have turned around rough U.S. neighborhoods, from New York City to Portland, Oregon. "I swear I don't mean to sound like I'm selling something," Sergeant Stephen Deboard says. "But what the Marines are doing out there in the city is amazing. They are so integrated in the community. The first time I stayed at one of the stations, I awoke to the sound of an Iraqi baby crying and the smell of the neighbor's eggs cooking. They're living right there with the Iraqis."

The results of the Anbar Awakening and the surge are plain to see. Since the Fifth Marine Regiment's Third Battalion rotated into Fallujah in September 2007, not a single American has been wounded there, let alone killed. Hardly anyone even tries to start a fight now. A handful of people have taken potshots at Marines; one man threw a hand grenade in the neighborhood of Dubat; some fool blew himself up when the Iraqi police caught him planting an IED outside their station. Every attack has been ineffective. Of all Iraq's cities, only nearby Ramadi has experienced so many dramatic changes in so short a time.

"We tell people that we're in our third battle of Fallujah," First Lieutenant Barry Edwards says. "The first was in April of 2004, which we'll say we lost. November and December of 2004 we kicked ass. Al Qaeda in Iraq promised televisions, refrigerators, and air conditioners, [but] they did not follow through. Al Qaeda was trying to take them back in time. The Iraqis said, 'No, we don't want that. We want televisions, refrigerators, and air conditioners.' They see that the Americans are actually providing [these things]. We tell them that if they can get their area secure, we can get their televisions and air conditioners running and keep them running. When they see that, things improve."

Edwards concludes: "Now we're in that third battle where if we back off right now, Al Qaeda in Iraq will get back in. They want Fallujah. It's a very influential city. It's their first clubhouse."

Not that Fallujah is going to be a tourist attraction anytime soon. There was a time when Fallujah had money, and most of its houses are still quite large, even in the poor neighborhoods. Almost all of them are riddled with bullet holes, however, and some are just piles of rubble. The city's infrastructure is shot, half of its citizens are unemployed, most factories in its industrial district are closed, and its culture is stultifying even by conservative Arab standards. I see no bookstores, libraries, movie theaters, or any other public place where culture can be consumed, but only a handful of men-only cafés serving identical glasses of tea. Alcohol isn't banned, but only one bar exists in all of Fallujah, and it's on a side street next to a boarded-up building. The owner doesn't dare put up a sign.

During the war years, nobody collected the city's trash, and though today the Marines pay residents to pick it up, the city is hardly clean. It takes a long time to dispose of the buildup and to persuade residents to change their habits and use the new dumpsters, so every street has at least one dump site, and the market smells of rotting garbage and urine. Raw sewage contaminates the streets, too. Unlike some Iraqi cities, Fallujah once had a functioning sewer system, but the insurgents, bent on demonstrating the Americans' inability to govern, destroyed it by burying hundreds of IEDs beneath the streets and detonating them. A new water-treatment plant is under construction in the poorer southern district, but it will likely take years to rebuild the whole system, even if the war doesn't start again.

Most vexing, in a country where ferociously hot summers make sleep all but impossible without air conditioning, is the chronic electricity shortage. Traditional houses were relatively easy to cool even in August, but Iraq's modern homes are designed to be cooled with electrical power. If the power is out or intermittent, they're heat traps for six months of the year—a fact that the insurgents understood well when they paid desperately poor people to sabotage the electrical grid. Now that the power lines are finally secure, Fallujah's electrical system is slowly being repaired, and residents get about 12 hours of electricity per day—an improvement, but still brutal during the summer. The outdated system is a rat's nest of sizzling wires and overloaded transformers even when it is not being messed with; what it really needs is to be scrapped and rebuilt from scratch.

It's difficult to assess how truly safe Fallujah is. On the one hand, while I didn't meet any Marines who were nervous, all agreed that I would be crazy to walk the streets without their protection, since a small number of insurgents still lurk in the alleys. I'd be kidnapped or worse if I were unlucky enough to stumble on them alone.

On the other hand, Fallujah isn't as mean as you might expect—at least not on the surface. I walked the streets every day on foot patrols with Marines, and the only mobs we ran into were screaming children who wanted candy, soccer balls, high-fives, and photographs. Whatever Iraqi adults think of Americans, the kids really like us. But the adults seem friendly, too, or indifferent at worst. Several Marines told me that they had met Iraqis who said, in no uncertain terms, that Americans should leave their country at once, but it never happened while I was around. Arabs are among the world's most polite and hospitable people, so it would be a mistake to assume that Fallujans are pro-American just because they smile and wave. But in 2006, no one smiled or waved at Americans here. Marines could count themselves lucky if a cold shoulder was the worst they got.

"This summer, I ate dinner just about every week out there," Lieutenant Edwards tells me. "I couldn't have done *that* back in January [2007]. They would have lit my tail up. You couldn't go 100 feet down the road that runs along the river without getting hit by an IED. Now we can sit there with our flak jackets and helmets off like we're sitting right here. We go out there and eat chow with the guys who were shooting at us a year ago."

Corporal Brandon Koch, who fought in al-Fajr, has returned to Fallujah after three years' absence. "It's good to see the city the way it is and to go to the same neighborhoods," he says. "They're so much cleaner now. These people are doing things on their own; they're taking care of their own stuff. When I was here three years ago, I never would have imagined this place would ever be like it is now."

When American soldiers and Marines abandoned Fallujah in the early days of the war, it wasn't ready to stand on its own. They are more certain now that their work is nearly finished. Almost all the army soldiers have left, and only two jobs remain for the Marines: repairing the city; and preparing the local authorities to stand on their own. Most of the effort goes into training the Iraqi police.

Fallujah's police officers are in better shape than their Baghdad counterparts and in much better shape than they were themselves even six months ago. But they still have a long way to go. Incompetence and corruption are nearly intractable. In the end, only their teachers may save them from their enemies and from themselves. "They will emulate you, gents," one American officer says to his men. "They. Will. Emulate you. Why? *Because we came over here twice and kicked their ass.* I do not trust the Iraqi police today. Our job is to get them up to speed. They don't need to be up to the standard of Americans. But they do need to be better than they are right now."

Lieutenant Brandon Pearson, a military police officer and the resident expert in American criminal justice, takes a longer view than anyone else I speak with. "They're where the American police were in the late eighteenth and nineteenth centuries," he says. And though the Iraqis are more than a century behind, they are teachable. "Different agencies within the Marine Corps. . . . . train the Iraqi police," Captain Stewart Glenn explains. "How to conduct a proper investigation, CSI-type stuff, how to be a detective. We can train the Iraqis on how to handle their weapons properly, how to load and shoot their weapon straight, how to move out in the city, how to enter a house. Some of the rule of law things: for example, when you go into someone's house it is *not* okay to go to the refrigerator and take a drink. You know what I mean? It's a small thing, but they're supposed to be the good guys and this is how good guys act. It's small stuff, and I know it isn't real sexy. But this is how you make a country."

"We've already seen a pretty significant difference," Specialist Brian Henderson says. "When we first got here and went on patrols with the guys from the Dubat station, they were just looking around. Now they're trying to work on their intervals, their staggers, the stuff that we've taught them. They're putting this stuff into play more and more."

I sit in on a training class in the town of Karmah, an area on Fallujah's outskirts that was pacified even more recently than the city proper. First Lieutenant Eric Montgomery is lecturing Iraqi police officers about the high standards expected of them, focusing specifically on the proper rules of engagement, the Law of Armed Conflict, and the United Nations Code of Conduct for Law Enforcement Officials. "If they become like a police state, people are not going to support them," he tells me afterward. "If we can get them not to beat detainees, that's a big step."

No one knows how seriously the Iraqis will adhere to such basic principles after the Americans leave. Every one of them grew up in the shadow of Saddam Hussein; none was exposed to international ethical standards of policing and warfare until now; a civilized police force is an alien concept to them.

"These guys aren't the sharpest tools in the drawer," a trainer says quietly to me after Montgomery's lecture is finished.

"Well," I say, "hopefully some of it sticks." Some of it does, he tells me.

Not all the Marines would agree. "Some of them will tell you straight up that the only reason they are Iraqi police officers is because it pays better than the insurgency," one sergeant says. "I hear that and I want to say, 'Hold this guy while I go get my pistol.'"

Optimists slightly outnumber the pessimists, though. "The Iraqi police can almost take over now," says Lieutenant Eric Laughlin. And Lieutenant A. J. DeSantis asks me rhetorically: "Are they Marines? No, but they don't need to be. They just need to keep their neighborhood safe."

The Marines' final mission is the make-or-break mission, as all final missions must be. The third battle for Fallujah will be decisive. After the Americans leave, the city will either transform into a relatively normal backwater that nobody cares about—or tear itself apart. If Fallujah goes, Baghdad goes, and all of Iraq will follow.

A particularly pessimistic U.S. Army soldier I met in Baghdad last summer was certain that Iraq was too dysfunctional and conflict-wracked to be fixed. "Iraq will always be Iraq," he said. Fallujah, likewise, will always be Fallujah, and Fallujah is difficult. One should not be starry-eyed at the news of its "awakening." The city is not yet open to the modern world and its ways. Only desperate necessity granted Americans a reprieve from Fallujah's fear and loathing of outsiders, which it now directs at Baghdad, Iraq as a whole, and international as well as local jihadism. Jeffersonian democracy has not yet come to the banks of the Euphrates.

That said, Fallujah's worst days are likely behind it. "The Al Qaeda leadership outside dumped *huge* amounts of money and people and arms into Anbar Province," says Lieutenant Colonel Mike Silverman, who oversees an area just north of Ramadi. "They poured everything they had into this place. The battle against Americans in Anbar became their most important fight in the world. And they lost."

City Journal
Spring, 2008

Fourteen

The Rings on Zarqawi's Finger

"I am a ring on your finger." — Al Qaeda in Iraq member Abu Anas to
Abu Musab Al-Zarqawi

Since Abu Musab Al-Zarqawi formed the Al Qaeda in Iraq franchise, the terrorist group that destroyed the World Trade Center has fought American soldiers in Iraq and Afghanistan instead of American civilians in the United States. This may be good for Americans, but it has been a catastrophe for Iraqis—especially in Baghdad, Ramadi, and Fallujah.

I had lunch with several Iraqi police officers and spoke to them about the searing conflict that raged for years in their city and only quieted down a few months ago. The trauma of war is still fresh enough that they don't want me to publish their names or their pictures, nor do they want me to identify their police station. So I'll just say they work somewhere in the vicinity of Fallujah, and I'll call them Omar, Mohammed, Ahmed, and Mahmoud—generic Arabic names which I'm using as pseudonyms.

"What did you think of the Americans a few years ago when they first got here?" I said.

"The United States made a big mistake when they invaded Iraq," Omar said. "They destroyed the Iraqi army. They destroyed the whole army when they invaded. They lost their right hand against the insurgents. They lost a good partner that could have really helped in the future. In the beginning if they had just kept the Iraqi army and the Iraqi police, somebody would have been backing them."

"Do you think invading Iraq was the right decision, or was it a mistake?" I said.

"It was a surprise invasion for both the Americans and the Iraqis," he said. "They had no ability to analyze the actions they were taking. Neither the Iraqis nor the Americans could understand what was going on. All the casualties during the invasion were Americans and Iraqis. None were the third party. We were both losers. If we had just started with political methods to accomplish the mission, it would have been far better than the military action. As a result, the Iraqi people and the American people were losers."

Omar noticed my camera.

"He's a journalist?" he said to Tom, our interpreter.

"Yes," Tom said.

"We are not authorized to talk to journalists about politics," Ahmed said and glared at Omar, who had just given me some opinions about politics.

I knew what Ahmed meant. They have to stay in their lane, as American soldiers and Marines like to put it. The Americans in Iraq aren't supposed to talk to journalists about politics either, unless they are talking about local politics they're involved with as part of their job. Talking above their pay grade on the record isn't allowed—although sometimes they do so off the record. Privates can talk about their basic job as a private—which is why I rarely quote them. Most privates are reluctant to say anything to me whatsoever. Sergeants can speak about platoon-level issues. Lieutenants and captains can get into the nuts and bolts of local politics because they deal with it constantly. "But I can't talk about why President Bush invaded Iraq," one high-ranking officer said.

They have to be careful when they talk about high-level politics even indirectly. One mid-level officer, whom I shouldn't name so I won't get him in trouble, strongly recommended that I read the book *Fiasco*. by Thomas Ricks. "Especially make sure you read the chapter called *How to Create an Insurgency*," he said. "Ricks gets it exactly right in that chapter. But you can't quote me by name saying that because it's another way of saying the insurgency is Paul Bremer's fault. And Bremer outranks me."

Talking above pay grade isn't the only thing the Iraqi police officer I call Ahmed was concerned with. "The Iraqi police in this area are considered enemies by some people because we work with the Americans against the insurgents," he said. "So we don't want our pictures to be shown in any newspapers."

"Does everyone here at this table want me to refrain from publishing their picture?" I said. Lots of Iraqi police officers want me to publish their pictures, but some ask me not to, and a smaller number are so worried about it that they won't let me take their picture at all.

Everyone at the table nodded. None wanted their photographs published.

"They are a little bit scared, you know," Tom said. "Their pictures might be seen in this country."

"Tell them if they don't want me to publish their pictures, I won't publish their pictures," I said to Tom. "It isn't a problem."

Tom is a 60 year-old Palestinian who lives in Jordan, and his real name isn't Tom. He, like all the other interpreters I've met in Iraq, goes by an American name to conceal his identity. There is a chance he could be hunted down by terrorists and murdered even in Jordan if he could be traced.

He once invited me to have coffee with him in his room back at the station. Of course I accepted. We discussed Middle Eastern politics and his job with Americans.

"I love the Marines," he said. "They are like my second family."

I almost thought better of it, but I had to ask: "Have you ever been to Israel, Tom?"

"Yes!" he said, beaming. "It is my country. It is beautiful. I have family there. The first time I went to Israel, after the 1967 war, I was afraid the Jews might eat my flesh. But they were so nice to me in Haifa. They welcomed me into their homes even though I am Palestinian. We hated them, you know, after all that had happened. But I was welcome as a Palestinian. The Jews are good people. Like you."

For all the hatred in the Middle East, there is also forgiveness and moderation. Where are the moderate Muslims? ask many Americans. I find the question bizarre. I meet them every day in Iraq, and everywhere else in the Middle East, too. The problem is they have a hard time getting attention in newspapers and magazines that wallow in sensationalism.

"What happened before, happened," said Omar, returning to the discussion of the American invasion with the Iraqi police. "One mistake was committed, but it's gone. Let's just close it and not keep analyzing the same problem again. According to our analysis, American troops are now here to help Iraq."

"We have promised to work with the Americans against Al Qaeda," Ahmed said. "And that's it. That is all we are allowed to say about politics."

"Can you describe what Al Qaeda did here?" I said.

"The Al Qaeda organization is the enemy of Iraqis and of Americans," Mahmoud said. "We are Muslims. Sunnis. Al Qaeda came through Islam and used it to enter Iraqi lands. They are killers, insurgents, they don't respect humanity. They don't belong to Islam or have religious beliefs. They have no kind of religious beliefs."

Don't assume Mahmoud is dissembling when he says this. It may appear that some Muslims are being overly defensive by saying Osama bin Laden is not a real Muslim, but there is a solid case to be made that radical Islamism is, in fact, a totalitarian cult unhinged from the religion as it is actually practiced by the majority. After all, it is they, and no one else, who blow up mosques in Iraq.

Every mosque in the Fallujah area—and there are more than 200 of them—broadcasts pro-American messages from minaret loudspeakers. The messages inside the walls are as pro-American as the ones outside. The Marines have fluent Arabic-speakers listening in so they can keep their ears close to the ground of public opinion. If the mosques turn against Americans again, the Marines need to know.

When Mahmoud says Al Qaeda does not belong to Islam, he is not speaking theologically. I'm afraid Al Qaeda *does* belong to Islam theologically even if it isn't the mainstream. Mahmoud is quite right, though, that Al Qaeda does not belong to his Muslim community.

"In Western Iraq we have been a part of this big game," Mahmoud said. "The Sunnis here are very simple people, very innocent people. It is easy to win their hearts. Al Qaeda tried to go through the religion to earn their affection. People can get enrolled in those types of Islamic organizations for that reason."

"Al Qaeda is like a mafia or any other secret organization in the world," Ahmed said. "If you enroll in that organization, that's it. You're gone. Nobody can get you out of that business. You're lost. It's a matter of trapping the man after letting him in. Then he's trapped, he's lost forever. He cannot go back because the Al Qaeda organization will get him."

They are not just like a mafia. They are also like a murderous cult.

"The Al Qaeda organization has a core philosophy," Ahmed continued. "When you join the Al Qaeda organization the first thing you have to do is get your parents far away from your mind. Your father and mother have to be away from your thinking. There can be nothing else. Only the Al Qaeda organization. Your kids, your wife, your family, your parents, your beliefs, all have to be out. Only then can you enroll in the Al Qaeda organization."

An Al Qaeda member in Fallujah named Abu Anas was punished by Abu Musab Al-Zarqawi when he accidentally revealed to a journalist that foreigners came to Fallujah from somewhere else to fight the Americans. Zarqawi placed Anas under house arrest and only released him when he pledged his fealty not to Islam or God, but to Zarqawi himself. "I am a ring on your finger," he said.

"If an Al Qaeda officer gives you an order to kill your father," Ahmed continued, "you have to do it. Your father, your mother, your neighbor, no matter who it might be. It's a simple way to get anybody killed—American, Iraqi, any civilian, any local, anyone. It's a matter of ideological indoctrination from the organization itself."

According to the conventional narrative, Al Qaeda was rejected by Iraqis because it murdered Iraqis. It was far more vicious and hateful than the American army it vowed to expel. The narrative is correct, as far as it goes, but Al Qaeda is detested for more than mere thuggery. Other armed groups have been able to maintain at least some popularity even though they also murder Iraqis. None of the others, however, violent though they may be, are so thoroughly totalitarian, and so alien to the traditions of Iraqi culture. Al Qaeda in Iraq tears at Iraq's centuries-old social fabric as viciously as Pol Pot's Khmer Rouge did in Cambodia.

If you want to understand Al Qaeda in Iraq—its methods, its rise, and its fall—you'll find their story has more in common with the Shining Path's guerrilla and terrorist war in Peru than with the Islamic religion as it is practiced today in the conservative mosques of Fallujah.

Nowadays we can analyze what is going on," Ahmed said. "In the Sunni area, in the Western area, we have people being killed by Al Qaeda. The tribes and locals civilians here are standing up to fight the Al Qaeda organization because of that. We have been moving one step forward and two steps backward. We are no only semi-literate people. We need some more education.

"Were all the insurgents here Al Qaeda, or were there other organizations also?" I said.

"The Al Qaeda organization is the major one," said Omar. "They made some smaller sub-organizations for themselves to assist them by another name. But, in fact, they are all Al Qaeda."

"Al Qaeda's main task was to kill Iraqis," Mohammed said. "That's all. No matter how or when or why. They just want to kill people in Iraqi lands."

"Well, what was their real objective here?" I said. "Surely they had an objective other than just killing people. They wanted to accomplish something."

"Of course," Omar said. "This organization belongs to somebody, somebody outside the country. I blame Syria and Iran. There are small cells running around in this country in favor of those two countries."

The Syrian and Iranian regimes may or may not use Al Qaeda cells for their own reasons, but the fighters who make up Al Qaeda are not fighting for Alawite Baathism or for Persian Shia theocracy.

"Don't you also have problems here with Islamist extremists from Saudi Arabia?" I said.

"Actually, yes," Omar said. "They have been here in this area. But they aren't right now for the time being. If you look at Al-Anbar Province, it's becoming a stable and safe area. This image is being projected to the other provinces. Kirkuk and Mosul appreciate this and are trying to achieve the same thing."

"How long do you think the Americans should stay here?" I said. "And I mean here in the Fallujah area, not in the whole country."

"I anticipate that the American forces will be withdrawn to major bases in Iraq," said Ahmed. "They will finish their mission here in, let's say, one or two years. Maybe one and a half years."

"A lot of people say that the Americans are here to benefit from the oil and the Iraqi economy," Omar said. "They want to do business in this country. But the Americans could have just asked Saddam Hussein for that."

"What do you guys think of Saddam Hussein?" I said. The overwhelming majority who live in and around Fallujah are Sunni Arabs, as is Saddam Hussein. The Kurds—who also mostly are Sunnis—and the Shia Arabs did not enjoy the relative sense of security felt in this area.

"We appreciated the leadership of Mr. President Saddam Hussein," Ahmed said. "Because now we are sacrificing a lot. Because of the Al Qaeda organization. Saddam was painful. I admit that. But it wasn't as bad then as it is now.

"During the leadership of Saddam Hussein," he continued, "you could say he was a one-man commander, or a dictator. He was only representing himself. But at least during that particular time, we felt safe."

"We were secure in our homes and our properties," Omar said. "We can't compare that to the situation we have now with all these different types of organizations running around all over the country. Before there was nothing like an Al Qaeda organization here. I mean, they were here, but they were secretive, they were not in the field, they were not recognized yet. But now we feel that they are serious, that something big is going on."

Did the American invasion of Iraq inadvertently unleash this terror on the country? It would seem so. Would it eventually have happened anyway, albeit later? Who knows? At this point, it may not even matter.

"The presence of American forces here proves that there is an Al Qaeda presence in this country," Omar said. "This is why the American forces are here. Their purpose here is to fight the Al Qaeda organization. If the Americans want to accomplish any future missions, they need to support the Iraqi army and the Iraqi police with weapons and money and other things. Just get us so we can stand and fight side by side and accomplish our missions for the Iraqi lands. The more equipment you give us, and the more people you can get enlisted in the Iraqi army, the more support you will have from our side.

"Iraqi soldiers and the locals here are very brave," he continued.

"Americans know it, because they have given them the authority to take action against Al Qaeda. It's dangerous, but they are very good soldiers. You can count on them. But they cannot control Iran. Iran is the most important resource for the terrorists in this region."

"Is it true that the local people here welcomed the insurgents at first?" I said. It's hard to gauge how many locals were, as Lieutenant Colonel Patrick Malay put it a few years ago, "friendlies, fence-sitters, or fuckos."

"Yes," Mahmoud said. "And there was a reason for that. First, they were afraid of the insurgents. They were really scared. They didn't want to support them, but they didn't have any choice."

"Why did they have no alternative?" I said. "The Marines were here, too."

Weren't they? I didn't quite believe the probably face-saving argument that no one supported the insurgents except out of fear, or that the "awakening" alliance between Iraqis and Americans could not, at least in theory, have started earlier than it did.

"Actually," Mohammed said, "the Marines came, achieved their mission, and left. The insurgents lived in the city with the civilians, at home, in every part of the town. The American forces did not get involved."

January 2008

Fifteen

The Dungeon of Fallujah

Next to the Joint Communications Center in downtown Fallujah is a squalid and war-shattered warehouse for human beings. Most detainees are common criminals. Others are captured insurgents—terrorists, car-bombers, IED-makers, and throat-slashers. A few are even innocent family members of Al Qaeda leaders at large. The Iraqi police call it a jail, but it's nothing like a jail you've ever seen, at least not in any civilized country. It was built to house 120 prisoners. Recently it held 900.

"Have you seen that place yet?" one Marine said. "It is absolutely disgraceful."

"The smell," said another and nearly gagged on remembering. "God, you will never forget it."

I hadn't seen or smelled it yet, but I was about to.

"Come on," American Marine Sergeant Dehaan said to me. "Let's go take a look."

I picked up my notebook and camera.

"Leave the camera," he said. "The Iraqis won't let you take pictures."

"Don't you have any say in it?" I said. This was the first and only time during my trip to Fallujah that somebody told me not to take pictures.

"Nope," he said. "The jail is completely run by Iraqis. They'll freak out if you show up with that camera. If it were up to me, yeah, you could take 'em. But it's not."

If the Marines wouldn't mind if I took pictures, I think it's safe to say the No Photograph policy is not a security measure. The Iraqis, it seems, don't want you to see what I saw.

Sergeant Dehaan and I were joined by Rich Crawford, a civilian law enforcement professional who works with the Marines and helps them train the Iraqi police.

"It's bad in there," he said as we walked toward the jail. "But I've seen worse."

"Where have you seen worse?" I said. He looked like someone who had been around. The hard lines in his face looked as though they were carved by sobering experience as much as by time.

"In Latin America," he said. "In Colombia. I was a DEA agent there. The jail here is bad, and it might be the worst you'll ever see. But you need to know it isn't the worst in the world."

"Actually," I said. "This will be the first time I've ever been inside a functioning jail."

Sergeant Dehaan rapped on the gate. An Iraqi police officer grinned when he saw us and let us in.

"I brought you something," Sergeant Dehaan said and handed him boxes of instant oatmeal and toothpaste.

"Is this food?" the Iraqi said as he squinted at a box of oatmeal. It was a Quaker Oats Variety Pack. Iraqi stores do not sell oatmeal.

"Yeah, you mix it with water," Sergeant Dehaan said.

"It's good," I said.

The officer did not understand, so Sergeant Dehaan pantomimed pouring boiling water into a cup and stirring the oatmeal with a spoon. I don't think the message got across, but one of the Iraqi police officers at the jail probably figured it out eventually.

"And this?" the Iraqi said as he held up the toothpaste. He made a brushing motion across his teeth with his finger.

"Yep," Sergeant Dehaan said. "It's toothpaste."

Our Iraqi host grinned again, put his hand on his heart, and bowed slightly. He then led us into the back toward the prisoners.

"This guy is great," Sergeant Dehaan said, referring to the Iraqi officer. "He has two wives and six daughters. Al Qaeda murdered four of his brothers."

I didn't know what to say. For years in Fallujah, every day was September 11.

"Can you believe this building is only three years old?" Sergeant Dehaan said to me.

"*What?*" I said.

No, I didn't believe it. The building looked at least sixty years old, and it looked as though no maintenance work had ever been done. Floor tiles were broken, the foundation was cracked, the stairs were uneven, and the walls were utterly filthy as though they hadn't been painted once since I've been alive.

"A really bad contractor built it," he said. "It was during the war."

"I guess it's been hit a lot, too," I said.

"Yeah," he said. "This place was hit constantly by insurgents."

A handful of Iraqi police emerged into the hallway and greeted Sergeant Dehaan with hugs and kisses on his cheeks. They shook my hand and said welcome. One offered a cigarette. Iraqis are always offering cigarettes. It was strange to think that these people ran such a terrible jail. Did they ever offer cigarettes to prisoners?

Frankly, I doubt it, although I did not think to ask at the time.

Sergeant Dehaan led me and Rich Crawford to Major Ibrahim's office. The major is the warden, so to speak, and has worked as an Iraqi police officer in cities all over Iraq. We sat in plush chairs set up in a semi-circle in front of his desk. A young boy brought us hot glasses of sweet tea.

"How many prisoners are here right now?" I said.

"320," Major Ibrahim said.

So the jail is "only" at triple capacity now.

"It's a jail," Rich Crawford said. "Not a prison. None of them have been tried yet. Later they'll move to a prison if they're found guilty."

"I can fill you in on all this stuff," Sergeant Dehaan said. "These two have business to discuss. Come on, I'll show you the cells."

We left the major's office and Sergeant Dehaan rapped on the door of another office. A prison guard emerged with a key ring in hand and led us through a secure door and into the hallway that took us to the prisoners. I didn't feel like we were in a jail. The doors to the cells looked like doors leading to offices or sleeping quarters. There were no bars. I could not see the prisoners from the hallway.

The guard opened the first door and walked right in. He didn't even slow down. I gingerly stepped inside and found myself surrounded by children. They lounged on the floor. Some stood up when they saw us.

What the hell?

"This is the room for minors," Sergeant Dehaan said. "They're treated better."

They are? The cell was the size of my living room. Two dozen children lived in this place. They slept on the floor on blankets and had no personal space whatsoever. The kids were grubby, but they didn't appear beaten down or even in bad spirits necessarily.

"Some of them are related to wanted men," he said.

"Is that the only reason they're here?" I said. "What are they, hostages?" This would be a real scandal if Americans were running the jail.

Sergeant Dehaan ignored my question, but he seemed to sympathize with what I was getting at.

"You see this kid here in the Adidas shirt?" he said.

The kid stood in front of us, smiled, and admired Sergeant Dehaan's rifle. He did not have the look of a hostage about him, but he was in jail even though he hadn't committed a crime.

"He's the little brother of a high-up Al Qaeda guy," he said. "The other day he was being kicked around in the yard by some of the others kids who hate him because of his brother. But he hasn't done anything wrong. We saw what was happening and put a stop to it. We took him aside and gave him some cake to make him feel better."

Another cell lay beyond a door at the back of the kid's room. The guard turned the key and opened it. He and Sergeant Dehaan entered first. I followed and braced myself for what I might see.

"Holy shit," I said when I stepped through the door. This was not at all what I expected.

A hundred and fifty men were smashed together in a single windowless room the size of my house.

"This is the biggest cell," Sergeant Dehaan said.

No kidding.

There was no furniture. Most men sat on blankets and carpets. A few near the door cautiously stood up to greet us, but they did not shake our hands. They seemed slightly wary and had a weird look of innocence on their faces, almost like the kids in the previous room who really were mostly innocent.

Sergeant Dehaan and I must have been genuine novelties. The Iraqi prisoners weren't used to seeing foreigners. That much was obvious. The men looked at us like we were a curious yet benign alien species. I didn't feel threatened, but I was shocked to find myself standing there with nothing in between me and such a huge number of prisoners. I expected small cells with bars on the doors. I expected that no one would be able to touch me no matter how hard they tried if I stayed clear of the bars, but without any bars, any one of them could have reached out and touched me at any time. We were surrounded and vastly outnumbered.

The heat in the room was suffocating. It was winter outside and very cold at night, but it was easily 85 degrees Fahrenheit in that room. The warmth came from everyone's ambient body heat. Amazingly, the "cell" didn't smell bad even though I was told that it did.

It must be awful in August, though. The building was made of concrete, which made it a heat trap.

"There's no air-conditioning in this building during the summer," Sergeant Dehaan said. "And there's nowhere for the prisoners to take a shower."

The place probably smells like a zoo during the hot months of the year.

Sergeant Dehaan gestured toward a small room off to the side.

I stepped through the doorway and found a single Arabic-style toilet—basically a hole in the floor. It was, of course, filthy. The room smelled of strong sour urine. There was no wall or curtain for privacy. Dirty cooking pans and dinner plates were stacked in the toilet itself.

"There are six cells total," Sergeant Dehaan said. "The others are all a lot smaller."

"They once crammed 900 people into this place?" I said.

"They did," he said. "And it was standing room only. There was no room for them to sit down. They had to sleep standing up."

Every single person in that "cell" was a man. Was one of the six cells for women?

"They don't arrest women," said Sergeant Dehaan. "Ever. That just is not done in this country."

That seemed right to me. Women are treated badly overall in Iraq. Their social roles are strictly proscribed. There are so many things they aren't allowed to do in this culture. Crime is one of them.

Iraqi Arab culture is slowly reverting back to itself now that the totalitarian regime of Saddam Hussein has been replaced. *His* government arrested women every day. They were often raped and viciously tortured by his *mukhabarat* agents.

I didn't feel nervous, exactly, standing there with all those suspected criminals around me. Sergeant Dehaan and the Iraqi guard seemed pretty comfortable. I wondered, though, if I should be. I didn't exactly feel at ease, either.

"Are there any insurgents in here?" I said.

"No," Sergeant Dehaan said. "They're kept in their own cell. They are way too dangerous to be left in here with these guys."

I wasn't sure it was wise for me to ask this, but there was no helping it: "Can I see them?" I said.

"Sure," he said.

Before we went to see the insurgents, several more Iraqi police officers joined us with weapons. The guard with the key unlocked the door. The Iraqis went in first and yelled at the prisoners. I gingerly followed and found myself in a smaller and equally crowded room jammed wall-to-wall with suspected terrorists. Nothing stood between me and them except the Iraqi cops and their guns.

"Salam Aleikum," Sergeant Dehaan said to the prisoners as he stepped inside. *Peace be upon you.*

I refused to say that to the men of Al Qaeda. Politeness has its limits.

It was darker in there. The men hadn't shaved. They sat on the floor and squinted up at the police. And they squinted at me. Unlike the suspected criminals in the previous room, none smiled or greeted us in any way. They did not seem curious. They looked at us as if we were bugs.

"They're extremely violent," Sergeant Dehaan said as though they weren't sitting right there in front of us. He patted his rifle. "They're treated the same as everyone else, but they have to be segregated."

My skin tingled and I felt flashes of heat. These men would kill me if I met them anywhere else.

Not all Middle Eastern terrorists are alike. I have been inside Hezbollah's headquarters south of Beirut. I brushed shoulders with Hamas leaders in the Palestinian parliament in Ramallah. Never once did I worry that Lebanese or Palestinian terrorists would actually harm me. Al Qaeda is different. These guys are like Arabic Hannibal Lectors.

"Is it safe to be in here?" I said.

"Well," Sergeant Dehaan said. "There's five cops. And me."

Last summer in Ramadi I met a handful of detainees who were suspected of being Al Qaeda. They looked like doofuses who couldn't get a date or a job.

Most of the men in this room looked like they were perfectly willing to murder us all with their hands. I could see it in their eyes, in the sinister way some of them squinted at me, in the tightness of their jaw muscles. I wished I had a gun of my own.

Should we have even been standing there in the first place? More than 50 potential killers all but surrounded us. They sat on the floor, but some of them were less than three feet away.

"The nastiest ones are the little guys," Sergeant Dehaan said. "The little rat-looking bastards. They're the ones who have done the worst things to people."

I've seen how cruel Iraqi kids can be when they fight over candy the Marines hand out to them. The little rat-looking insurgents most likely were mercilessly picked on as children. When they joined Al Qaeda their bottomless hatred was unleashed against Iraqis even more than it was unleashed on the Americans.

"We have to get out of here," Sergeant Dehaan said. "The cops are getting nervous."

He was right. They were. Their hands twitched. Their eyes darted rapidly around the room.

"Let's go then," I said. If the cops are nervous, I'm out of there.

We left and I shuddered. There would be no interview in that room.

"Human rights organizations would have a cow if they saw this place," I said to Sergeant Dehaan. I felt little sympathy at the time. It was just an observation.

"Well, what should the Iraqis do?" Sergeant Dehaan said. "Let them *go*?"

"Of course not," I said. "That would be idiotic. It's just so….nasty in here. And people think Gitmo is bad."

Sergeant Dehaan was comfortable with his mission in Iraq and the flaws of the Iraqi police he was tasked with training and molding.

"I prefer these small and morally ambiguous wars to the big morally black-and-white wars," he said to me later. "It would be nice if we had more support back home like we did during World War II. But look at how many people were killed in World War II. If a bunch of unpopular small wars prevent another popular big war, I'll take 'em."

The jail in Fallujah is the only functioning jail I have ever visited. I did, however, go inside one of Saddam Hussein's former jails in Iraqi Kurdistan.

The famous "Red Building" in the city of Sulaymaniyah is a horror show. It's a museum of sorts now, in the way Auschwitz is a museum. Perhaps *monument* or *memorial* are better descriptions.

Before it was liberated by the Iraqi Kurdish Peshmerga, resistance fighters and their family members were arrested, interrogated, and sadistically tortured inside its walls. A free-standing rape room with large windows was built just outside. Bloody women's underwear was found on the floor after the Baath regime agents were ousted. Inside some of the cells are messages carved by children into the walls. "I was ten years old. But they changed my age to 18 for execution." "Dear Mom and Dad. I am going to be executed by the Baath. I will not see you again."

More than 10,000 people were murdered in the Red Building alone by the previous government of Iraq. All died during torture. Formal execution actually took place in Abu Ghraib.

I wrote about and photographed that hideous place on my first trip to the country, and Martin Kunert left the following note in my comments section:

"Two years ago, I produced the documentary film *Voices of Iraq*, where we sent 150 DV cameras across Iraq and allowed Iraqis to film their own lives. The cameras got into the prison you visited and others. I viewed several hours of video and testimony detailing the horrors of Saddam's torture. One woman recalled tearfully how her newborn baby was fed to dogs in front of her eyes. Another video shows floors stained with blood and fat that liquefied off torture victims and poured onto the tiles below them. What transpired in those chambers is beyond belief. It takes a strong stomach to go through the tours you're experiencing."

It seems somehow inadequate, tone-deaf, and perhaps even wrong to say Fallujah's disgraceful warehouse for humans is progress. But it is.

February 2008

PART FOUR

BAGHDAD REVISITED

Sixteen

On the Hunt

If your men conduct any raids," I said to Captain Todd Looney on the outskirts of Sadr City, Baghdad, "I want to go."

"We might have something come up," he said. "If so, I'll get you out there."

Less than an hour later Haji Jawad, one of the most dangerous terrorist leaders in all of Iraq, was spotted holding a meeting at a house in the area. An arrest warrant had already been issued by the government of Iraq, and Captain Looney's company was the closest to his location. They would be the ones to go get him.

"Do you still have room for me?" I said.

"Get your gear," he said.

Last time I was in Baghdad, I was told that most suspects surrender the instant they realize their house is surrounded. Fighting would be suicidal, and most terror cell leaders do not seek martyrdom. But the man we were after was far more committed and vicious than usual.

"Is he the kind of guy who might shoot at us during a raid?" I said to Captain Clint Rusch.

"Oh yeah," he said. "He's definitely the kind of guy who will shoot at us. He's a really bad dude. A few weeks ago he and his men lobbed huge bombs at a JSS in the area and almost destroyed it, then called up the commander and asked him how was his morning. And he said if we don't stop chasing him, he'll start wearing a suicide vest wherever he goes."

The tip-off came in over the phone late at night when the terrorist leader's meeting was almost scheduled to be finished. By the time everyone had their gear and was ready to go, we had seventeen minutes or less to drive across a portion of Sadr City and break down the door before the meeting was over.

We ran to the Humvees.

"Go with Sergeant Gonzales," Captain Looney said to me. "When we dismount, catch up to me and stay on me." He looked angry all of a sudden, but mostly he was just being serious. Any of us might be killed in less than an hour.

Our convoy of Humvees roared down Baghdad's streets in the dark without headlights. I checked my watch. No time to waste. We had eleven minutes to catch the bastard before his meeting was scheduled to end. Hopefully he and his pals were on "Arab time" and would hang out and drink tea for a while before heading out.

Almost every house we drove past was dark. Few streetlights worked. It was hard to believe I was in the middle of a city of millions. Iraq's electrical grid is still in terrible shape. Baghdad is only marginally better lit than the countryside. It produces perhaps only one or two percent as much ambient light after dark as cities in normal countries. Baghdad at night from the air looks more like a gigantic constellation of Christmas lights than the brightly lit circuit board of Los Angeles.

The Humvee in front of mine suddenly stopped. Our driver slammed on his brakes.

"Dismount!" Sergeant Gonzales said from the passenger seat in the front.

Here we go.

I got out of the Humvee. Even hopped up on adrenaline it's impossible to throw those doors open quickly. They weigh hundreds of pounds because they're thickly up-armored with inches of steel.

Every soldier could see better than I could. They all had night-vision goggles. I had to rely on my eyes in a near-pitch black corner of a dark city. It takes thirty minutes for a man's eyes to adjust to darkness, and we had left the brightly lit interior of the base less than ten minutes before.

Sergeant Gonzales motioned for me to follow him alongside a wall toward an opening that led into the neighborhood. I stepped in a deep puddle of mud. At least I hoped it was mud. Sewage still runs in the streets in much of Baghdad, and we were in one of the most decrepit parts of the city. But I hardly cared *what* had just splashed up onto my pant legs. Any second now I might be shot at or worse.

One at a time we poured through the hole in the wall. Every single house on the other side was cloaked in darkness. I had no idea which house we were about to storm into, but the soldiers knew and I followed them up to the gate.

It was locked. One of the soldiers—I couldn't tell anyone apart in the dark—kicked it with everything he had. Twice. And it did not open.

"Goddamn it!" Captain Looney said.

He pulled out an enormous hammer and swung it hard against the front of the gate.

BANG.

The gate merely shook.

BANG.

The metal gate shuddered, but it didn't break.

BANG.

Everyone in the neighborhood must have heard us by then.

If a meeting was still going on in that house, they knew we were coming. I kept as close to the wall as I could in case we were shot at. No one inside the house would be able to hit me as long as I didn't back up into the street.

Taking the house would be much more dangerous now, but the soldiers brought flashbang grenades. Flashbangs stun and blind everyone in a room for up to ten seconds. All the soldiers had to do was toss one of those babies into the rooms ahead of them. Ten seconds is an eternity in room-to-room combat. And American soldiers can do whatever they want in a room full of terrorists in less than two seconds.

BANG.

The hammer came down on the gate once again, but it still didn't break.

"Keep busting it open while we're climbing the wall!" Captain Looney said.

BANG.

The wall was about seven feet high and made of cement. Most of us couldn't get over it without some kind of boost. I'm not used to throwing myself over walls taller than I am, and the soldiers were weighed down with 80 pounds of armor and gear. Someone crouched on all four and let everyone else use his back as a step ladder. That effectively knocked two feet off the height of the wall. It's easy to climb five feet.

"Keep going over!" the captain said. "Keep going over!"

The gate was locked from the inside. Those on the other side desperately tried to unlock it, to no avail.

"Bolt cutters coming over!" somebody yelled and tossed a pair of cutters over the gate. They came prepared.

And yet still the gate did not open. We had wasted almost a minute while making one hell of a racket.

I felt useless just standing there and tried mostly in vain to take photographs in the dark. What was I supposed to be doing? I'm not trained for kinetic raids. I didn't know the procedure.

So I selected a soldier at random and asked. "Is everyone going over the wall? Do I need to go over, too?"

At that point I was ready to take orders from even a private.

"Yes, sir," he said, whoever he was. "You need to go over."

Can't say I was thrilled about that. Unless they got that gate opened, I'd be pinned in the tight enclosed courtyard in front of a suspected terrorist's nest. There would be no running away if something happened. But that was preferable to being left all alone on the street in front of that house while the soldiers—my *de facto* bodyguards—were inside and over the wall.

One of the soldiers who had gone over ahead of me kicked in the front door of the house with his boot. The sounds of smashing glass and twisting metal surely alerted anyone in the house who somehow might not have heard the banging on the gate with the hammer.

If the target inside was indeed wearing a suicide vest, this was most likely when he would martyr himself and take some of us with him, so I waited a moment before climbing onto the wall. I had cover from an explosion as long as I stayed where I was. But I didn't hear anything

The soldier crouching in the mud was waiting for me to use his back as a step ladder, so I planted my muddy boot in the small of his back. I felt slightly bad about that, but he was plenty filthy already. I had five more feet of wall to clear, and for an absurd moment I worried that I might humiliate myself by not being able to make it over the top. That was ridiculous. It was only five feet, and besides—I had so much adrenaline in my body at that moment that I could have thrown a car.

As soon as I pulled myself onto the wall I realized that every single one of us climbed up in the wrong place. Climbing straight over would have put us in the neighbor's yard. I had to shimmy along the top of the wall several feet so I could drop down in the courtyard of the house we were raiding. I could barely see, and I was terribly exposed.

Yes, he's the kind of guy who will shoot at us.

I was more exposed than anyone else while I crawled along the top of that wall.

Get down, get down!

I dropped into the courtyard of the target house.

"Top floor's clear!" I heard someone yell from inside.

No one had fired a shot yet. No one had exploded a suicide vest.

Then the gate broke open and five more soldiers poured through.

Lights were on in the house when I ran inside. The front door had been violently kicked off its hinges. It leaned up against the couch in the living room.

Shards of glass crunched under my feet. Mud and nasty muck from outside was tracked all over the carpets—and Iraq is a country where almost everyone takes off their shoes before stepping inside. We might very well be in a terrorist leader's house, but a small part of me still felt bad about the mud and the door.

My digital voice recorder was turned on inside my pocket. It recorded everything, but I have no idea who said what.

"Where's the terp at?"

Terp is short for *interpreter*. Our interpreter, Eddie, was an Iraqi from Baghdad who had spent the last several decades in San Diego.

"They've over there at the next house."

"Go! Go! Next house! Let's go!"

"Out! Out the gate!"

Every soldier in the house ran out the gate. I followed. The house we had just hit was empty. No one was sure exactly which house in a row of three Haji Jawad was supposed to be in. So we went house to house.

Some poor bastards would soon return home from wherever they were to find their door broken down, mud all over their carpets, and no explanation.

We ran to the next house and had no trouble unlatching the gate. Each soldier took up position. I stood near the front door and away from the windows. My eyes were beginning to adjust to the darkness and I could sort of see.

"Hit it," someone said. "Go right fucking in there."

A soldier kicked the door in with all his might. It crumpled like an empty 7-Up can. Glass shattered. A woman inside screamed. Soldiers streamed into the house.

Someone flicked on the lights.

The woman in the front room screamed again and put her hands on her head. Small children ran behind her for protection.

"Get down! Get down!"

She looked at me in wide-eyed animal terror as if she had just seen Godzilla, and she said something to me in Arabic that I did not understand.

"La etkellem Arabie," I said. *I don't speak Arabic.*

I wanted to say "it's okay," but it was not okay. I had no more an idea what was about to happen than she did.

"Go upstairs," said one of the soldiers.

"Hey, you, in there," said another to the woman who had just spoken to me. "Get in there."

They were rounding up all the women and children into one room and all the men into another.

"Get in there now!"

Two soldiers led three Iraqi men down the stairs. The men looked frightened and disoriented, but much less so than the women and children. Two were turned around and flex-cuffed.

The Americans were *not* fucking around. Odds were high that we were in a terrorist's safe house and still might be shot at any moment from any direction.

The one Iraqi man who had not yet been flex-cuffed spoke to me calmly in Arabic.

"I am a police officer," he said. "I have a badge."

I understood him perfectly, but I nevertheless told him I didn't speak Arabic. He needed to explain himself to somebody else.

Men were taken into the front room of the house. Women and children were herded into the back.

Then the power went out and the house plunged into absolute darkness.

Eddie, our interpreter, screamed at the Iraqis like he was prepared to beat any and all of them. His thunderous voice demanded instant obedience. While it was possible he spoke to them this way for effect, I suspect his anger at mass-murderers who had car-bombed his home town for years was totally genuine.

Flashlights came on and I could see again.

Captain Looney stood before the Iraqi man who said he was a police officer and asked whether he knew anything about Haji Jawad.

"I've never heard of him," the man said.

"Hey!" Captain Looney said. "Everybody knows who he is. Saying you've never heard of him is like saying you've never heard of Moqtada al Sadr."

I stepped outside the front door and into the courtyard for some air. Glass crunched under my feet again. The door hung at a crazy angle from the only hinge that didn't twist off when it was kicked in.

Two men from inside the house had been taken outside and planted face down in the mud with their cuffed hands behind their backs. They trembled in fear.

I went back inside. Captain Looney was speaking to another Iraqi man in a wife-beater T-shirt whom I hadn't seen before. What did *he* know about Haji Jawad?

"I've never heard this kind of name," he said. His hands shook and he looked at his feet.

Two soldiers in the kitchen briskly opened every cabinet and drawer and searched for anything that was not supposed to be there—weapons, intelligence, anything incriminating or out of the ordinary.

They didn't mess the place up, but they rifled through everything with a practiced thoroughness.

I heard Captain Looney's voice in the back room where the women and children had been corralled. The woman who had screamed when the soldiers broke down her door was crying hysterically.

"I've been in Iraq too long for your crying to affect me," Captain Looney said in a hard, even, and no-bullshit voice.

She stopped crying instantly. She didn't even continue to sob. She just stopped as if the captain had flipped off a switch.

"I've lost too many of my own soldiers in this country," he said.

In COP Ford's Tactical Operations Center hang three photographs of American soldiers in his company who were killed in Sadr City by Shia militias. All were personal friends and comrades of every American soldier I was with that night on the raid. "We fight for the men next to us," the captain had said to me earlier that evening in his office before we set out.

The woman who was somehow able to stop crying instantly also said she had never heard the name Haji Jawad. Everyone in the room knew she was lying.

"Do you know what this guy *does*?" said one of the soldiers. "He *rapes* women like you. He *cuts* off the heads of men like your husband. And he *murders* children like yours."

He also kills American soldiers, but that went unsaid.

Every person in that house did one of two things that night: they either covered up for Haji Jawad, or they revealed they were deathly afraid of him. There is no chance that none of them had ever heard of the guy. He is a notorious mass murderer on the loose in their own city. Imagine meeting an adult American who says he or she has never heard of Timothy McVeigh or Osama bin Laden. It just doesn't happen.

"I have a daughter," the woman said. She did, indeed, have a daughter. The little girl held onto her mother's leg for dear life.

"Lots of insurgents have daughters," Captain Looney said. "Having a daughter does not make you innocent."

The two soldiers searching the kitchen moved into the living room and started opening closets and cabinets.

"I had better not find anything other than one Glock in this house," Captain Looney said.

One of the soldiers found the Glock pistol that apparently had been declared. The man who told me he was a police officer said it was his. But everyone knew that police officers in Iraq sometimes moonlight as terrorists or insurgents. It meant something that he was a police officer, but it didn't clear him.

I stepped out of the house into the courtyard again, not quite sure what to do with myself. So I paced. And I needed some air. There was a tremendous amount of emotional violence in that house. All of us felt it. All of us knew we might be shot or even blown up at any moment. But I noticed, only in hindsight, that no one had been struck or even shoved by a single American soldier. The raid was intense, but it was also restrained.

Nobody was arrested. Haji Jawad wasn't in there. We would have known. He lost a foot in a fight and now limps around on a prosthetic. Captain Looney said it was time to go back to the base. The residents of each house that had been raided could file some paperwork and get a cash reimbursement for the damage caused on the way in.

Then a call came in over the radio.

A suspect with a bad foot had just been spotted limping away from the house a few streets over. So instead of going back to the base we circled around to where the suspect had been spotted.

After rounding a corner I was back in near-total darkness. My eyes had adjusted to the dim light in the house, so I could hardly see again in the darkness that is Baghdad after midnight. This neighborhood was dark even compared with most of the others. Only the faint outlines of homes against the cold dark sky were visible. Still, I could see that the housing conditions dramatically deteriorated as we walked. The homes we had just broken into appeared to be more or less middle class, but behind them were slum dwellings. What little I could see resembled hillside *favelas* in Latin America.

My boots squished and sucked in the mud and the muck. The street obviously was not paved. All of Baghdad is strewn with trash, but this area choked on it.

I followed Captain Looney.

Slum dogs barked and charged from every direction. Captain Looney pointed his rifle at one. I saw a red laser dot on its side.

Please don't shoot the dog.

I didn't want to see a dog shot right in front of me, and I didn't want to hear any gunfire. We were possibly homing in on one of the most dangerous terrorists in the world, and I could hardly see a damn thing. Whoever it was we were chasing probably couldn't see any better than I could. That was a good thing. Gunfire would reveal our location.

If I hear gunfire too close that isn't ours, I thought, *I'm throwing myself onto the ground and planting my face in that muck.*

"The target's pushing southeast," someone said. "That's back behind us."

But then we heard a gun shot a few blocks ahead of us on the other side of some houses.

"Shot fired," someone quietly said into the radio.

It sounded like a rifle shot, not like a pistol. But it wasn't close enough that I needed to face-plant in the mud just yet.

There was no return fire, but I knew this whole thing could turn kinetic and violent at any second.

The mud got deeper, and I had to navigate around giant holes in the road. It wasn't even really a road. It was more like an alley. Most cars were too wide to drive down it.

"Look at that big-ass rat," somebody said.

I couldn't see the rat without night vision. I wondered whether I would accidentally kick it.

I kept near the walls more than the soldiers did. They had night vision goggles and rifles. I didn't have either, and I felt more vulnerable.

Stars shimmered above us. They were the same stars that shine above my house in Oregon. That surprised me on some irrational level. Sometimes Iraq feels like a distant planet. Somewhere overhead I heard the roar of a jetliner, probably on its way to Kuwait. That put me back in the world. Kuwait is clearly on the same planet as Oregon. And though it's right next to Iraq, it seemed remote because it's so civilized and luxurious. Trust me: unless you're Iraqi, if you fly from Iraq to Kuwait you will feel like you're home.

No one was walking around except us—and the person up ahead we were about to detain. The night was as silent as if we were camping out in Alaska.

Just ahead on the left was a dump site where an enormous amount of garbage had been tossed. I gave it a wide berth. Insurgents sometimes bury anti-personnel IEDs in those piles and detonate them as platoons of soldiers walk past. For all I knew, the entire neighborhood was laced with booby traps.

More dogs barked. I faintly heard men speaking in English up ahead and saw the black outlines of motionless soldiers a hundred feet or so up ahead. It seemed they had caught the fleeing suspect with the bum foot.

"They got him," Sergeant Gonzales said. His job was to monitor the radio with an ear piece and listen to chatter.

"*Him*?" I said.

"They got the guy who matches the description," he said. "We don't yet know if it's him."

The area got more and more slum-like as I moved toward them. Then I realized I was inside a junk yard.

A small Iraqi man sat on the ground. Three American soldiers stood over him.

"Stand up!" Captain Looney said when we reached them.

Eddie translated.

"Why were you running?"

"I did not run away," the man said.

"We were watching you," Captain Looney said. "We watched you run. Only the thief fears the judge. Why were you running from us? Why were you hiding? We saw you hiding. How do you think we found you?"

The man mumbled something in Arabic. I could hardly hear him. I don't think Eddie heard him either because he didn't translate.

"Somebody bring some zip strips," Captain Looney said.

Someone brought the zip strips and flex-cuffed the suspect.

I noticed another man had also been captured. "He's shaking like a dog shitting razor blades," somebody said.

The identification cards of both suspects were checked and called into the base. Someone in the Tactical Operations Center compared their names with those in the known terrorist database.

"You still haven't answered my question," Captain Looney said. "Why were you running? Are you a Muslim?"

"Yes," the man said.

"Do you read the Koran?"

"No," the man said.

"You know," Captain Looney said, "that it says only the thief fears the judge, right?"

A loud and low military plane roared overhead.

"We were scared," the man said.

"Why were you scared?" Captain Looney said. "Look at me."

The man looked up at Captain Looney. The captain shined a flashlight in the man's face and checked his appearance against a color photograph of Haji Jawad.

He wasn't the guy.

But the other captured man, the man standing just a few feet away and trembling violently, bore a more striking resemblance to the man we were after. He was the one with the bad foot. Was it the prosthetic that Haji Jawad hobbled around on?

Captain Looney approached him.

"Why were you running?" he said.

"We were scared," the suspect said.

"Well, you know what?" Captain Looney said. "When the police come into my neighborhood, I don't run. You know why? Because I haven't done anything wrong."

"I am afraid of you," the man said.

"Why?" Captain Looney said. "Why do you fear us? We don't just go running around here *killing* people like Saddam Hussein did."

"I am afraid because of the explosion," the man said.

"What explosion?" Captain Looney said.

"It was four months ago," the man said.

"What does that have to do with *now*?" Captain Looney said.

"I am sorry," the man said. "I apologize."

A soldier frisked the suspect firmly and thoroughly in a way you do *not* ever want to be searched. This wasn't your typical airport security line pat-down where the TSA guy knows very well that you almost certainly are not a terrorist.

On the other side of a chain link fence was a van surrounded by enormous piles of junk yard refuse.

"Are you living in that van?" Captain Looney said to the suspect. "Go check out that van," he said to one of his men.

Two soldiers climbed over the chain link fence and poked around inside the van.

"What the fuck are you doing out here, man?" the captain said.

"We are security guards."

"Yeah, but what are you *guarding*," Captain Looney said.

"There are air conditioners out here," said Eddie, our interpreter.

"It's junk," Captain Looney said. "It's just junk."

Almost every encounter I have ever seen between an American soldier—especially an American officer—and an Iraqi has been polite. Terrorist suspects, especially terrorists with American blood on their hands, get treated differently. No one had physically harmed either of these men, though. I didn't even see either of them get shoved, let alone struck.

"He's shaking pretty good," one of the soldiers said, referring to the second suspect.

"I was a prisoner in Iran," the man said. "I have the flu and a bad heart."

He matched the physical description of Haji Jawad, but he was just a random guy who coincidentally had a bad foot. And he got spooked and ran. The fact that he wasn't actually *missing* a foot was all the proof we needed that he wasn't the target. At this point he was only being interrogated because he ran from American soldiers. In and of itself that's not a big deal, but he ran right after the soldiers raided a house that was thought to be a meeting place for terrorist leaders. He picked a bad time to freak out.

Captain Looney asked him the same questions over and over again and could not get a straight answer. All he got were stock responses larded with filler words like "Inshallah."

"Inshallah" means *God willing* in Arabic, and it's often associated, from the American point of view, with the evasion of responsibility. "I'll see you tomorrow at three o'clock, Inshallah," is often correctly interpreted as meaning, "There is a good chance I won't be there." Earlier that day I heard an American soldier tell an Iraqi bureaucrat that his wristwatch didn't come with the word *Inshallah* on it anywhere.

It's often difficult to get a straight answer out of Iraqis. Evasion is a habitual survival mechanism that evolved in a society that was ruled for decades by a totalitarian police state. It survived the destruction of Saddam Hussein's regime because so many neighborhoods have been ruled by psychopathic militias. It is still not clear to some Iraqis that American soldiers aren't just another psychopathic militia. Canned boilerplate is all you can get out of some people.

"I'm tired of this Iraqi talk," Captain Looney said to the suspect. "I'm going to hand you over to the interrogators. That's what they get paid to do. I'm tired of hearing *Inshallah*. Listen up. You can have this conversation with me, be honest with me, and stop giving me these bullshit answers like *Inshallah* and *Wallah adim*, or I'm going to take you to the interrogators and let them talk to you."

The man mumbled something and ended his sentence with "Inshallah."

"You're saying it," Captain Looney said. "You're saying *Inshallah*. I don't want to hear that word."

A pair of blackhawk helicopters flew overhead. Military air traffic over Baghdad is constant, partly so insurgents and terrorists will always feel like they're being watched from the air as well as the ground. And they *are* being watched from the air and the sky as well as the ground.

My Kevlar helmet was beginning to make my head hurt. I wanted to take it off, but I didn't dare in the slums of Baghdad. The air smelled of garbage and piss. Home felt not only thousands of miles away, but years away.

Captain Looney asked the suspect what he knew about Haji Jawad. The man said he had never heard of him, which was a lie.

"That's like saying you don't know who Ali or Mohammad is," Captain Looney said. "What *do* you know?"

The suspect kept talking in platitudes and had nothing of substance to say.

"I'm tired of these motherfuckers," one soldier said.

Captain Looney spoke into his radio. "These two individuals are living in squalor," he said. "They're pretty uneducated. I don't think either one of them would be smart enough to even hit the switch on an IED. But we can still bring them in for interrogation, over."

No one, including me, seemed to think either of them should be brought in and questioned.

"Ugh," said one of the soldiers and stepped back. "This guy breathed on me and I just about dry heaved."

"Don't get so close to him," said Sergeant Gonzales.

"I was worried I was going to have to shoot a dog back there," Captain Looney said to me.

"I thought you might," I said, "when I saw one painted with the red laser dot."

"I was just trying to scare them away," he said. "They're only doing what comes naturally. Dogs don't make a choice. People make a choice to be good or bad."

The radio squawked and he answered. "I think it was bad intel," he said. "I don't think these guys have anything to do with who we're looking for."

One of the soldiers who was searching the van stepped out with something in his hand. "Sir," he said. "We found three M4 magazines and a military map of Fallujah."

A military map of Fallujah?

"Let me see that," Captain Looney said.

The soldier produced the map and unfolded it. Sure enough, it was exactly like the maps I had seen on the walls inside U.S. Marine bases in Fallujah. An American Marine sergeant's name was written on top of the map with a red pen. How did these guys get that map?

"It's not wise to have U.S. military stuff in your house, bro," Captain Looney said to the suspects.

"Okay," said the first.

One of the soldiers scrolled through the names in each suspect's cell phone.

"What's your boss's name?" Captain Looney said to the second.

The man mumbled Abu something-or-other. I could not quite make it out.

"Abu" means *father of.* Arab men often adopt a second name for themselves after they have a son. Palestinian Prime Minister Mahmoud Abbas is also known as Abu Mazen, for instance, which means his son is named Mazen.

"Abu..." Captain Looney said. "What's your boss's *real* name?"

"I think it's Mohammad."

"You *think* it's Mohammad?" Captain Looney said. "Seriously? You don't even know who you work for? Listen. If you keep acting this god-damn stupid, I'm going to detain you for the simple fact that no one can be this stupid unless they're hiding something."

It is not at all apparent from this exchange, but Captain Todd Looney has a lot of respect for Iraqis in general. I have spoken to him at length, and I've seen him interact with Iraqis who aren't being detained on suspicion of terrorism. It's only fair that I point that out.

It's also only fair to point out that these Iraqis may not be as dumb as they come across. I've pretended to be stupid while being questioned by foreign authorities. They usually get sick of it and let me go without extracting any information from me whatsoever.

It's common knowledge that Iraqi police officers frequently abuse those they arrest. Not everyone in Baghdad knows or believes that American soldiers rarely do so and will get in serious trouble if they are caught. And you'd be scared, too, if you were flex-cuffed and aggressively questioned. No one wanted to say anything about Haji Jawad because they were rightly afraid that he would retaliate.

And don't be shocked by the profanity. Military men don't talk like accountants, and they never have. "I don't trust an officer who doesn't cuss," I heard Captain Looney say to another officer earlier that same day. "We have a nasty job. Our job is killing people."

He really does not like to kill people. "I'm a pacifist, man," he had told me in his office. "At least I'd like to be. Of course I know *how* to fight any time that's what the enemy wants. I'm ready whenever they are. But it's not what I'd rather be doing."

Some soldiers and Marines I've spoken to feel slightly uneasy in Iraq now that they rarely get into firefights. Many don't feel comfortable with nation-building and peacekeeping, partly because it is not what they trained for, and also because it is not the kind of thing warriors generally do. Nation-building is political work. Most soldiers don't join the army to become politicians.

One night I asked Captain Looney which he prefers: kinetic fighting or nation-building?

"I vastly prefer this," he said. He meant nation-building. Killing people does not make the would-be pacifist happy.

"Some soldiers tell me they prefer fighting," I said.

"They're immature," he said.

"That's a good answer," I said. And it was. Killing people really is a nasty business, no matter how necessary it sometimes may be. So is raiding the wrong house in the middle of the night and scaring old women and children. It had to be done, but I felt horrible watching it happen.

"Get up," Captain Looney said to each of the suspects who knelt in the mud in the junk yard.

"I am at your service," said the second suspect, the man who had been shaking in fear the entire time. "If I'm guilty, take me."

"Get out of here," Captain Looney said. Then he cut the man's flex-cuffs.

The other man's flex-cuffs likewise were cut. Both were free to go.

They were afraid of American soldiers that night, so they ran. God only knows what they think of Americans now. Did they feel humiliated? Or were they more surprised that they weren't arrested and beaten up? The Iraqi police might not have been nearly so lenient. And the Iraqi police today are extraordinarily lenient compared with Saddam's Iraqi police that these men had grown up with. The two suspects might have an even lower opinion of American soldiers than they once did, or they might think better of them today. I have no idea.

All of us—Captain Looney, Sergeant Gonzales, the rest of the soldiers, and I—walked back toward the waiting and idling Humvees that would return us to base. We had come up empty. We did not have the most-wanted terrorist flex-cuffed and blindfolded in the back of one of the trucks. All we had was more mud and muck on our boots to show for the effort.

"Why the *fuck* are you here voluntarily?" Captain Looney said to me.

I didn't know what to say.

"Do you do this kind of shit all the time?" said another soldier to me on the way back.

"Not exactly," I said.

"Pretty heavy, I guess," he said. "We were ready to go kinetic back there."

"I could see that," I said. "And yeah, it's kind of heavy. But it's not too dangerous here anymore, at least not in general."

"But it sure has the potential to be," he said.

December 2008

Seventeen

The Future of Iraq

Captain Todd Allison slipped off his helmet and tucked it under his arm as he and I walked on a dusty residential street in a Shia quarter of Baghdad.

"This is the safest place in the city," he said. He no longer needed his helmet or body armor, and neither did I. "This street is protected by JAM."

Not much remains of Moqtada al Sadr's *Jaysh al Mahdi* militia. The Iraqi army purged Basra and Sadr City of Shia insurgents last spring, but Sadr and his men still have clout in some areas.

I joined Captain Allison and captains Todd Looney and Clint Rusch for dinner at Iraqi army General Nasser's house to discuss politics and security. General Nasser greeted us at the door and welcomed us warmly in Arabic. After introducing us to intelligence officer Major Kareem, he invited us to sit and drink black tea with sugar.

"We've also got a JAM guy joining us tonight," Captain Allison said.

Hajji Jasim, our JAM companion, was from the Organization of the Martyr Sadr, the supposed "political wing" of the Mahdi Army. The distinction between the Mahdi Army's "political" and "military" wings is a diplomatic invention. The U.S. military came up with it partly as an excuse to meet with members of an enemy militia, and partly to signal to Sadr that he can dissolve his militia without having to retire from politics.

The British government is trying a similar approach with Hezbollah in Lebanon, but Hezbollah refuses to play along and makes it abundantly clear that no distinct "political wing" exists. "All political, social and jihad work is tied to the decisions of this leadership," said Hezbollah's Deputy

Secretary-General Naim Qassem. "The same leadership that directs the parliamentary and government work also leads jihad actions in the struggle against Israel."

The Mahdi Army, though, is a bit cannier than Hezbollah and is willing to go along with the ruse because it's expedient. "We're all part of the same hypocrisy," Captain Allison said. "Hajji Jasim is using us, and we're using him."

General Nasser sat in a high-backed chair in front of the window and wrapped himself in a heavy robe as thick as a blanket. "We wear this type of outfit in winter," he said, "to keep us warm." It was December and still cold in Iraq. At least Iraqis felt cold. I did not need a jacket, let alone a thick blanket.

Saddam Hussein threw General Nasser in prison during the 1991 Gulf War. Now that Saddam's regime is out of the way and Nasser's own Shia community dominates Iraq's politics, he's angling to be picked as the minister of defense.

I asked him what most Iraqis really thought about the new Status of Forces Agreement (SOFA) signed by the United States and Iraq. The American military is welcome to stay in Iraq for a few more years, but is obligated to evacuate most Iraqi cities by the middle of 2009 and retreat to bases out in the countryside, leaving both governing and security to Iraqis.

"Most people here are in favor of SOFA," he said, "but JAM and Iran try to prevent people from knowing what it is really about. Iraqi journalists explain it well, though. We in the security department try to make sure everyone knows about it. The only people who don't accept it are uneducated."

"That describes most people in Sadr City," Captain Heil said.

Major Kareem joined the conversation. He's an intelligence officer in charge of the Iraqi army's 44th Brigade.

"They've been brainwashed for five years by JAM," he said. "But people have been turning against them. Even regular people in those areas are beginning to cooperate. Even many JAM members themselves understand reality and are starting to talk to us. The end is now very obvious."

"Our concern," Captain Heil said to Major Kareem, "is that those who are left really just want to keep on fighting. They're the ones aligned with Iran. Are they going to keep fighting?"

"Now we're at the core of the problem," Major Kareem said.

"If we weren't here," Captain Heil said, "they couldn't attack us. This is part of the problem. Even when JAM has been defeated, there are groups that just want to attack coalition forces. They all want to claim that they drove us out of Iraq."

If American forces withdraw from Iraq under fire from Shia militias, two contradictory things would happen at the same time. The militias' excuse to exist would be yanked out from under them, but their credibility would be bolstered thanks to their perceived victory. Iraqi "resistance" groups therefore have mutually exclusive goals. They must resist the Americans, but they'll be useless the instant they win.

"I've been an intelligence officer for seventeen years," Major Kareem said, "and I've been working with Americans for five years. The JAM Special Groups are linked in a straight line to Iranian intelligence and Khameini's office. They want to achieve Iranian interests in Iraq. As security forces working with the Americans, our job is to find and eliminate them."

Ryan Crocker, who served as the U.S. ambassador to Lebanon from 1990 to 1993, and to Iraq from 2007 to 2009, compared Iran's sponsorship of Shia militias in Iraq to its Hezbollah program in Lebanon. "Iran is pursuing," he said in testimony to the U.S. Congress in the spring of 2008, "a Lebanonization strategy, using the same techniques they used in Lebanon to co-opt elements of the local Shia community and use them as basically instruments of Iranian force."

"Three weeks ago," General Kareem said, "an American brigade ambushed three Special Groups members. An op was discovered. These three members paid 20,000 dollars to a guy to go onto an American base and kidnap American soldiers. Where did they get the 20,000 dollars? I don't have that kind of money. Hardly anyone in Iraq has that kind of money. That means they have strong financial support. We have to find these groups and detain them."

Hajji Jasim, General Nasser's guest from the office of the Mahdi Army's "political wing," sat next to Major Kareem on the couch. "Understand something," he said to Captain Heil. "In the media, JAM only pretends to oppose the Status of Forces Agreement. Privately, we like it. It helps Sadr more than anything else. Those committing violence are going against Sadr's orders. You wanted the occupation to last 20 more years. Now, under SOFA, it's down to three years. That's great for us."

When I met military correspondent and author Tom Ricks a few weeks ago, he relayed to me an interesting anecdote from his book about the surge called *The Gamble*. "Sadr's people entered into secret negotiations with the United States in, I think, 2007, about whether or not to have negotiations," he said. "They said before we begin any talks, we have to have a date certain when you will withdraw from Iraq. The American policy said we can't do that. So the Sadrists said well, then we can't have talks. Then the Americans said, well, just out of curiosity, what was the [withdrawal] date you had in mind? The Sadrists said 2013. Which put them on the right-wing of the U.S. Congress."

If the Sadrists, two years ago, wanted the United States out of Iraq after six years, of course they're privately happy now that the United States has agreed to be out in three.

"Iran supports violent groups," Hajji Jasim, the JAM guy, said. "But they are small and scared. They aren't scared of you or the Iraqi army. They're afraid of the Iraqi people. I was in Sadr City today. People were happy. The situation is very calm there. We want safety for your people and ours."

"Hopefully you and your people can start doing more and we can do less," Captain Heil said.

"After you withdraw," Jasim said, "we will double our efforts." When he said "we," he meant Iraqis, not necessarily JAM. "We will prove to you that the Iraqi soldiers can do this."

Not even in an alternate universe would a Hezbollah official say anything like that to an Israeli officer. There is absolutely no chance that Hezbollah will cooperate with the Lebanese army to stamp out anti-Israeli terrorist cells in South Lebanon.

I didn't know what to make of this guy Hajji Jasim. Whose side was he even on? The lines were not clear. One thing, at least, however, was clear: the similarities between the Mahdi Army and Hezbollah were fewer than ever.

Jasim then had to excuse himself. He couldn't stay long at General Nasser's house because he had an appointment with some of his JAM friends.

I wanted to ask General Nasser more about the new Status of Forces Agreement. Everything the American military will and won't do in Iraq will be determined, at least in part, by that agreement.

"If you pull out of here and leave us," General Nasser said, "we know the remedy for Iraqi people. We will use force."

Iraq has never been successfully governed by anyone but a strongman. You might even say Iraq has never been successfully governed at all. Who today sincerely believes the use of force by Saddam Hussein's Baath Party regime was an effective "remedy" for the Iraqi people, as General Nasser put it? Still, despite my unease with what he was saying, I don't think he necessarily meant a totalitarian system is the solution to what ails Iraq.

"Twelve JAM members were brought to court recently," he said. "They asked to be put under American justice because you are softer and jail people under better conditions. Iraqis are not like Americans. You are educated, we aren't. Without force, Iraqis cannot be civilized. Americans don't use real force. You talk to people nicely and worry about human rights."

This is how many Iraqi optimists talk, I am sorry to say. Most Iraqis who think the worst is over, that the surge was more or less the end of the war, don't believe Iraq is going to look anything like the post-communist nations in Eastern Europe. Baghdad is not the next Prague. Iraq may be less brutal from here on out than it has been, but that hardly means it will be a model democracy.

"Do you think," I said, "the Iranian government can dial up the violence here whenever it wants to?" Iran might very well wish to ramp up attacks against American soldiers in Iraq if Israel strikes Iranian nuclear facilities later this year or next. But Iran can't retaliate significantly in Iraq if the Shia militias are a spent force.

"The Iranians," he said, "have already used all the violent force in Iraq that they were able to use. Iraq was caught in the middle between Iran and America. This war has been a proxy war fought inside Iraq. Iraqi Shias could only get support from Iran, but Sunnis have all the Arab countries to help them. If Sunni countries stop supporting Sunnis militias, Shias will stop seeking support from Iran. You know what Al Qaeda did to the markets here. We were forced to seek support from Iran."

Maybe General Nasser is right, and maybe he isn't. I heard a different answer earlier from an American military officer who asked not to be quoted by name. "Iran has been restrained," he said. "Tehran doesn't want to trigger an open war with the United States. They can turn up the violence if they want to, but if they do, we might be forced to do something about it. So they don't want to."

"If the U.S. solves three problems," the general said, "American-Arab relations will be very good. First, resolve the Arab-Israeli conflict. Second, promote democracy in the Arab world. Third, destroy the Wahhabis. If you solve these problems, all will be well."

"What kind of solution do you want to see for the Arab-Israeli conflict?" I said.

"1967 borders," General Nasser said. He did not want to dwell on that, though, and I was surprised he even mentioned it. The Arab-Israeli conflict is peripheral, if not entirely irrelevant, to Iraq's problems.

"We need to have a good relationship with the U.S.A." he said. "The militias have bad slogans. If we finish them off, we will be okay. We need a strong relationship because the U.S.A. is powerful, educated, and prosperous. We are not against Israel or the U.S.A. Americans are my friends. A bad guy can get 40,000 dollars for killing me because they say I'm an American agent." Then he laughed. "A JAM guy, though, the number two JAM guy after Moqtada al Sadr, recently told me don't worry, I will protect you."

Sometimes it's hard to tell if Iraqis with their pro-American talk are sincere or if they're just blowing smoke. General Nasser, I think, was sincere. His body language and tone of voice said so, as did the naked calculation of his own interests.

"I had Iraqis here at my house recently," he said. "I told them Americans are better than you because they keep their word and they are disciplined. American people are not profiteers. Their wisdom led them to this. I want Iraqis to learn about American honor."

The first time I visited Baghdad, I only stayed for a week. The place stressed me out. The surge was only just then beginning, and though I was never shot at personally, I often heard the sound of gunfire in the background. One night, shadowy militiamen stalked me and a U.S. Army unit I was out on patrol with. Car bombs exploded miles away, but sounded as though they were detonated just blocks away. You have no idea, really, how terrifyingly loud those things are until you hear one yourself.

I left Baghdad and headed out to Anbar Province—which just months earlier was one of the most dangerous places on earth—because I wanted to relax. That part of Iraq had just quieted down for the first time since Fallujah exploded in 2004. The big question on everyone's mind in 2007 was whether or not it was possible to export the Anbar Awakening—the reconciliation between Iraqi tribes and Americans who forged a united front against terrorism—to a gigantic and hypercomplex city like Baghdad.

Nobody knew the answer, and many had doubts. I had doubts, too, but the doubters were wrong. The Awakening, or something that looks a lot like it, has now swept across every last corner of Iraq's capital city.

I spoke to Major Mike Humphreys at a medium-sized base in Northern Baghdad while on my way to the Sunni-dominated Adhamiyah area and the former Mahdi Army stronghold of Sadr City. He told me about the Sons of Iraq program, the institutionalization of the successful Awakening model in Baghdad.

"Sons of Iraq is something the U.S. government adapted from what started as a Sunni movement," he said. "It started in Anbar Province about two years ago."

"You're talking about *Sahawa al Anbar*," I said.

"Yes," he said. "The Awakening, which is what *Sahawa* means in Arabic. It's very much a political movement," he said. "What you had were Sunni tribesmen who were tired of the violence, tired of Al Qaeda in Iraq. These Sunnis said 'we've had enough and we're not taking it anymore.' They stood up to protect their own neighborhoods from these

Sunni extremists that were terrorizing their people. Then it spread, and it spread very rapidly throughout Iraq."

Baghdad has suffered terribly since the insurgency exploded after Saddam's regime was demolished, but the physical war wreckage I've seen in the capital is insignificant compared to what I saw in Anbar's provincial capital Ramadi. Ramadi was more wracked with destruction than even Fallujah. Ramadi looked like World War II had recently ripped through the place. Two American colonels I spoke to there compared the Battle of Ramadi to Stalingrad. It's no wonder Iraq's muscular anti-terrorist movement began there.

"From the point of view of the Shia-controlled government," Major Humphreys said, "the Awakening movement could be considered threatening because you basically had what amounted to a Sunni militia. Now the way we've tried to adopt that was by considering it as a Sunni-led *political* movement operating along political lines instead of military lines. So we've incorporated that movement into something that could be used to protect the people in Adhamiyah. We took these members who called themselves Awakening and we gave them a job for 300 dollars a month to stand guard in their neighborhood."

Adhamiyah is mostly Sunni and was a stronghold of support for Saddam Hussein's Baath Party regime. More recently, it was a stronghold for Al Qaeda in Iraq. Not until Al Qaeda thoroughly ravaged the place did local residents decide the Americans were the lesser of evils.

"Now many of these people," Major Humphreys said, "many of these Sunnis of Adhamiyah, were former AQI operatives. But the only reason they were out working for Al Qaeda is because they needed sustenance. They needed a paycheck to put food on the table, and AQI provided it. So we provided them with a stable job. Most of them already had their own weapons, so we weren't arming them. We were just giving them jobs. They go out and they guard their neighborhood. And they say, 'you know what? We've got a stable job here and we're tired of violence. And AQI, you're not welcome here anymore.'"

Some analysts have described this phenomenon as "buying off" or "bribing" the insurgency. This is half true at best. The insurgency did not go away. The leaders were never bought off. Only the opportunists and low-level operatives were. And they weren't even really bought off. An authentic anti-terrorist movement took hold in Iraq, and some former low-level operatives were given jobs as long as they were deemed to be loyal to the local authorities. Al Qaeda in Iraq still exists. *It* was never bought off. Its leaders remain fanatically ideological and can't be bought off or bribed for any amount of money.

"The *Sahawa* movement is Sunni," Major Humphreys said, "but the Sons of Iraq program is divided between Sunni and Shia, about 60-40. It's 60 percent Shia and only 40 percent Sunni. This is what bugs me about the media. Sons of Iraq is constantly referred to as a Sunni movement, but it's not. The Sons of Iraq are functioning very well in North Adhamiyah, and they are Sunnis and Shias working together. It's not being well reported at all, and I've tried on numerous occasions to get reporters to see that, but people at the bureaus still see Sons of Iraq as the Awakening movement. But it's not true."

My Spanish colleague Ramon Lobo from *El Pais* in Madrid joined me for the interview and had some questions of his own.

"If American troops leave in one, two, or three years," he said, "do you think the situation will be stable? Is the progress we're seeing real progress?"

"In most of our area the Iraqi army or the national police are already in control," Major Humphreys said. "We are very much in an overwatch position. We observe what they do and assist them. They don't have the intelligence infrastructure that we have. They don't have the aerial reconnaissance platforms that we have or the human terrain teams. So we support them with that. But they do have a very good intelligence network. I mean, the Iraqi army and the national police both, in our area especially, have developed such a rapport with the people in the neighborhoods. People are telling them what's going on."

Unlike Major Humphreys, I wouldn't describe the relationship between civilians, the police, and the army as a "rapport." Many people in the neighborhoods don't actually like the police or the army. I heard a number of complaints from Iraqi civilians, some second-hand from American officers and others directly from Iraqis themselves. But Iraqis like terrorist and insurgent groups even less. Some Americans find this hard to believe, but imagine how you would feel if political extremists exploded themselves at shopping malls in your neighborhood. It would hardly matter *what* you thought of the local police, you would almost certainly cooperate with them if it got the bombers off the streets and in prison.

Turning Adhamiyah around was a major development, but it was minor compared with the pacification of Sadr City last spring. Sadr City is one of the worst places in all of Iraq—and that's saying something. It's a vast slum. It's a vast slum in *Iraq*. Millions of people live there. And until recently it was a stronghold of Sadr's militia. It was to Iraq what Hezbollah' *dahiyeh* south of Beirut is to Lebanon—a ramshackle militia-ruled state-within-a-state where neither the police nor the army dare tread.

Early last year militiamen fired rockets into the Green Zone from the Jamilla Market area in South Sadr City and the U.S. Army took it back. At the same time the Iraqi army seized the northern portion of Sadr City. Both areas in Sadr City remain quiet today. The U.S. military isn't allowed in the northern part of Sadr City, but the Iraqi army and Iraqi police have the place under control.

"It's hard for us to see what goes on in north Sadr City," Major Humphreys said, "because we don't go there. We only know what we see from aerial reconnaissance platforms and what we hear from the Iraqi army. But journalists go in there sometimes by themselves. A reporter from the *Washington Post* recently followed around a former member of the *Jaysh al Mahdi* Special Groups. And this former JAM member said he is constantly on the run. He can't go home anymore because his neighbors report on him. He can't go into his old hangouts because there are Iraqi army checkpoints there. The guy was completely flustered. And this was a *Jaysh al Mahdi* leader. If they're still fighting, we call them "Special Groups" members because we don't affiliate them with Moqtada al Sadr's office that still says they're in a ceasefire. So if they're fighting, they are not aligned with Moqtada al Sadr."

It's not necessarily true that those who fight aren't aligned with Moqtada al Sadr. The U.S. military is giving Sadr a door. The Americans are trying to convince him to exchange bullets for ballots. Those who fight Americans or Iraqis are therefore politely described as "Special Groups" members even if it isn't true. Theoretically, it allows Sadr to stand down and wash the blood off his hands without losing face.

"We've seen enormous progress in our area in the last six months," Major Humphreys said, "and a lot of it is because of what happened in Sadr City. We had a very young Iraqi army brigade—and by that I mean a lot of relatively young new recruits, not a lot of experience. They had checkpoints around Sadr City. This was the 42nd Brigade. When fighting in Sadr City broke out, most of these checkpoints were overrun by the Mahdi Army militia. Iraqi army soldiers either ran or were killed. It was pretty bad initially. We ran in real quick, shored up all the checkpoints, and sealed off Sadr City so the violence couldn't escape. That emboldened the Iraqi army leaders. They knew we had their backs. And they immediately moved back up and resecured their positions. As long as they knew we had their backs, they were much more bold, more brave, and more capable."

Iraqi army soldiers passed right through American lines on their way into north Sadr City where they smashed the Mahdi Army in battle. If the Lebanese army were to try this in Hezbollah's *dahiyeh* south of Beirut, they'd lose. Hezbollah would clobber the Lebanese soldiers, and civilians in the area would help them. But Sadr City's civilians were sick nearly to death of being ruled by violent fanatics, and they tipped the balance.

"Immediately there was this snap back like a rubber band," Major Humphreys said. "What started out as clearly a *Jaysh al Mahdi* initiative quickly became a coalition forces joint initiative with the Iraqi army. And the Iraqi army really started fighting back and doing a remarkable job. We were fighting side by side in the southern part of Sadr City, as well as around the outskirts of Sadr City from where they were firing the 107 millimeter rockets at the Green Zone.

"I look at it as similar to our War of Independence," he continued. "We had militia units, small organizations, that were formed out of the ashes of the American Revolution. Some of those units are still alive today in our active army. They began their heritage then. And now these Iraqi units, because of what happened in Sadr City, they have begun their heritage, their history. And as they develop through time and grow, they will always have that. If you look at our brigade flag, there's all these streamers hanging off it. Each one of those streamers represents a campaign that unit fought in. These Iraqis are now doing that. These new Iraqi units that just got their start in Sadr City can put a streamer on their flag that says they were there, they were there at the Battle of Sadr City."

Iraqis didn't think the Mahdi Army was beatable. As the battle began, neither did most American journalists or foreign policy analysts. It's hard sometimes to be optimistic about Iraq. It takes effort for me even today. But pessimists have been proven wrong repeatedly during the last couple of years just as optimists were proven wrong again and again during the first half of the war.

"Before Sadr City broke out," Major Humphreys said, "the *Jaysh al Mahdi* was seen as this mystic, mythical beast that was beyond the realm. It threatened them every day. It was incredibly vicious and undefeatable. So when these Iraqi army units started moving, they were overcome by fear. But then they realized they *can* stand up to these guys. They have the capabilities. They have the training. They have the equipment. And they have the support from coalition forces to actually win. They can actually fight and win."

"And without that support," Ramon Lobo from said, "it would be very difficult."

"Then yes, now no," Major Humphreys said. "They needed our direct support. They needed us to shore them up. They needed us to put our arms around them and hold them up. But now, not so much. They operate independently in Sadr City right now. They own north Sadr City, which is two-thirds of the entire city."

"How long did it take them to take it back?" I said.

"They moved into north Sadr City in about two months," he said. "We've made enormous strides in the last six months, and I am not talking baby steps. I'm talking about enormous strides in developing a capable and competent Iraqi military."

Major Humphreys works at a large base in Northern Baghdad. He doesn't go outside the wire into the streets very often. There's nothing wrong with that, and in some ways it's an advantage. He sees a big picture, yet he's not so far up the chain of command that he lives "echelons above reality," as some lower-ranking officers put it.

Still, the street level view of Iraq is more detailed and nuanced. Those who grasp it best, in my experience, are the NCOs, lieutenants, and captains. They understand strategy as well as tactics, and they go out in the streets every day with their men to either fight or forge relationships with Iraqis.

Two of the most hospitable officers I've met yet in Iraq are Captain Todd Looney and his XO Captain A.J. Boyes at Combat Outpost Ford. Looney and Boyes' company did most of the fighting last spring in Sadr City. They were out there every day, and they, too, were shot at.

I felt slightly depressed when I arrived at their outpost. I had heard what seemed like a relentless torrent of negativity at Combat Outpost Apache next to the famous "Gunner Palace" in Adhamiyah, which is now an Iraqi army base. Many Americans at Apache sounded gloomy about the future of Iraq once I probed beneath an optimistic façade. They made a strong case that Iraq is too dysfunctional to keep it together when they leave. After watching Lebanon's slow-motion descent in the years since the Syrians left, I was at least partly persuaded by their dark assessment. Lebanon is much more advanced than Iraq, and if Lebanon is doomed (and, believe me, it is, at least for the short and medium term), it's difficult sometimes to see how Iraq won't be.

Iraq is ahead of Lebanon in a few key ways, though, and Looney and Boyes found the pessimism of some of their fellow Americans rather annoying. They made an equally strong case that Iraq will be more or less fine, and I found their arguments just as persuasive.

We drank army coffee in their quarters late one night when most of their men were asleep.

"How do you guys feel about what will happen after you're gone," I said, "when everyone from the U.S. is gone, when Iraqis are running the country themselves?"

"Will Iraqi democracy look like democracy in the United States?" Captain Looney said. "No. But a form of democratic government in Iraq will serve as an example for others. When people get a taste of freedom, they want to keep it. There is no person in the world, man or woman, who does not want to be free to make their own choices, free to choose their own government, free to exercise the rights we have under the Bill of Rights. Everybody wants that. There's not a culture on earth that doesn't want that. If they don't want that, it's because they haven't been exposed to it. Once it gets seeded here, and once freedom is able to spread, and people see it working, I think it will start catching in other areas and begin to spread there. For me to be able to look back on that and say, hey, I had a part in that, I was partially responsible for the freedoms these people now experience, I think that's something to be proud of."

"You think that's a likely outcome?" I said. "Or a possible one, at least?" I am not sure. Sometimes I think so, and sometimes I don't.

"I do," he said. "I think it's likely that it will happen. A critical time, of course, will be when we begin the drawdown our president is talking about. When that happens, we'll see. But the potential for success is definitely there."

"What I've been hearing at Apache," I said, "from both Americans and Iraqis, are real concerns about the nature of Iraqi society. Looking beyond the security improvements, which at this point are obvious, there are still so many problems that might not be fixable. The corruption, the sectarianism, the tribalism, the backwardness, the religious extremism, the fact that so many people here lie all the time, the laziness. All that stuff. You know how it is here."

"I think people see what they want to see," Captain Boyes said. "Everybody looks through some sort of lens. If you look back at historic counterinsurgencies and nation-building as a whole throughout contemporary history, when you have large powers going through and conducting nation-building—not colonialism, but nation-building—it's generational. It doesn't happen overnight. You don't go from having Saddam on the streets and the statues still up on April 8 to having Saddam gone and a Starbucks and a McDonald's on April 9."

"Here's an example for people to understand the time line," Captain Looney said. "Let's use our own country. The Emancipation Proclamation was signed in 1863, but we didn't finally sign the Civil Rights Act until 1964. It took 101 years for us to go from no slavery to equal rights. And I would argue that not even up until the early 1990s did we actually begin to achieve racial equality. So people are disappointed that after five years in Iraq we haven't gone from a dictatorship to America in the Middle East? Isn't that a little unrealistic?"

"And we had a democratic government for 100 years *before* the Emancipation Proclamation," Captain Boyes said. "Our democracy was uninterrupted for the entire time between then and now. In Iraq they've had either monarchy or fascism. All those things you mentioned are real problems. But at the same time, we can show you Iraqis who literally pulled themselves up by their bootstraps and are now extremely successful. They're the antithesis of every Iraqi stereotype out there. They're hard-working. They're forward-thinking. They do everything at what you and I would consider a high standard of work. It's already here. Until the 1960s, this place was considered the pearl of the Middle East. This was the place to be. They've had 50 years of bad luck and bad leadership. Hopefully that will change and they'll stay on this path of democratization. I think there is truly a budding democracy here. The judicial process, the legislative process, the executive. We're seeing coalitions forming in government. We're seeing true debate. They've had to jump-start some of these things with international help, but at the same time they've really come a long way. So I think the future isn't bright yet, but the possibility is there for this to become a well-functioning society."

"Look at the resources available in this country," Captain Looney said. "They have, relatively speaking, an unlimited supply of petroleum. They have great agricultural capabilities. Iraq is not a desert like Kuwait or Saudi Arabia. Those countries have oil and sand. Unless they're going to start becoming major exporters of mirrors and glass, that's not going to do them a lot of good. Iraq, on the other hand, has huge amounts of resources. Have you seen how lush the palm groves and orange groves are on the Tigris and the Euphrates? The orchards? They have unlimited capability to produce agricultural products, and combined with textiles and oil they could use those revenues to bring in other industries. Somebody just has to bring it all together. Their military, too, has the potential to be great again. Before Desert Storm they had the fourth largest army in the world."

"It was far from the fourth best army, though," I said.

"But their military education is based on the British system," he said. "They are not as unprofessional as we think, it's just that they were not led in the best manner."

"The Iraqi Military Academy," Captain Boyes, "was looked upon very highly in the Middle East as a great place to send junior leadership for development. It could go back to that."

"The problem is when you have a despot," Captain Looney said, "a dictator who runs an army like Hitler ran Germany's during World War II. When you cut off the head of the snake, it dies immediately. Our army is so decentralized that we can succeed at junior officer and non-commissioned officer levels. They can't because they haven't developed those levels. It's a very stove-piped organization."

"What happened to the old officers when Paul Bremer dissolved the Iraqi army years ago?" I said. "Did some of them come back, or are they still purged?"

"Some of them came back," he said. "Colonels and below were allowed to come back. Very few senior military leaders were allowed to return to the new Iraqi army. Some of them didn't want to come back. Some of them didn't want to be in the service in the first place. They were conscripted. The issue is how you said they weren't the fourth best. What is the difference between our army—which I would say is the best the world has ever seen—and the British army and the Australian army and the Canadian army? What do we all have in common? We're all volunteer forces. None of us were drafted. People join because they want to, because they feel a sense of duty, because they feel a sense of national pride. They're going to fight more aggressively and be more dedicated to the cause than those who were pressed into the service."

"Now it's an all volunteer army," Captain Boyes said. "And they're receiving better training and better equipment. They are better supported."

"It's also a good idea to have an all volunteer army because of the all the radicals running around here," I said. "If they had conscription, all those radicals would end up in the army."

"Yes," Captain Boyes said. "The Iraqi Security Forces have made leaps and bounds, and that's not only because they've been partnered with us. People are able to trust them again. It has been five years since Saddam was in power, and during that time people did not trust the security apparatus."

"They still don't in Adhamiyah," I said. "I've had Iraqis tell me themselves that they're afraid of the police and the army."

"It's changing, though," Captain Boyes said. "And it has to because we won't be here to facilitate that for very much longer. In our area, and in other areas, people are cooperating far more with the Iraqi Security Forces. The ability of the Iraqis to now direct their own operations, plan their own operations, execute their own operations, all based on intelligence they've collected from the locals, is truly a sign of real progress."

Sadr City is overwhelmingly Shia, and I wondered if these two captains had ever worked in Sunni areas which are much less friendly to Americans generally. Iraq's Sunni Arabs overwhelmingly opposed the invasion and demolition of Saddam Hussein's regime, but Shias on average have been much more supportive. Saddam Hussein brutalized them almost as viciously as he did the Kurds.

"Have you guys worked in Sunni areas?" I said.

"Yes," Captain Boyes said. "Previously."

"His platoon did the cordon on Abu Musab al Zarqawi and hit him," Captain Looney said.

"Our company had an area in Diyala Province," Captain Boyes said, "on the border of Salahhadin Province. It was on the west of Baqubah. It was a large territory with a diverse population. Sunni towns, Shia towns, towns with mixed population. We operated in Sunni areas. We operated in Shia areas. And this time we have about a 99 percent Shia area."

"Can you characterize the differences between one and the other?" I said. "Most of my time has been spent among the Sunnis. Opinion polls have showed the Kurds to be more than 90 percent pro-American, the Sunni Arabs around 90 percent anti-American, and the Shias about 50-50. Can you feel the difference, and does that affect your ability to work with the population? Those numbers suggest it might be easier to work with the Shias."

"I don't think so," Captain Boyes said. "Well, maybe in *other* Shia areas. Here, before the fighting in the spring, *this* Shia area was extremely anti-American aside from the safe neighborhood of Beida. We had this bastion of a safe neighborhood in Beida, and we had the area in north Adhamiyah that was predominately Shia and only somewhat negative toward Americans."

I wasn't surprised to hear that Beida had long been a safe area. I found it much cleaner and better developed than much of what I had seen in Adhamiyah and—especially—in Sadr City itself.

"On my previous tour," Captain Boyes said, "Hibhib was a 95 percent Sunni town where Zarqawi was killed. It was extremely anti-American and anti-Iraqi government. They wanted a Sunni-dominated powerhouse in the Middle East. And they were not cooperative with us in any way whatsoever. Within six months I could walk through that town by myself with an interpreter, leave my four gun trucks several hundred meters away, go to a tea shop, and have breakfast with the town. At first there would be six guys, and then an hour later there would be 300 people gathered around asking questions."

"You actually did this?" I said.

"Yes," he said.

"You had a weapon?" I said.

"Yes," he said. "It was on the ground. I sat there, surrounded by Iraqis, and just talked. We didn't even talk business all the time. I asked how everyone's family was doing, asked what was going on in the town. I went to Jedida one time and watched a World Cup match in the town on TV."

"Could you do that here?" I said. We were wedged between Beida and Sadr City.

"Yes," he said. "I would feel perfectly comfortable doing that here."

"Now, what if I were to walk around here by myself without a weapon, without you guys protecting me?" I said.

"I don't think you'd have too many issues," he said.

"You know, the chances of you getting struck by lightning are not that great," Captain Looney said, "but in the middle of a lightning storm you probably shouldn't go outside with a steel pole and stick it in the air. That's what you'd be doing, my friend."

"There are people who are anti-American in nature, and anti-Western in nature," Captain Boyes said. "But it is a safer area now. And after six months of walking around and talking to the shop owners, we were able to change the atmospherics. We didn't do anything special. It was just a matter of getting down into the population and talking to them, opening a dialogue. And we weren't just coming in once a month. It was constant."

"When people aren't familiar with each other," Captain Looney said, "they think the worst about each other. They don't realize how much they have in common. I'll sit down with people and say, 'okay, let's talk about our differences. And then let's talk about what we have in common.' We want to have a safe environment for our families to live in. We want our children to have a better life than we did. We want to be happy in our profession. We want to be happy with our family. What beyond that makes us so different? Okay, they're Muslims and I'm a Christian. But we talk about this stuff and they realize we aren't that different."

Insurgent and terrorist groups feel threatened by even this basic level of cultural interaction. When I visited the Lebanese border from the Israeli side a few months before the 2006 war, a Turkish-Israeli Kurd named Eitan showed me a destroyed building just over the fence on the Lebanese side. "Look over there," he said and pointed toward Lebanon. "That's the old French customs house It, too, was used when the Lebanese-Israeli border was open. Hezbollah blew it away. [Secretary General Hassan] Nasrallah wanted to make sure there was no contact at all between our two peoples."

Contact between peoples really does reduce tension and can help reduce the chances of war. That's one reason why Hezbollah prohibits contact between Lebanese and Israelis. (The other reason, of course, is that they know many Lebanese spy on Hezbollah for Israel.)

Eitan is an Israeli. He is therefore, at least technically, at war with the people of Lebanon. But he waved hello to them every day, and sometimes they waved back even though they weren't supposed to. They were friends when the border was open, and they didn't feel—or act—any different even after the border was closed.

"You've seen *Dances with Wolves*?" Captain Looney said. "Remember how when they don't know each other, they're scared of each other? But as they get to know each other, they realize they're not that different? They want the same things in life. They want peace. They want prosperity. They want a better life for their children. What culture in the world does not want those things?"

"And unfortunately," Captain Boyes said, "until recently, and still when you get farther out of the cities, a guy from one village may not travel very far in his lifetime."

"Maybe not at all," I said.

"Maybe not at all," he said. "Especially in a place like Afghanistan and the frontier region of Pakistan. They really don't travel very far. Here a guy may not leave his province more than a couple of times during his life. And when he does, it's usually on some kind of religious pilgrimage. So he's almost always surrounded by people of his exact same faith and culture. So do they ever really experience what it's like to meet and talk to a Sunni, a Kurd, a Shia, or somebody else? There is a generational gap. If we take a snapshot of Iraqi politics, security, and governance right now in 2008 and come back two generations from now and compare them side-by-side, I think we'll see a huge difference. I think it will be almost entirely better."

That sounded right to me. Even when I feel like Iraq is a doomed country, which I do around half the time, that still sounds right to me.

"But what is it going to be like in one year?" I said. "Or two? That's the big question."

"Well yes," Captain Boyes said. "It is. Any time something new happens in a counterinsurgency, when there are new security forces, there is an immediate spike in violence because the insurgents are testing the ability of the new element."

"Iraq is about to experience a power vacuum," I said, "when you withdraw from Iraqi cities."

"Exactly," he said. "When we leave and transition all of what we do now to the Iraqi Security Forces will there be a spike in activity? Absolutely. One hundred percent."

That stopped me cold. Captain Looney and Captain Boyes are the most optimistic American officers I've spoken to recently in Iraq. And they think the odds of a spike in violence are 100 percent.

"You guys are the optimists," I said. "And yet you think this."

"Yes," Captain Boyes said. "There will be a spike in violence. They're going to want to test the new Iraqi Security Forces. What is their reaction to an attack going to be compared with what it is now? How will the Iraqis operate independently? It should be up to the media to portray this as something expected. There will be a spike in violence because the insurgents are going to test the Iraqi Security Forces, but I have complete faith that the resolve of the Iraqis will be there."

"You guys expect a spike in violence," I said, "but think Iraq will be okay anyway?"

"We're realists," Captain Looney said.

"You're optimists compared with some of the people I talked to last week," I said.

"There's going to be a spike in violence because it's only natural," Captain Boyes said. "Those who think otherwise aren't being realistic. And those who say there's going to be a spike in violence and another civil war are too pessimistic. It will be somewhere in the middle. Eventually the bad guys will understand that the Iraqi Security Forces are here to stay. They are improved. They are vastly superior to anything we have seen in the past. "

The United States didn't fight a single war in Iraq. It fought two consecutive wars and won both, the first unambiguously and the second a bit tenuously.

Saddam Hussein's Baath Party regime is finished forever and has no more chance of returning than does a communist party dictatorship in Russia. The war against his government was easy and short.

The second, against various insurgent militias and terrorist organizations, was hard and long, but it, too, is more or less over. None of the insurgent or terrorist groups can declare victory or claim Americans are evacuating Iraq's cities because they were beaten.

America's most modest foreign policy objectives there have been largely secured. The toxic Saddam regime has been replaced with a more or less consensual government even if it is unstable. Iraq is most unlikely to seriously threaten the United States or its neighbors again any time soon. Nor is it at all likely to be ruled by terrorists as it probably would have been if the United States had given up at virtually any time between

2004 and 2007.

Even so, a large number of Iraqis and Americans in Iraq have a hard time feeling optimistic about the future. Iraq remains, in some ways, a threat to itself, and there's no guarantee a third war won't break out sometime soon. There are plenty of pessimistic Americans and Iraqis in Baghdad, and they have a case.

The reduction in violence, even if it is only temporary, allowed me to see Baghdad a little more clearly than I could the first time I visited. And I'm sorry to say that the city is still as run-down and dysfunctional as it was when what passed for daily life was punctuated by gunfire and car bombs. Iraq is backward and messy not only by Western standards, but also by Arab standards.

"A lot of people want us to stay or they will leave," Sergeant Nick Franklin told me. "They don't care where they go. They want to go to America, to Europe, or even to Jordan or some other Arab country. They don't care. They just want out."

You would probably want out, too, if you lived there. Violence has been drastically reduced, but sectarian tension remains just as bad, if not worse, as it is in Lebanon—and the possibility of renewed civil strife hangs over Lebanon like a Sword of Damocles. Iraq is still violent compared with most countries, and the entire government and security forces are shot through with corruption. Electricity still doesn't work half the time. Sewage still runs in the streets. Neighborhoods are still clotted with an appalling amount of garbage. Police officers steal from citizens and often beat suspects not during but *before* interrogations.

Back at Combat Outpost Apache, next to "Gunner Palace" in the Sunni Adhamiyah neighborhood just north of the city center, I asked several American soldiers if it was safe enough to walk the streets on my own without armed protection. Few thought that would be wise.

"I wouldn't try it," Sergeant Manuel Juarez said. "I wouldn't even think of it. Who is to say that these Sons of Iraq guys don't still have some ties to Al Qaeda? Once in a while we get reports about one of them being shady."

"Sons of Iraq is shady as hell," said another soldier who overheard our conversation and preferred not to be named. "I know as a fact that they're shady as hell."

"What do you know?" I said.

"I don't know anything," he said and looked away. That was all he was willing to tell me.

Staff Sergeant Christianson said he didn't think I'd be much safer when I later moved into the Shia parts of the city even though Shias, overall, are friendlier toward Americans.

"Hezbollah kills civilians as well as Americans with total disregard for Iraqis," he said.

He was referring, of course, to Hezbollah in Iraq, not to Hezbollah in Lebanon. Iran's Revolutionary Guard Corps, though, is a patron and armorer of both. A crucial difference between the two is that the Iraqi branch of Hezbollah, unlike the Lebanese branch, doesn't have anything that looks even vaguely like a "political wing." Its members don't build hospitals, schools, or anything else. They just kill people.

"*Jaysh al Mahdi* is much more careful and only tries to kill us," he continued. "I don't know why Hezbollah is so much more ruthless, but they are. When we pull out of this country, this place is going to burn."

No one can know if it really will burn. Many think it will, but not everyone does. Certainly nobody I spoke to hopes that it does. Even the relative optimists, though, are concerned that it might.

"I sure hope this holds," Sergeant Pennartz said, "because we're going to pull out soon. I think it's a mistake. This country is going to need help for years. But at the same time I really really really don't want to come back here. That's how a lot of us feel. We don't want to pull out, but we also don't want to be here. I just hope the peace holds so we don't have to come back and fight for the ground we already won and abandoned. Again."

American soldiers have since withdrawn from most of Iraq's urban areas. We'll have a better idea soon enough whether the optimists or the pessimists turn out to be right.

"On the surface everyone will tell you Sunnis, Shias, we don't care, we're all Iraqis," Sergeant Pennartz continued. "But talk to them for a while and they'll tell you what they really think. 'Do you know what those Shias did?' Et cetera. Some Sunnis say Shias were never in Iraq until the Iran-Iraq war. Some are totally ignorant and say they'll never live next to Shias. It's worse among the older generations, like back in the States."

I joined Lieutenant Eric Kuylman and his men on a foot patrol in Adhamiyah. Our convoy of Humvees parked near a traffic circle and we stepped out to talk to people who lived in the neighborhood.

The lieutenant approached a group of young men and asked if they lived in the area.

"I'm from Fallujah," said the first in good English. "I go to college here and commute three hours each day."

"It takes you *three hours* to get here from Fallujah?" I said. If Iraq were a normal country, it would only take an hour or so to drive in from there.

"The security checkpoints slow us down," he said.

"Okay," Lieutenant Kuylman said. "You guys aren't from around here. I'm curious, then, what you think of the area."

"The security is good," the man said. "I had to quit college in 2006 because it was too dangerous. But I was able to come back this year because it's safer. I'd like to see American forces here as guests, not carrying weapons or wearing armor."

"Me, too," Lieutenant Kuylman said and laughed. He wasn't indulging the man. He was serious.

"I hope you can leave Iraq soon," the man said.

"Me, too," said the lieutenant.

We moved on and I asked our interpreter Tom what the Iraqis in Adhamiyah really think of the American military. He's an Iraqi who grew up in Baghdad. "Tom" is the nickname he uses to conceal his identity, and it's only coincidentally the same nickname used by the Palestinian I met and wrote about earlier who worked with the Marines in Fallujah.

"Eighty percent in this area don't like Americans," he said. "Some want American forces to stay, but most want them to leave."

"How would you characterize their negative feelings?" I said. "As irritation? Hatred?"

"Both," he said. "It depends. You have to understand that this was a favored area when Saddam Hussein was the president. It was a Baath Party stronghold."

"Do they credit Americans with improving security?" I said.

"Yes," he said. "But they still want American forces to leave. You heard what that guy just said."

The Sunnis of Adhamiyah have rational reasons to dislike Americans. Sunni Arabs make up only 15-20 percent of Iraq's population, but they were Saddam Hussein's base of support. Iraq's democratic elections have empowered the country's Shia majority—an ancient foe of the Sunnis—for the first time.

Rational anti-Americanism, however, is compounded by the conspiratorial and phantasmagoric anti-Americanism that persists in much of the Arab world. One of Iraq's various insurgent groups recently tried to fire an improvised IRAM rocket at a joint American-Iraqi security station, but the trigger man botched the job and blew up the rocket on the launch pad. He killed himself and destroyed nearby houses. Most residents of the neighborhood think American soldiers dropped a bomb from a helicopter.

An Iraqi man walked up to Lieutenant Kuylman and me. His friends followed.

"I want to say something," he said in English. "Please don't hand us over to the Iraqi army. We've been working with you for over a year."

He was part of the Sons of Iraq program and was worried about what might happen to him if he had to rely solely on the Iraqi army for protection from terrorists.

"Look," Lieutenant Kuylman said. "We're not running away. We aren't just going to abandon you."

It's true that the Americans aren't running out of Iraq. But they are withdrawing from the cities and will no longer be available to provide security as they did during and after the surge.

From the look on the Iraqi man's face, he was not at all convinced by what Lieutenant Kuylman said. He probably doesn't know what happened to the anti-Hezbollah South Lebanon Army in 2000 when Israel withdrew its armed forces from Lebanon, but he was clearly worried he and his men might suffer a similar fate. Many South Lebanon Army soldiers ended up as refugees in Israel when Hezbollah took over the area. Most will never see the country that raised them again.

S ergeant Nick Franklin took me with him when he visited the home of an Iraqi woman named Malath who is in charge of a Sons of Iraq search unit. She invited us to sit on couches in her living room. Incense wafted in from the kitchen. It smelled lovely, unlike Baghdad outside which often smells of rotting vegetables, diesel, and piss.

"This is your house," Malath said.

"If this is my house," Sergeant Franklin said and grinned, "where's my room?"

She laughed.

Her house was much nicer inside than the army outpost at Apache. Her living room was cozy. Peach-colored lights cast a soft glow on the wall. Arabic music videos from Egypt and Lebanon played on the television.

"You could even put me on the roof," Sergeant Franklin said.

The roof would be more comfortable than the cramped conditions back at the base. Living conditions for American soldiers in Iraq are uncomfortable at best and sometimes horrific. Unlike Iraqis, they get 24 hours of electricity every day, which means they have air conditioning, but every Iraqi house I have ever been in is vastly more comfortable over all.

Malath's colleague Sermad Mahmoud sat next to her on the couch. Sergeant Franklin sat next to me on the other side of the room.

"Malath's family is liberated," he said, which meant no male family members imposed a strict code of behavior on her. Nor did she wear a headscarf. "She's not married, but she helps take care of her family's kids. Her brother was recently killed. Somebody poisoned him."

He asked her how things have been in the neighborhood lately.

"Quiet," she said.

And it was. The only gunshots I heard were fired by Iraqi police officers into the air.

A young boy, presumably Malath's nephew, brought us glasses of tea, fruit juice, and cigarettes.

Franklin and Malath engaged in idle chitchat for a while. Socializing often takes up the bulk of the meeting time when Americans and Iraqis get together to talk business. Iraqis prefer it that way, and Americans yield to their expectations and culture.

I was given a bit of time to talk to Malath myself.

"Is Baghdad ready to stand on its own?" I said.

"No," she said, "of course not," as if my question was frankly absurd. None of the American soldiers in the room argued with her assessment, neither in front of her nor later after we left. "We won't be ready until young people replace the older generation in the Iraqi army and Iraqi police," she continued. "They need to replace the old Baath Party members who are still inside."

Paul Bremer dissolved what remained of the Iraqi army after he was made the head of the Coalition Provisional Authority by the Bush Administration in 2003. He wanted to purge Iraq of its Baathists and old regime loyalists. A large number of Baathists, though, were Baathists in name only. They weren't ideological. Party membership was required of government employees, and a huge number of Iraqis worked for the government. Bremer's dismissal and blacklisting of these people radicalized many. Some joined the insurgency. Many think it was a bad call on Bremer's part, and he did it despite warnings from his advisors about what might happen if he went through with it.

He faced a formidable problem, even so. What is to be done about Iraq's leaders and functionaries who cut their teeth in a totalitarian political system? Keeping them around on the payroll surely would have been problematic, as well. Malath, like many others, thinks Iraqis will just have to wait for them to retire or die.

"What should the American people know about Iraq that they don't currently know?" I said, addressing my question to both Sermad and Malath.

"Iraqi people are friendly and follow the old Iraqi traditions," Malath said.

I can vouch for that. There should be no question that it is true.

"What is the local opinion of the Iraqi police?" I said.

"People here don't feel comfortable talking to them," she said. "They are Shias from Sadr City, and they are corrupt."

She's right about that. Shia officers were brought in from Sadr City to police Sunnis. In Fallujah and Ramadi, the Iraqi police were much more trusted and effective because they worked in the same community they lived and grew up in.

"How, exactly, are the Iraqi police here corrupt?" I said.

"If we ask them about detainees," Sermad said, "they don't answer unless we pay them to answer. A guy was recently released from jail because he bought his way out."

"When did Al Qaeda move in?" I said.

"They came in November of 2005," Malath said. "They used young people and jobless people, and they lured them in with money."

"Has public opinion here changed about American soldiers since Al Qaeda came in?" I said.

"Yes, definitely," Malath said. "Many people here like American soldiers now."

That's not exactly what our interpreter Tom had told me earlier, but either way it was clear that vastly fewer people in the neighborhood were interested in fighting American soldiers than they used to be.

"Al Qaeda used to control people's minds," she said. "They said Americans just wanted to control Iraq, and we believed them. We know now that it isn't true. Americans have been helping a lot."

"So public opinion changed about Al Qaeda, as well?" I said.

"Yes," she said. "I mean, we didn't like them before, but we agreed with them about some things. And anyway we couldn't talk about them before, not until Sons of Iraq was created."

Her nephew brought more glasses of tea.

"Iraqi elections have all been corrupt," she said.

"How so?" I said.

"Terrorist groups and outside organizations threaten people and assassinate their political enemies," she said.

"Speaking of outside organizations," I said, "what do people here think about Iran?"

"Iran has lots of influence," Sermad said. "They support the militias, *Jaysh al Mahdi*, and the Badr Corps. They support some of the Iraqi parliament members. Iran is going to invade Iraq as soon as American soldiers withdraw."

"He's talking about a sort of generalized fear," Sergeant Franklin said. "They don't necessarily believe that is going to happen, it's just something they are afraid of."

Sunni Arabs like Malath and Sermad all over the Middle East are instinctively wary of Iran, which is Persian and Shia, not only because of Tehran's support for anti-Sunni militias, and not only thanks to the memory of the horrific Iran-Iraq war in the 1980s—which killed a million or so people—but also for ancient reasons going back more than a thousand years. Islamic civilization split into its warring Sunni and Shia halves shortly after Mohammad founded the religion, and Persians and Arabs have been foes for almost as long as Persians and Arabs have existed.

"The Iraqi parliament members will invite the Iranian army," Malath said.

Malath and Sermad had good as well as bad reasons to fear and loathe Iran, but they were both being slightly hysterical. Like many Iraqis, they inflated threats all out of proportion to their actual size. Iraqis did the same thing when American soldiers first came. The U.S. invasion was compared, in the minds of many, to the vicious Mongol invasion in the 13th century.

"Do you think Prime Minister Maliki is an ally of Iran?" I said.

"He didn't used to do the best thing for Iraq," Malath said. "He is better now, but only because Americans forced him to conduct the operations against Shia militias. He used to say the Sons of Iraq was a Sunni militia."

"I have one more question about a completely different topic," I said.

"Okay," Malath said.

"Is there any chance that Iraq will have normal relations with Israel in the future?" I said.

Sergeant Franklin leaned over and whispered to me. "Most Iraqis don't think that far outside the box," he said.

I knew that already, but he was right to remind me. Israel is about as far removed from Iraq's problems as Sri Lanka.

"Iraq has no issues with Israel," she said, "but it depends on the next Iraqi president." Then she paused and gave me a more honest answer. "Personally, I don't want normal relations with Israel."

"Why not?" I said.

"Do you know about the situation with the Palestinians?" she said.

"Of course," I said. "Everyone does."

"I disagree," Sermad said. "We should have normal relations with Israel. There is no reason we shouldn't."

Because of Israel's remoteness to Iraq's problems, the topic isn't nearly as much of a red line there as it is elsewhere in the Middle East. Every Iraqi Kurd I have ever spoken to about Israel wants peace, normal relations, or even a strategic alliance. Arab opinion is mixed, but Arab Iraqis don't seem to be afraid of arguing with each other about it. Some Lebanese want normal relations with Israel, but they don't dare say so in public because anti-Israel opinion in some quarters there is ferocious.

The electricity went out all of a sudden. The room went dark. This was Iraq, and Iraqis still don't get anywhere near 24 hours of electricity.

A huge demonstration broke out just south of Malath's house shortly after we left. Thousands of radical Shias streamed out of Sadr City and surged up the main road into Sunni Adhamiyah, screaming slogans in support of Moqtada al Sadr and what's left of his Mahdi Army militia.

American soldiers can't do much more in Iraq. General David Petraeus' counterinsurgency program is finished. He achieved a major breakthrough when he embedded his soldiers in Iraqi neighborhoods and ordered them to prioritize security for Iraqi civilians, but the new Status of Forces Agreement requires American soldiers to vacate Iraq's cities and hole up on remote bases. Iraq's urban areas—where most Iraqis live—will stand or fall on their own.

Before the withdrawal, Lieutenant Eric Kuylman invited me to join him and his men again while they conducted a foot patrol in one of the older districts of Adhamiyah. We came across a rubble-strewn site where it appeared a building might have once stood. Two soldiers swept for IEDs with a wand that whined like a metal detector in an airport.

An elderly Iraqi man nervously sidled up to Lieutenant Kuylman. "Is there a bomb in there?" he said.

"Nah," the lieutenant said. "We check empty lots like this just in case. Don't worry about it. There's no more reason to think there's a bomb in there now than there was five minutes ago."

The man watched as the soldiers continued sweeping the pile of rubble.

"Hey," Lieutenant Kuylman said to the man. "I'm trying to learn a few things about the neighborhood here. Can you tell me who has been living in the area the longest?"

"I have been living in this house," he said and gestured toward the dwelling behind him, "for forty years."

"Can we speak to you in private?" the lieutenant said.

"Of course," the man said. "You are welcome."

He opened the door and beckoned us in.

"Thank you," I said. He shook my hand warmly with both hands.

"Please," he said and gestured for us to sit on his couch.

His wife smiled and brought us tea. I didn't see any children or younger adults.

The couple seemed genuinely friendly. Almost all Iraqis I've met are at least superficially friendly, but these two seemed especially so.

"I like to find the people who have lived in the neighborhood the longest," Lieutenant Kuylman said. "If there are any people you don't feel comfortable with around here, I will go talk to them. And I want you to feel comfortable telling me."

"It's quiet here," the man said. "And if there are any problems, we will solve them amongst ourselves."

"Really?" Lieutenant Kuylman said. "Who's the mediator?"

"We have a guy who is like a sheikh," the man said. "He settles these problems between people. Sheikh Zawi."

"Ah," the lieutenant said. "I know him. He's a good guy."

The elderly couple had a striking hand-made Persian carpet in the living room that would fetch around 6,000 dollars in the United States.

"When Americans come into our houses," the man said, "people outside want to know what's going on."

"What do people think is going on?" I said.

"That Americans are investigating or exchanging information," he said. "Our traditions require us to welcome Americans into our homes."

"Does it cause a problem for you if we come into your house?" I said.

"No, no," the man said. "Everyone here knows me and knows my personality."

An enigmatic response. Adhamiyah is predominantly anti-American. Was the man saying his anti-American credentials were solid, that no one would be concerned he was cooperating with the enemy? Or was I reading too much into it? The man did approach us in the street. He introduced himself voluntarily and was concerned about bombs.

"There are going to be a lot of changes all across Baghdad," Lieutenant Kuylman said. "We're trying to push the Iraqi army and Iraqi police and get your system to work. We're here to help, but we try to make sure the Iraqi army and Iraqi police have first done everything they can before we step in."

"I want to relay a message to you," the man said. "Hopefully the Iraqi forces will join us together. No Sunnis. No Shias. When I go outside Adhamiyah, I don't trust the Iraqi forces."

"Why not?" I said.

"You have to check the backgrounds of men in the Iraqi army and the Iraqi police," the woman said. "There are a lot of bad people trying to work for them."

"Do you have any names for me?" Lieutenant Kuylman said.

She didn't have any names. Neither did her husband. All they had was a sense of dread and foreboding.

"When I hear about the schedule for American forces leaving Iraq," the man said, "I get scared. I hope we get a nice life here in Iraq and that you can make it home safe."

Lieutenant Kuylman winced. "There might be some growing pains."

The woman flung her hands toward the ceiling.

Getting an accurate reading of Iraqi public opinion is hard. It might not even be possible. I've seen Iraqis cheer American soldiers, and I've seen Iraqis *hug* American soldiers, but hundreds of thousands celebrated when the U.S. evacuated Iraqi cities as stipulated by the Status of Forces Agreement.

Perhaps there's no contradiction. Some Iraqis are pro-American. Others are anti-American. Those who celebrated when the American soldiers left and those who greeted American soldiers warmly may well be different individuals, at least for the most part.

Maybe not, though. Iraqi public opinion is famously contradictory. And Iraqi public opinion as relayed by Iraqis themselves is notoriously unreliable.

Most Iraqis, like most Arabs everywhere, are extraordinarily hospitable and polite. It's a guidebook cliché, but it's a guidebook cliché for a reason. Their culture requires them to welcome foreigners, and they take that requirement seriously. Most will conceal any negative opinions they may have against a visitor or even a visitor's country—and this is true even for visitors from enemy countries. They don't mean to be deceptive. They're just being nice.

There's another problem with picking up the mood of the street— politics. For decades Iraqis have lived either in fear of the state or in fear of militias. They had to learn to keep their opinions to themselves if they wanted to live.

Not many Iraqis today are afraid of the state, but everybody was terrified of Saddam Hussein's totalitarian government. Speaking their minds could get them imprisoned or killed. It could get an entire family dragged off to prison, tortured, and painfully executed. Before the Baath Party regime was demolished, it was extremely difficult for journalists who showed up in Baghdad to read the mood of the street. Everybody appeared to be fanatical supporters of Saddam Hussein even though few Iraqis actually were.

That's not true anymore, but habits of mind go down hard. Concealing opinions from the authorities became a survival mechanism, whether the authorities were Saddam Hussein's *mukhabarat*, militiamen in the neighborhood, or American soldiers.

Before the Status of Forces agreement kicked in, I asked U.S. Army Colonel John Hort if and how he and his men took all this into account. Effective counterinsurgency isn't possible when counterinsurgents have no idea what the general population is thinking.

"How do you measure public opinion?" I said to him. "How do you know what people really think? We all know about this tendency in Iraq where people tell you what they think you want to hear—or what *they* want you to hear, which isn't necessarily the same thing. If you ask what

Iraqis think of the American military while you're standing there with guns in your hands, they might say *oh, we love you guys*. Then someone from the *Guardian* newspaper comes along and asks what they think of the imperial occupation forces, and the same people might say *we hate them*. So what's their real opinion? Do you take this sort of thing into account? Do you have Iraqis feeling out the opinions of people for you?"

"We do," he said.

"And they report back to you?" I said.

"Right," he said. "We have the Iraqi Advisor Task Force. They aren't spies. That's illegal. But they're hired to measure atmospherics. They monitor the mosques. They hit the restaurants, places like that. And we get these reports almost every other day. Over time we've seen the atmospherics and compared them to what you were talking about, the guy on the street talking to the U.S. soldier. Do they match up? And if they don't match up, we have to figure out what we need to change about the way we're presenting ourselves."

Colonel Hort worked at War Eagle, the medium-sized base in Northern Baghdad. After I left the FOB and moved to a small combat outpost deep in the city, I asked Sergeant Nick Franklin if he could help me arrange an interview with one of the Iraqis the Army trusts to provide real information. I was tired of trying to learn about Iraq through the lens of the United States military, and I was tired of asking Iraqis what they thought while they were in the presence of American soldiers.

What were Iraqis saying when Americans weren't in the room? *That's* what I really wanted to know. Even if I had disembedded myself from the Army and wandered around Iraq by myself, I still wouldn't be able to figure that out because I'm an American, too.

"You're right," Sergeant Franklin said. "You practically have to beat a straight answer out of people. I'll take you to meet this guy Sayid who works for us and tells it just like it is."

"How did you meet him?" I said.

"He's been around for a while," he said. "He's been a source for the Army for years. Each unit that rotates out hands him over to the next unit as a known good guy who tells it to you straight and really knows what's going on."

So Franklin took me outside the wire to Sayid's house. Sayid isn't really his name. That's just what I'm calling him here because I need to conceal his identity.

I needed help from reliable straight-shooting Iraqis to see the truth behind the façade. I can't know if everything Sayid told me was true, but what he told me was a lot more interesting and substantial than the "America good" boilerplate I often heard from random civilians.

What I wanted from Sayid was a glimpse into the Iraqi psyche, and he delivered. He also shared with me his vision of Iraq's future. And I should warn you that his vision is not pretty.

Four of us sat on couches in his living room—me, Sergeant Franklin, Lieutenant Eric Kuylman, and our Iraqi interpreter "Tom." We didn't need to bring Tom with us, though. Sayid speaks near-perfect English.

"They say you're a good guy to talk to because you give straight answers," I said. "It's hard to get straight answers in Iraq."

"It's the formula of our community," he said. "There are many kinds of people. I will give you a straight answer, but it's Iraqi like me. Just 20 percent of our people are good. 80 percent are bad. You should know that."

I had heard that before. The Iraqi interpreter at War Eagle with the code name of Hammer said something similar.

"The bad people won't give you a straight answer if you ask them about anything," Sayid said. "For example, if you ask them about electricity. Is it good or bad? If they have 12 hours of electricity a day, they will say they have just one hour. They don't tell the truth about this stuff. And that's just an example. And if you ask a deeper question, you can imagine the kinds of things they will say."

"Why is that?" I said. "Why is it hard to get a straight answer out of people? Is it cultural, or is it political?"

"The main reason," he said, "is because our community is too selfish. They love themselves very much. All they think about is their stomach. They want to enjoy themselves, and everyone else can go to hell. You should know that."

He sounded depressed, like he desperately wanted to live somewhere else, but was resigned to the fact that he would spend the rest of his life in Iraq.

"What percentage of the people do you think are bad in a way that causes security problems?" I said

"I will answer you honestly," he said. "I'm shocked at the number of people who supported the Al Qaeda organization. It was about 60 percent. In the past. Not now. A lieutenant came yesterday and showed me a picture of a terrorist he was looking for. I know this man. He is a good person. I am shocked. I asked the lieutenant what this guy did, and he told me all kinds of bad things. They are normal humans, you know. They look like me and you."

Of course they are humans and look like me and Sayid. I've seen some of them. The first suspected Al Qaeda members I saw in a holding cell in Ramadi looked like losers who couldn't get a job at a gas station. A larger group I saw in Fallujah, however, looked like a gaggle of psychopaths. The hatred on their faces was unmistakable. It was human, but it was unmistakable.

"What do people here actually think about the American forces?" I said. "I hear contradictory things. They seem friendly on the surface, and there is a lot less violence now. So anti-Americanism must be somewhat reduced. And yet I hear from some Iraqis that 80 percent of the people in this area don't like the American forces and want them to leave. So I'm not sure how to sort all this out."

"The American forces help people in this area, you know," Sayid said. "There was a time when the militias ruled this area. They were shooting people. When the Americans came, they could no longer do that. The Americans secured the area. And of course anyone who gives security is loved. He is a friend.

"But in the depths of their minds, no. They don't have any love for American forces. They always say Americans are bad people. They know the truth, but still they say this. They know Saddam Hussein caused a big mess in the region, but they ignore that. They ignore the truth. They hang all the responsibility on the American forces. But American forces secure them, give them help, give them money, give them a job. All the people in Adhamiyah working for the municipality, the Iraqi army, and the Iraqi police is because of the American forces. And they know that. But when you sit with them and talk with them, face to face, Iraqi to Iraqi, they don't say that. They say all bad things come from America. If you give them money and jobs, they're good. If you cut the money, you will see another face. You will see the guns and the roadside bombs again."

But where does the anti-Americanism come from? Is it because the United States invaded Iraq, or is it older and more elemental than that?

"In Adhamiyah they loved Saddam Hussein too much," he said. "I'm not from here. I moved here about four years ago."

"Are you Sunni also?" I said. Then I checked myself. "I'm sorry. I probably shouldn't ask you that."

"I don't believe in that," he said. "I believe in God, but it's just that."

Lieutenant Kuylman cut in. "As far as the current sentiment toward us right now," he said, "I think we're seeing a hangover. It's like the morning after. We've been here for five or six years, and now that violence isn't an issue, militias aren't patrolling the streets, and people aren't tearing each other apart, it's all about money. It's all business. *Gimme gimme.* 'If you're here and occupying the country and cutting me off on my roads, what are you going to give me now for it?' They've seen how much money we have, and now they just expect it. So if we're not going to do anything good, we're just going to piss them off more the longer we stay."

Sayid nodded. What Lieutenant Kuylman said sounded right.

"Everyone was glad that the Americans were here," he continued, "that *Sahawa* was here, as long as there was a bad guy out there to fight. Fast-forward a year later to when the violence is down, and you have *Sahawa* on the street corners acting like gangs and militias."

Sayid nodded again. "They are gangs," he said.

"You're talking about the Sons of Iraq?" I said.

"The Sons of Iraq, yeah," Lieutenant Kuylman said. Higher ranking American officers didn't like to discuss the dark side of the Sons of Iraq, or the dark side of anything, really, with the media. Lower ranking officers were a little less concerned about public relations. "Depending on which area you go to, people have a different view of them. And now with us, we pumped all that money in shops and into *Sahawa*, so they know we have money. But if they don't see constant improvement, then they wonder why we're still here. They look at us and say 'what have you done for us lately?'"

"What do people here think of Al Qaeda now?" I said to Sayid.

"They don't love them," he said. "In the past they helped them and even opened their hearts to them. Al Qaeda are really bad people. They even rape women, and you can't do anything. They kill people right in front of your eyes, and you can't do anything."

"What were people here expecting from those guys?" I said. "They must have known Al Qaeda was doing this sort of thing in other places, in Afghanistan, in New York City. Maybe they liked Al Qaeda for what they did in New York City."

"It's a religious thing," he said sadly. "They think if they kill someone like me, someone like you, they will go to heaven. If they have a big bomb and they kill us all, they'll go to heaven. They fill people's minds with this crap, that there are beautiful chicks in heaven."

"Were people here expecting Al Qaeda to kill only Americans?" I said.

"No, no, no," he said.

"I'm trying to figure out what kind of mental shift went on here," I said.

"They love to kill people like me," he said.

And so they do. The overwhelming majority of people who have been killed in Iraq by Al Qaeda are Iraqis.

"Yesterday I showed a lieutenant a house of Al Qaeda leaders in Adhamiyah," he said. "He didn't know where they lived. I have many relationships, and from those relationships I can collect information about them. So I showed the lieutenant two houses. One of these guys killed his sister's husband."

"Why did he kill his sister's husband?" I said.

"Because his sister's husband was Shia," he said.

If Al Qaeda in Iraq strictly limited its targets to American soldiers and Shia civilians, the organization might still be popular among Iraq's Sunnis. A disturbingly high percentage of Sunni Arabs outside Iraq in places like Egypt cheered Zarqawi's people not only for fighting American soldiers but for murdering Shia "apostates."

"It's not so much that people here have turned against Al Qaeda," Lieutenant Kuylman said. "If people in Adhamiyah are against anything, it's the *Jaysh al Mahdi* militia and the 'Special Groups.' They will vehemently blame everything on *Jaysh al Mahdi* and Iran because they're Sunni. So you don't see too many explicit denunciations of Al Qaeda.

"Look at the Abu Hanifa Mosque," he continued. "I wouldn't say it's a breeding ground, but it's a haven. It's a nice place to hide. We can't go in there. The imam was detained. He doesn't like us very much. I wouldn't say he's a radical, but he's not cool."

I turned toward Sayid. "You were saying the Sons of Iraq is like a gang," I said. "What did you mean, exactly? There are different kinds of gangs."

"I'll tell you something," he said. He sounded so sad, like a man who has completely given up on his culture and his society. "Maybe this isn't the answer you're looking for, but I know why you're asking. And I'll tell you something. If the American forces leave this area before two or three years, the people will start fighting each other. You should know that."

"That's the big question right now," I said.

"I see that,"he said. "I know it will happen. I live here."

"Does everybody here think this is what's going to happen?" I said.

"No," he said.

"Is it a majority opinion, or a minority opinion?" I said. Among the Americans I talked to, around half were optimistic and half were pessimistic, but Sayid was talking about Iraqis.

"Minority," he said.

"Most people think it will be okay?" I said.

"Simple people," he said. "Uneducated people. The same 80 percent of people I was talking about before. They don't see beyond their own nose."

"Is there any way to avoid this?" I said. "Assuming you're right. I mean, nobody really knows what will happen until it happens."

"It's complicated," he said. "I'll tell you something. We're Arabs. But first we are selfish and greedy. If you visit a house, a neighbor, you will see that if someone's neighbor is driving a nice car, he doesn't feel good. He feels bad because the neighbor has a nice car. So, of course, he is envious of him. He will do anything to hurt him. When the civilian war happened, neighbors threw away their own neighbors. They said 'if you don't leave your house right now, we will kill you and your family.' They said this to people who were their neighbors for thirty or forty years. You can't imagine. We don't have honest politicians. Politicians are bad. They just give the ignition to start it. The community does the rest. A small child could tell you that."

I turned to Tom, our interpreter, who seemed to give it to me straight earlier about what Iraqis in the area truly felt and believed.

"Do you think that's true?" I said.

"Yeah," he said and nodded. "I do."

Sayid did not want the American soldiers to leave Iraq. In his view, they have only finished around a quarter of the job. Whether he's right or wrong about that is immaterial—there was no way either the American or the Iraqi publics would tolerate more than a decade of continued occupation. Americans were sick of the cost and the casualties, and Iraqis were sick of foreign soldiers on their streets and in their neighborhoods. Whether it was foolish or wise, Americans were on their way out.

"Believe me," he said. "Maliki is a dictator in Iraq. If the American government doesn't watch him, he will become a dictator in no time. In four or five years, he will look like Saddam Hussein. Keep on him. He wants to rule. He wants to have the power. Everyone who works in his office are his relatives. He will bring all his tribe."

"That's how it is everywhere," he said.

"No, no," he said. "In the States?"

"I mean, in this region," I said. "It's like that everywhere in this region."

"In this area?" he said. "Yeah. It is." It's hard to convey just how depressed Sayid sounded. If he ever felt any optimism or hope, Iraq had beaten it out of him a long time ago. "Except Israel and Lebanon. They have democracy. But the rest of them? Syria? Damn." He laughed darkly. "Iran, too. If they evacuate the forces from this block, I will be the first one killed. The first one.

"I'm a friend of Americans. The Americans are my family. They saved my life. The Iraqi army arrested me and hit me until I was unconscious. They kidnapped me from my house. They were dressed as Iraqi army. Well, they are Iraqi army. But they also belonged to the militia. They wanted to kill me. But an American, the bravest man I know, saved my life."

"What did he do?" I said.

"He is a captain," he said. "He got me out. He knew me from before because he visited me. And we had a kind of bond. And since then I feel that the American people are my family. Not the Iraqi people. People here want to kill me. They kidnapped me to kill me. And Americans saved my life."

He reminded me of Hammer, the Iraqi interpreter I had met years before in a different part of Baghdad at War Eagle. He desperately wanted out of Iraq, and he finally did make it out when he was issued a Green Card. He and his son live now in Florida. I have no idea what became of Sayid. Maybe he made it out, too.

"I want to leave this country," he said. "I have suffered a lot. When my dad died, it was hard when I buried him. I couldn't go to the cemetery because of the shooting. If I took him to the cemetery, they would shoot me. But I went anyway and hoped no one would try it. The cemetery is across the river. There was a sniper shooting at us. We've seen hell. We've seen hell. And that hell, if the American forces evacuate, will repeat. I hope it won't repeat for me. I'm wondering what I can do with my house and my family. I don't know. If Obama forces an evacuation from Iraq soon, everything will turn against him in this land."

"Yeah," Lieutenant Kuylman said. "Sit on that, Mike."

"Sayid might become an interpreter for us," Sergeant Franklin said. "And if so, he'll be able to go to the States. He, and most of the rest of them, will be happy to turn their backs on Iraq and just go."

As we drove back to COP Apache in Humvees, I asked Sergeant Franklin what he thought of Sayid's analysis now that we could talk privately.

"Do you think Sayid was basically right?" I said.

"I do," he said and nodded. "There will be a power vacuum here after we leave. They're going to jockey for power. Someone will take over and be dictatorish or an outright dictator, and Iraq will either flourish or it won't."

"I think he's right, too," said our Iraqi interpreter Tom.

Prime Minister Nouri al-Maliki fought with Americans against Iranian-backed Shia militias and won. What I didn't know then, and still don't know now, is whether or not Iran can ramp that violence back up again, or if Tehran's proxy militias have been truly defeated. I asked a number of American military officers what they think about this, and their answers were all over the place. Maybe nobody knows. Predicting events in the Middle East is a mug's game.

Sergeant Franklin, though, was not optimistic.

"I think Iran is laying low right now and is riding us out," he said. "They're still killing our guys, though, and we know it. You know it. But we pretend they aren't so we don't have to open another front. When we pull out, though, and they know we're almost out, it will be game on here in Iraq."

July 2009

Afterword

Open rebellion broke out in Iran just a few short months after my last trip to Baghdad. Millions of furious citizens took to the streets and demanded their vote be counted after the government declared Mahmoud Ahmadinejad the winner of an obviously rigged presidential election. The authorities sent men with riot gear and truncheons into the streets. Dissidents disappeared into dungeons. Demonstrations spread throughout the country, and for the first time in its history, Iran's Islamic Republic regime faced a revolutionary threat to its very survival.

It survived, however, at least through the summer of 2011 when the first edition this book was published, but the upheaval may have produced at least one good result even if it wasn't regime change. Iran's government had less time, energy, and resources to spend on Iraq once it got sucked into street fights at home.

Iraq didn't blow up when the Americans withdrew to bases out in the desert. Maybe it's partly because Ahmadinejad and Iran's true head of state Ali Khamenei couldn't be bothered with Baghdad while Tehran was burning. Perhaps the pessimistic Iraqis and Americans got it wrong, that Iraq was in better shape in early 2009 than they thought. And maybe the country won't come apart until later. Few things in that region happen on schedule.

The Kurds might still break away. Most of them, after all, want to. The Sunnis and Shias could start fighting again at any time. Just because they more or less stopped in the late 2000s hardly means a rivalry more than a millennium old is finished forever. Prime Minister Maliki may well turn into an outright dictator who rigs elections and jails his opponents, and if he doesn't, perhaps his replacement will. In August of 2011 he tepidly supported Bashar al-Assad's murderous crackdown on peaceful demonstrations in Syria. Iraq might suffer a terrible fate that no one can see coming in 2011. But the world is forever surprising, and it's possible, just possible, that slowly, fitfully, and in very small increments, Iraq will become a country that prospers and grows instead of explodes.

Portland, Oregon
August 2011